Gender &
Racial Inequality
at Work

Cornell Studies in Industrial and Labor Relations Number 27

Gender &
Racial Inequality
at Work

The Sources & Consequences
of Job Segregation

Donald Tomaskovic-Devey

ILR Press
Ithaca, New York

Library of Congress Cataloging-in-Publication Data

Tomaskovic-Devey, Donald, 1957–
Gender and racial inequality at work: the sources and
consequences of job segregation/Donald Tomaskovic-Devey.
p.   cm.—(Cornell studies in industrial and labor relations;
no. 27)
Includes bibliographical references and index.
ISBN 0-87546-304-5.—ISBN 0-87546-305-3 (pbk.)
1. Discrimination in employment—United States.   2. Sex
discrimination in employment—United States.   I. Title.
II. Series.
HD4903.5.U58T66   1993
331.13'3'0973—dc20   93–16551

Copies may be ordered through bookstores or
directly from

ILR Press
School of Industrial and Labor Relations
Cornell University
Ithaca, NY 14853-3901

Printed on acid-free paper in the United States of America

5   4   3   2   1

To my father, Donald P. Devey, who through much of his adult life has labored for racial and gender equality in the workplace and the community

CONTENTS

TABLES AND FIGURES

TABLES

FIGURES

ACKNOWLEDGMENTS

I HAVE DISCUSSED THE ISSUES in this book with many fine people. I owe a particular debt of gratitude to Cynthia Anderson, Luisa Maria Bianco, Jerry Jacobs, Arne Kalleberg, Barbara Kilbourne, Kevin Leicht, Jeff Leiter, Dave Maume, Toby Parcel, Barbara Reskin, Barbara Risman, Rachel Rosenfeld, Barbara Tomaskovic-Devey, and Cathy Zimmer, all of whom made helpful suggestions and generous criticisms at various points in the research and writing process. Barbara Risman, in particular, took the time to read and critique the entire manuscript. Parts of this research were presented at various university seminars and academic conferences. Now-anonymous participants in these seminars and conferences were valuable sources of new ideas, interpretations, and improved methods. I am in their debt.

The North Carolina Employment and Health Survey was paid for by the College of Agriculture and Life Sciences at North Carolina State University in support of research on the quality of life in North Carolina and graduate methodology training in the Department of Sociology, North Carolina State University. I thank my graduate methodology seminar for help in pretesting items and discussing the survey design. Particularly important in this regard were Sara Curran, Carolyn Herman, and Rosemary Ritzman.

In terms of the big issues, I thank Evelyn Glenn for introducing me to the study of sex segregation in employment and S. M. Miller for supporting my initial attempts to integrate the new structuralism in sociological studies of inequality with sex and race segregation research.

*Gender &
Racial Inequality
at Work*

CHAPTER 1
SEGREGATION, INEQUALITY, AND DISCRIMINATION

MEN AND WOMEN RARELY work in the same jobs in the same workplaces. Most men work in jobs only with other men, and most women work in jobs only with other women. The majority of white Americans work in jobs filled only by others of their own racial group. African-Americans, because they are a minority of the total labor force, are more likely to have white co-workers, but they still tend to work in organizations where many, if not most, of the workers in similar jobs are also African-Americans. Even among jobs that are integrated by sex or race, token integration is much more common than demographic balance. Job-level segregation by sex and race, although less common now than in the past, continues to be the norm rather than the exception in U.S. workplaces.

Sex and racial segregation at work are intimately linked to sex and racial inequalities in the labor force. White women, black women, and black men tend to earn substantially less than white men. Similarly, white men tend to have profound advantages in their access to the most desirable jobs. Jobs that have high prestige and power over other workers, that are relatively autonomous, and that provide career ladders and skill training are all more likely to be filled by white men. In short, although there has been some erosion of white men's advantages in the workplace over the last two decades, they remain substantial.

As we shall see, sex and racial segregation are profoundly linked to the quality of jobs. This is because the best jobs in most workplaces are systematically reserved for white males. In addition, as a job comes to be thought of as "women's work" or a "minority position," it tends to be downgraded in prestige in an organization. We shall also see that this segregation is largely the result of workplace processes rather than the labor supply decisions of individuals.

If as a society we are to directly challenge sex and racial segregation and the resulting inequalities, we will have to do it in workplaces. Such a change will require not only reeducating and redirecting the behavior of employees, managers, and co-workers who perpetuate the segregation, but also changing the structure of organizations. Racial and gender segregation are intertwined with the very fabric of work, influencing not only the allocation of people to jobs but the character of jobs and workplaces themselves. They are organizational processes, independent of the race or sex of the individuals who populate workplaces.

Jobs can have gender. There are black jobs. There are also white male jobs, and these jobs often develop certain advantages in the workplace over and above the skill levels or even the organizational power of the people who hold them. Joan Acker has produced one of the most clear and provocative statements about this notion in a discussion of organizations as gendered processes:

> To say that an organization, or any other analytic unit, is gendered means that advantage and disadvantage, exploitation and control, action and emotion, meaning and identity, are patterned through and in terms of a distinction between male and female, masculine and feminine. Gender is not an addition to the ongoing process, conceived as gender neutral. Rather it is an integral part of the process (1990:46).

Jobs rarely have a gender- or race-neutral status. A white male can potentially hold a job that is fundamentally conditioned by its being typically held by a black female. In the building in which I work black women do the cleaning. The nature of these jobs, the pay, the level of supervision, the capital investment in the tools to get the work done are at least partially influenced by the racial and sex composition of their jobs. If you, the reader, somehow ended up in one of these jobs, you would thus get a wage and experience working conditions that reflect the organizational evaluation of work done primarily by black women.

You might object to the preceding scenario on at least two grounds. The first objection is a supply-side one that focuses on the importance of the individual characteristics, besides race and gender, that allocate people into jobs. According to the supply-side argument, you would not have one of those jobs not because of your race or sex but because, if you are reading this book, you probably have skills and educational credentials that qualify you for better jobs.

The second objection is a more structural one that focuses on jobs and organizations. It is that these cleaning jobs pay poorly, are closely supervised, and have little capital investment not because they are filled by black women but because they are low-skill jobs in the state sector of the economy. Low-skill jobs, particularly in the absence of unionization, typically pay poorly. Further, jobs in the state sector often have low levels of capital investment in tools and training since there are few organizational resources for either good pay or the investment in better tools.

These two objections mirror the two dominant social science approaches to discussions about the quality of jobs. The supply-side, individual approach focuses on the role of personal qualifications in sorting people into jobs of different skill and pay. Human capital theory in the academic field of economics and status attainment theory in sociology share models of job sorting in which individuals with more skill, experience, and advantageous credentials are assumed to be more or less efficiently sorted into better jobs. These supply-side approaches focus on the skills and motivations of labor market entrants to explain labor force inequalities. They tend to ignore, or at least downplay, the important role of sex and race in sorting people into jobs. Since jobs can have typical gender or race expectations, the process of sorting people into jobs can also involve the exclusion of women and African-Americans from desirable positions. Unfortunately, meritocratic social science theories leave much of the process by which people get jobs, and jobs get evaluated, unexplored.

The second objection to the race and gender explanation of how jobs reflect the status characteristics of typical incumbents is more closely associated with the "new structuralism" in sociological studies of stratification and with the dual economy, dual labor market tradition in economics. Proponents of these theories would agree that racial and gender inequalities are widespread and cannot be explained by differences in individual skills or human capital alone. These more structural, or demand-centered, approaches to labor markets focus their explanations of racial and gender inequalities on the organizational and job segmentation of the labor force along racial and gender lines. Proponents would argue that the quality of a job has to do with the power of the job in an organization and the resources of the organization in its regional and industrial environment. Race and sex, they would argue, are important sources of sorting, so that the best jobs in the most resource-rich organizations typically are reserved for white males, particularly white males with educational credentials. The actual quality of the job, however, would be conceptualized to be a function of the power of the job within its organizational context and the power of the organization in its industrial and regional environment. Patriarchy (systems of male advantage) and racism in this demand-side structural formulation are the result of labor market organization and perhaps direct face-to-face discrimination, but jobs and their quality are determined by power within and between organizations, not by the racial or sex composition of the jobs themselves.

It is my thesis that job-level segregation by sex and race is a fundamentally important source of black-white and male-female inequalities in employment. Supply-side explanations that focus on individual skills and demand-side explanations that focus on job and organizational power are unable to account for sex and racial inequalities because they treat sex and race as variables, not as organizational processes in their own right. It is the thesis of this study that jobs can be profoundly influenced by their sex and racial composition. In addition, the typical racial or sex composition of jobs is hypothesized to be a much more powerful determinant of sex and racial segregation than are individual's human capital or preferences. Stated theoretically, both labor markets and the concrete organization of work are profoundly influenced by processes of *status closure* and *status composition*.

Status closure refers to the workplace discrimination processes by which status characteristics, such as sex and race, determine who has access to valuable employment positions. Discrimination is not a constant; instead, social pressures for race- and sex-based exclusion rise as the quality of a job increases. *Status composition* refers to the process by which the typical sex or race of a class of jobs in workplaces becomes a fundamental aspect of the jobs, influencing the work done as well as the organizational evaluation of the worth of the work. Simply stated, the better the job, the more black men, white women, and black women are excluded, and the more a job is filled by black women, white women, or black men, the more it is devalued and deskilled by employers.

These observations about status closure and status composition produce new insights into our theoretical and social policy understandings of racial and gender inequalities. Discrimination is not something perpetuated solely by racist or sexist individuals but is fundamentally conditioned by competition for the best jobs. Inequality is not only the result of discrimination against women or minorities but also of the gendered and racial organization of production itself. These two processes—status closure and status composition—are fundamental sources respectively of the racial and sex *segregation* and *inequalities* that are so pervasive in our workplaces.

To understand racial and gender inequalities, we must first examine the social processes that lead to sex and racial segregation in employment. Theories of individual choice based on human capital invest-ments, labor force commitment, and prior socialization are explored for what they tell us about the process that creates sex- and race-segregated job structures. In the end we find that these supply-side theories tell us very little. Their emphasis on voluntaristic behavior obscures the reality that gender and race not only are individual attributes but also social processes that influence the struggle for social closure and job evaluation in workplaces. Organizational tendencies toward statistical discrimina-tion and social exclusion based on race and sex are found to be more compelling explanations of how segregated job structures evolve, as well as of those instances where they are absent.

This book is also about how sex and racial segregation affect gender and racial inequalities. Well-known social science explanations of in-equality based on human capital, organizational segmentation, and job-skill segmentation are supplemented with my argument that the very organization of production and pay may reflect the racial and sex composition of jobs. Organizations and jobs may be every bit as much the product of racial and patriarchal practices in the workplace as they are of power and efficiency considerations.

SEGREGATION AND STATUS CLOSURE PROCESSES

Jobs are important sources of personal welfare. They are important, often primary sources of income, security, challenge, and self-esteem. That jobs are profoundly segregated by sex and race has a great deal to do with the creation and maintenance of racial and gender inequalities in society. Jobs that are only or primarily populated by women or minorities tend to have low wages given their required skill levels. They also tend to have lower task complexity, autonomy, supervisory author-ity, and opportunities for promotion. For a given level of educational requirements, on average, jobs held by white males pay more and provide better intrinsic rewards to their incumbents. Thus, job segrega-tion is linked to and, as we shall see, is a partial cause of racial and gender inequalities.

Chapter 2 documents the extent of job segregation and briefly outlines some of its consequences. Chapters 3 and 4 explore the processes that lead to a segregated job structure. These two chapters form the heart of my evaluation of how jobs become segregated.

Chapter 3 evaluates the mainstream social science explanations of racial and sex segregation. There are basically two supply-side social science approaches to job segregation. The first stems from human capital theory and its current formulation in the "new home economics" literature. The most general argument is that individuals with high investments in human capital and high labor market commitment will work especially hard to reap returns in the form of earnings on those investments. What this suggests specifically is that full-time workers and workers with more education, experience, and tenure with their employers should avoid disadvantaged jobs. Logically, they should avoid jobs held stereotypically by minorities or women. Similarly, individuals with high motivation to earn, that is, those for whom income presumably has greater utility relative to leisure, should search more diligently for better jobs. This would suggest that full-time workers and workers with family responsibilities should be expected to aspire to jobs held typically by white males. Thus, some segregation should occur naturally if there are differences by race and sex in human capital, labor force commitment, or family responsibilities.

The new home economics literature develops this reasoning further by positing that family utility might include a division of labor between husband and wife in which the wife specializes in domestic work and the husband specializes in paid employment. This is seen as maximizing family utility based on prior socialization and the reality that women generally earn less in the labor force. Many women work in the paid labor force, of course, but may choose stereotypical women's work to have the flexibility to fulfill their primary domestic responsibilities. Thus, high levels of sex segregation in employment are posited to reflect the rational choices of wives specializing in domestic work and of husbands specializing in paid employment.

The second supply-side explanation focuses on childhood socialization. It argues that job aspirations and notions of the individual's appropriate "place" in society are learned through socialization. Women and men learn to expect and value sex-segregated roles as children. Similarly, although it is a weaker explanation, blacks socialized before the civil rights movement and whites socialized before the late 1960s and early 1970s, when public racism became illegal in U.S. society, might be more likely to select same-race employment.

These two approaches are examined because they are widely accepted. As explanations they are, however, inconsistent with the general theoretical argument advanced here. These supply-side approaches conceptualize race and sex as characteristics of individuals that may for reasons of taste or preparation for work lead to segregation. Although it is plausible that individual talents and tastes and domestic divisions of labor may play some role in creating segregation, this is not a very sophisticated explanation. As shall become clear in chapter 3, it is not an accurate one either.

The sources of segregation are explored further in chapter 4, where I turn to more structural explanations of the motivations of superordinate actors—employers and white male employees—to create segregation. Employers may be motivated to create a segregated employment structure to decrease labor costs or to control potential dissent by white male workers. There are two general theories that explain these motivations. The narrower approach, an attempt by neoclassically informed economists to explain the long-term persistence of segregation, is called statistical discrimination theory.

Statistical discrimination theory argues that employers may discriminate against all members of a status group based on their perception that, on average, the status group will be less productive or more expensive to train than the alternative status group. The argument is that if employers believe that black, Hispanic, or female labor on average is more costly because of its high training costs, high turnover, or low productivity then employers may rationally discriminate against all members of the status group.[1]

The statistical discrimination argument makes most sense when training costs or wages are high and thus the costs of bad hiring decisions are also high. It leads to a prediction that employers will tend to exclude workers of suspect status groups from jobs that incur high training costs or other high labor costs to their companies. As Glen G. Cain (1986) points out, there is a built-in naiveté in this argument since it assumes that employers cannot use other mechanisms, such as provisional status for new hires, to assess individual-level productivity. The argument also hinges on the assumption that females and African-Americans are more costly to train or will be less productive than comparable white male workers. As data in chapter 4 show, there is no strong evidence that this is the case.

Of course, if all or most employers believe there are group differences in productivity and act accordingly, the consequences will be the same whether or not their belief is accurate—white males will tend to be preferred for jobs with high training costs. In this case we should more properly say that the discrimination is based on a belief system rather than on rational economic calculations. In this case what looks like statistical discrimination is simply old-fashioned racist and sexist discrimination or, as I shall argue later in this book, a narrowly framed version of more general social closure processes.

Social closure refers to "the process by which social collectivities seek to maximize rewards by restricting access to resources and opportunities to a limited circle of eligibles" (Parkin 1979:44). Social closure processes are the means by which superordinate groups preserve their advantage by tying access to jobs or other scarce goods to group characteristics.

Educational credentials, capital ownership, ethnicity, race, religion, and gender are all group characteristics that are commonly the basis for formal and informal exclusionary rules.

Social closure processes are not simply historical or traditional privileges but active, ongoing attempts by the already advantaged to preserve privilege. People who own capital defend the "rights" of property. Those with educational credentials insist they are necessary to gain access to high-quality jobs. Active social closure is required to preserve advantage because the excluded tend to react to exclusionary rules by attempting to usurp valued positions. Colleges and universities for minorities and women and ethnic economic enclaves are examples of mild forms of usurpation. Over time, however, as Raymond Murphy points out, subordinate groups tend to fight back and to overturn or modify the rules of exclusion:

> Exclusionary codes are not permanent, however much they may appear so while they are flourishing. Caste, lineage, racial, ethnic, and religious exclusion (and indeed slavery) must have appeared virtually inevitable during long periods of history, but they were eventually attacked and replaced and the world images and ideas on which they rested changed. Gender exclusion rules were widely believed to be rooted in human nature until recently, but are now being contested and uprooted (1988:3).

The contemporary women's and civil rights movements are organized attempts to eradicate the exclusionary rules that have created and preserved white male advantage. Most of the formal legal restrictions regarding female and black labor in the United States have been repealed in the last thirty years. Although there have been substantial legal reforms, gender and race remain important bases for social exclusion in the United States. As Barbara F. Reskin (1988) points out in discussing sex segregation, employment segregation is currently one of the central rules by which male employment advantage is created and maintained. William Julius Wilson (1978) has argued that race-based exclusionary employment rules are declining in significance. As we shall see, both sex- and race-based job segregation remain widespread.

One clear advantage of social closure theory over conventional accounts of discrimination is that it points out clearly that historical and contemporary patterns of exclusion involve not only discrimination or market mechanisms of job allocation but also privilege. The conventional accounts read as if black or female disadvantage is the result of poor preparation or biased belief systems among potential employers but neglect to mention that social processes create the advantages white males possess and defend.

In chapter 4, I discuss the implications of social closure theory for understanding which jobs are reserved for white males. In general, social closure processes result in the preservation of the best positions for members of the dominant group and in status groups being segregated at equivalent levels in the job hierarchy. What I found is that as the desirability of jobs increases, they are less likely to have female or African-American incumbents. In addition, segregation by sex but not by race is greatest in the most desirable jobs. Segregation of demographically small groups, such as African-Americans, in higher-quality jobs may be much less practical than the segregation of large employee groups, such as women.

I also propose that attempts by dominant groups to create their own advantages are not fixed but vary by culture and organization. Neoclassical economics suggests, for example, that employers' freedom to discriminate, that is, to indulge their own tastes or those of white male workers so as to exclude women or African-Americans from desirable positions, should be limited by market forces. Firms in competitive markets should be forced by market pressure to hire cheaper minority or female labor. Over time this demand should drive up the wage rates of minorities and women.

Another force that may undermine tendencies toward social closure is the formalization of the employment relationship. When job requirements and personnel rights and duties are clearly spelled out in a bureaucratic environment, the informal exclusion of candidates from jobs and promotions based on their race or gender may be reduced.

Historical national and regional variations in cultural expectations may also affect the extent of social closure by sex and race. The degree of competition by racial groups for jobs as well as the intensity of traditional sex-role expectations should vary from place to place and certainly over time.

The final constraint on social closure is more purely demographic. Jobs and organizations with many incumbents may find total exclusion impractical.

Of these four potential sources of subordinate usurpation, all, except market competition, are found to undermine sex and/or race segregation. They are all discussed in detail in chapter 4.

INEQUALITY AND STATUS COMPOSITION

Although social closure processes are important constraints on who gets which jobs, it is also important to understand that gender and racial inequalities at work are also potentially built into the very fabric of the workplace itself.

Typical social science approaches to inequality focus on differences in the average qualifications between men and women or whites and minorities to explain racial and gender inequalities in work rewards. Human capital theory suggests that women have less favorable jobs than men because they have more interrupted careers, work in more part-time jobs, and take different courses in school (particularly in college). Human capital theorists have tended to focus on white-black differences in educational attainment and work experience. Human capital approaches explain some but not all of the observed inequality in U.S. workplaces.

Social closure explanations, which promote the view that the best jobs tend to be reserved for whites and males, suggest an additional set of explanations. Proponents of theories of split and segmented labor markets, although typically not using explicit social closure conceptualizations, argue that there is a general pattern of organizational and job segmentation by sex and race that produces additional sex and racial inequalities beyond that which we might expect given actual human capital differences between men and women and whites and minorities. Thus, existing theories of segmented labor markets lead us to expect women and minorities to be excluded from good jobs.

I argue that a third set of important social processes can result in workplace inequalities. Jobs can take on a gendered or racial character that is independent of their incumbents and that influences how such jobs are concretely organized—their level of complexity, autonomy, authority over other jobs, the manner in which they are controlled, and their level of earnings. Specifically, the status composition of a job—that is, the extent to which it is typically filled by males or females, whites or blacks—is intrinsically part of the labor process as well as the reward structure of the organization.

This notion of status composition has been most well developed in the burgeoning literature on the sex composition of jobs. There is now ample evidence that as the proportions of females in jobs increase, wages fall and working conditions deteriorate. This is not to say that power and skill are not important in influencing the quality of jobs but that there is a status composition process that may, at least in some circumstances, be as important in structuring the labor process and the organizational evaluation of the worth of a job.

The way this status composition process influences individual gender and racial inequalities is indirect; that is, it is a result of the disadvantaging of jobs that are typically but not always held by people of subordinate status. Social closure processes tend to sort women and minorities into low-quality jobs. When a job becomes socially associated with women or a minority group, status composition processes may further disadvantage that job relative to other positions with similar skill requirements or power resources. Both processes—status closure and status composition—together create the systems of advantage and disadvantage in workplaces that we call patriarchy and racism. Janet Saltzman Chafetz explores these issues:

> Is work done by women devalued on that basis, or are women, because of power inequities, only permitted access to devalued work roles? Both appear true. . . . Despite their differences, in both cases the fact that women do devalued and undervalued work results from superior male power. It is the power to *devalue* that which women do, and/or to ensure that women *do not gain access* to work that is highly valued (1990:60–61, emphasis added).

The devaluing of women's work is a *status composition process*. The denial of access is a *status closure process*. The latter is one of the primary sources of job segregation, while the former is one of the consequences of that segregation. Together they produce most gender and racial inequalities in the workplace.

This study extends existing feminist analysis to race issues in the workplace for two reasons. The first reason is that on general theoretical grounds we should expect that if both racial and gender inequalities are based ultimately on processes of status subordination, then a concrete mechanism that we know is important for female subordination—the sex typing of jobs—may be important for racial subordination as well. We certainly know that racial segregation in residence is a powerful source of racial inequality (Massey 1990), and it is also clear that race-based job segregation has been important in the past (Wilson 1978). It would not be surprising then to find racial composition effects on the organization of jobs that parallel the fairly well-documented gender composition effect.

We have good theoretical reasons to expect that the racial composition of jobs may be similar to the sex composition of jobs in its effects on the organization of the labor process and pay rates. Both should be governed by status processes of social closure and status composition. Following Wilson (1978), however, we might expect that gender closure and composition effects on jobs will be stronger than race closure and composition effects and that human capital explanations may be more powerful in explaining black-white inequality than they are in explaining male-female inequality.

Wilson (1978), in his controversial and influential study, has argued that race-based processes are being eroded and replaced by class-based processes (such as human capital formation, family class background, regional and neighborhood investment patterns) as the primary sources of black-white inequality. Wilson's *declining significance of race* thesis suggests that racial composition effects on the organization of jobs may be weakening over time. The study that follows is cross-sectional and cannot adequately address Wilson's historical interpretations. I found, however, that racial composition effects on earnings, although present, are substantially weaker than sex composition effects. It is also the case that human capital explanations of how individuals are sorted into jobs are more powerful in explaining black-white inequality than male-female inequality. Nonetheless, race-based status closure and status composition processes are still quite powerful.

The second reason to extend the status composition analyses to race is that most affirmative action programs and social movement activity have focused on higher-paying and higher-skilled jobs. Since the sex segregation of the labor force extends throughout the skill ladder and to workers of all educational levels, how gender composition has influenced the calculation of the social worth of jobs has been, if not self-evident, at least within the common frame of reference and investigation. Workplace policies labeled "pay equity" or "comparable worth" have become prominent goals of the U.S. women's movement. Race segregation, as we shall see in chapter 4, is not extensive among positions that require advanced educational credentials. Blacks with college degrees tend to end up in jobs with many white co-workers. Women with college degrees tend to end up in jobs with other women. Jobs that are typically held by blacks tend to be at the bottom in terms of job quality, and the effects of social movement activity and attention have been limited.

This focusing of attention on skilled work has led to affirmative action *and* comparable worth initiatives for women but primarily affirmative action agendas for educated or otherwise advantaged minorities. By establishing a pattern of racial composition effects on labor process organization and earnings inequalities, we should be able to shed some light on organizational and public policy attempts to reduce both gender and racial inequalities that take into account the broader range of discriminatory processes that create these inequalities. This includes bringing class back into the discussion of racial inequality and social policy.

Chapters 5 and 6 examine the three explanations—human capital, social closure, and status composition—of the processes that produce racial and gender inequalities. Chapter 5 looks at inequalities in access to high-quality work. The dimensions of work inequality explored include task complexity, workplace autonomy, supervisory authority, managerial decision-making power, and internal labor market (i.e., promotion) opportunities. Chapter 6 examines how the substantial pay inequalities between whites and blacks and women and men are created.

Both chapters weigh the relative importance of human capital, social closure, (organizational segmentation and job segmentation), and status composition processes in producing the inequalities. All the explanations have some merit, but they vary widely in the strength of their explanatory power. I found that both racial and gender status composition processes influence labor process organization and pay rates for subordinates and superordinates alike. That is, males in typically female jobs and whites in typically black jobs experience the labor process organization and are paid wages consistent with their jobs, rather than with their gender or racial characteristics.

THEORETICAL CONCLUSIONS

Although it is a bit premature to reach sweeping conclusions, and the reader is not relieved from responsibility to read the intervening chapters, I will briefly summarize the major theoretical conclusions offered in chapter 7. First, the competitive market models, which are derived from neoclassical economics, tell us very little about either the sources or the consequences of job-level racial and sex segregation. In particular, the new home economics model must be rejected. Older neoclassical economic models predict that market forces will undermine sex and racial inequalities in labor markets. Market forces, however, can be expected to undermine inequality only in the presence of competition. Since gender segregation is so nearly total that market competition barely exists, competition cannot be expected to have much effect on male-female inequality.

Second, although labor market segregation by race is less total and therefore market competition does occur more regularly between black and white labor, there are further fundamental flaws in the market model that lead to the prediction that inequality will be eroded and eradicated. Specifically, the model fails to conceptualize inequality as an active process of social closure on both the subordinate and superordinate levels. Discrimination is not only a matter of tastes or socialization or bad attitudes; it is also a matter of privilege and so will be strongly defended by the privileged.

Third, and finally, there is a classic error in the market model in its conceptualization of social structure. Social organization is described as a tightly coupled, dynamic, perfect information, competitive market system. The imagery is of all firms as always on the verge of collapse as market forces drive owners toward minimal profits. Thus, the cost of not hiring cheaper female or minority labor seems to be the difference between failure and survival. The reality is that market competition only occasionally disrupts normal economic life; it is not a constant condition of every market exchange. Further, markets are not tightly coupled all of the time. Dysfunctional practices, such as hiring high-priced male labor, only *occasionally* threaten organizational survival. Firms will often use cheaper female or minority labor to boost profits, as I shall discuss later in this study, but it is not a constant prerequisite to survival.

Although processes consistent with the statistical discrimination theory are associated with the racial composition of jobs, it is not possible from this study to say whether that process is associated with real differences by race in productivity and training costs or whether this is merely a widespread discriminatory belief with no empirical basis. Evidence from other studies is equivocal on this point. It is my position that for the time being we should reject the argument that there are differences in productivity by race and lay the burden of proof on its proponents. It seems more reasonable to suspect that, for historical reasons, including the growing importance of class in the definition of minority status, the patterns of social closure by race are most strongly manifest in skill-based exclusionary practices.

Gender-based social closure is more total. Women are excluded from jobs with high levels of training time, managerial decision-making power, supervisory authority, and opportunities for promotion.

Although race- and sex-based processes of social closure and status composition are widespread in workplaces, this does not mean that they are total or even permanent. Social closure is a process of struggle between subordinates and superordinates. Cultural change, formalized rules that discourage or prevent status processes from operating, and even demographic opportunity may reduce or increase the degree of race- and sex-based social closure. The civil rights and women's movements have reduced cultural and legal barriers to good-quality jobs. I found that urban communities, firms with more formalized work relationships between employers and employees, and jobs and organizations with larger work forces tend to be less segregated. I also found, however, that other bureaucratic mechanisms, particularly the proliferation of job titles in large organizations, are powerful forces for creating racial and sex segregation at the job level.

Compared with gender inequality, racial inequality is much more tied to class advantage and disadvantage. Whether or not there is a *declining significance of race*, it is clear from this study that race currently generates weaker status composition processes *in the workplace* than gender. Evidence from this study thus provides a novel insight into the experiences of Wilson's critics. The black middle class, who Wilson has characterized as advantaged and no longer imprisoned by racial status boundaries, have pointed out that they continue to experience racism in their daily lives. In general, however, the lower levels of job segregation by race mean that most black workers work with whites. Middle-class blacks work in extraordinarily white environments. There is evidence from this study and elsewhere that African-Americans often experience direct face-to-face discrimination at work.

I found that black employees seem to be more closely supervised than white employees not only because of the characteristics of the jobs they hold but because they are black. The near-total sex segregation of jobs means that even high levels of gender inequality become invisible because they are built into the jobs. By contrast, racial inequality is visible because most black workers, especially members of the black middle class, work in integrated environments. Social closure through job segregation is a method for producing status advantage. When segregation breaks down, as it has among educated blacks and whites, it would not be surprising to find less hidden attempts to display status dominance.

Finally, patriarchal relations in the workplace are both widespread and deeply ingrained in the patterns of hiring, the organization of the work process, and compensation policies. If there is some evidence of a declining significance of race in a comparison of the sources and consequences of racial and gender segregation, that same comparison suggests that patriarchal practices and processes are still quite strong.

Chapter 8 discusses the implications of this study for organizational and public policy. Although it is common to think of racial and gender inequalities as public policy issues, they are also organizational policy issues. This study should bring home the need for management and legislators to conceptualize the sources of racial and gender inequalities as broader than just relative preparedness and direct discrimination. Gender and racial inequalities are produced in workplaces by social closure processes and status composition processes as well.

LIMITATIONS AND SCOPE OF THE STUDY

This study is grounded in general social scientific theories of labor market allocation, job power, and status processes. These theories are specific to the advanced industrial capitalist economies they were formulated to analyze. They are probably most powerful in analyzing fairly unregulated labor markets such as that of the United States. The focus employed in this study is somewhat more limited, and that limitation should be faced but not exaggerated. White-black and male-female inequalities are examined in this study. Other ethnic inequalities, such as Hispanic-white, Asian-white, black-Hispanic, and Native American–white, are not examined. This is not because they are assumed to be empirically trivial. Rather, the focus on black-white status processes and inequality reflects the central importance of this particular inequality in both the historical and contemporary U.S. political economy. Other status closure and status composition processes linked to race or ethnicity should be examined in future work. It is my expectation that the same three sets of basic inequality-generating processes exist for other minority groups. The relative empirical importance of human capital, social closure, and status composition processes should be expected to reflect both local labor market practices and the historical relationship between different minority groups, white male employees, and employers.

This study uses as its primary evidentiary base a survey of employed adults in North Carolina. North Carolina is the tenth most populous state in the nation. It is also a state with a history of slavery, Jim Crow segregation after slavery, and a political economy wed to the exploitation of black labor. Although it is unlikely that the processes affecting *gender* segregation and inequality are much different in North Carolina than in the rest of the United States, the same cannot be said of the processes affecting racial segregation and inequality. When Wilson (1977) observed a declining significance of race, his field of vision was more clearly focused on regions of the country other than the old South and on the federal government. Although the civil rights movement and federal legislation have had important consequences in the South, change has probably been slower than in other regions. In addition, relative to the rest of the country, a much higher proportion of the population in much of the South is African-American. If status processes, in fact, involve the exclusion of status subordinates from desirable jobs, then the pressures for exclusion should be greatest where African-Americans are a larger proportion of the population. To generalize, then, the empirical estimates arrived at in this study, although they strictly speaking apply only to North Carolina, probably provide good first approximations of gender processes throughout the United States. Statements about racial processes and estimates of levels of racial inequality probably can be generalized to the southern United States. It may also be that similar racial processes exist in those urban areas of the

Table 1.1. Income penalties (in percent) associated with being black or female in U.S. metropolitan and nonmetropolitan areas, by region, controlling for human capital characteristics

Region	Metropolitan		Nonmetropolitan	
	Black	Female	Black	Female
New England	n.s.	−.34	n.s.	−.41
Middle Atlantic	−.05	−.35	n.s.	−.47
East North Central	−.07	−.42	n.s.	−.51
West North Central	n.s.	−.38	n.s.	−.42
South Atlantic	−.08	−.33	−.17	−.37
North Carolina	−.16	−.32	−.16	−.37
East South Central	−.16	−.38	−.24	−.40
West South Central	−.11	−.35	−.20	−.36
Mountain	n.s.	−.34	n.s.	−.42
Pacific	n.s.	−.34	n.s.	−.41

Source: March Current Population Surveys, 1987–88.
Note: Results are from a series of multiple regression equations by area by region for all positive earners, where logged earnings were regressed on race, sex, education (in degrees), experience and experience squared, weeks worked last year, and normal hours worked last year. An n.s. indicates a nonsignificant difference.

Northeast and Midwest where the competition by racial groups for jobs is most intense. As table 1.1 shows, the patterns of black-white earnings inequalities found in North Carolina are most similar to those in other parts of the U.S. South. Urban areas of the Northeast and Midwest show weaker but still significant levels of racial discrimination. The patterns of gender earnings inequalities show little regional variation; they are high everywhere.

Neither the black-white nor male-female status processes described in this study should be generalized to other status distinctions based on ethnicity, sexual preference, or physical handicap. Although certain similarities in process no doubt occur, these can be ascertained only through careful research using a full complement of theoretical explanations and historical knowledge. Marta Tienda and Ding-Tzan Lii (1987) have shown that processes of racial competition similar to those described in this study operate for Hispanics and Asians as well as for African-Americans. They show that as the size of all three minority populations rise, wage discrimination against these groups rises and that the penalties for minority status are higher for workers with more advanced educational credentials. Consistent with the arguments developed in the following pages, it is white males, particularly educated white males, who benefit from racial discrimination. From a workplace policy point of view, managers should expect that social closure and status composition–based discrimination against Hispanics, Asians, and other minorities are occurring in their organizations.

This study relies on cross-sectional data. Although the problems of tracking the sex and racial composition of jobs over time are large, a few studies have done this. Where appropriate, these more dynamic approaches, generally limited to occupational aggregates, will be brought into the discussion to help clarify and strengthen my inferences. The study is still limited to inferences about, rather than observations of, dynamic processes. The study nonetheless produces some important implications for change.

CHAPTER 2
EXTENT OF SEX AND RACIAL
SEGREGATION

THIS CHAPTER INTRODUCES THE reader to the survey data used in this study. It also explains how I have measured sex and racial composition and segregation. Finally, it documents the degree of job-level segregation by race and sex and its relationship to the sex and racial composition and segregation of occupations. Parts of this chapter are somewhat technical; even more technical detail on the sample and measures is provided in the appendix at the end of this book. Readers who are interested in issues of survey design, reliability, and validity should probably read this chapter and the appendix closely. Readers who are unconvinced of the utility of focusing on *job* rather than occupational segregation are encouraged to pay close attention to the final two sections of this chapter.

NORTH CAROLINA EMPLOYMENT AND HEALTH SURVEY

This study uses data collected in the North Carolina Employment and Health Survey (NCEHS) in 1989. Respondents were employed North Carolinians aged eighteen and older, who were sampled randomly and interviewed by telephone. The response rate was 72 percent, and comparisons of data on sex, race, age, occupation, and industry composition with Current Population Survey (CPS) data for North Carolina showed that the sample accurately represented the North Carolina labor force.

The NCEHS is an ideal source of data for examining the adequacy of theories about the sources and consequences of sex- and race-based employment segregation. The survey is a true random sample of jobs and workers, *and* it contains job-level information on the sex and racial composition of employment. Previous studies have been limited to organizational or occupational case studies (e.g., Cockburn 1988; Cohn 1985; Halaby 1979; Milkman 1980; Roos and Reskin 1984; Walby 1986), reliant on aggregate national data on *occupational* sex or racial segregation (Becker 1980; Glass 1990; Jacobs 1989a, 1989b), or based on nonrandom samples with incomplete information (Bielby and Baron 1984, 1985, 1986).

It is from the ogranizational and occupational case studies that we have learned most of what we know, or think we know, about the processes by which firms create segregated employment structures. It is this case study literature that has led us to expect that general processes of social closure based on patriarchal and racial status privilege are important forces behind the creation of segregated jobs. The particular strength of case study approaches is that historical and contemporary work processes can be studied in depth and in context. Their weakness is that the generality of findings is unknown. When Cynthia Cockburn (1988) concludes that the exclusion of women from skilled jobs is an active strategy of male employees, we do not know whether that is true in general or just of her sample of British engineers. When Jerry Jacobs and Ronnie Steinberg (1990) conclude that the economic theory of compensating differentials is wrong, we cannot reject out of hand the criticism that the evidence is based on non–market sector case studies (Filer 1990). The case study approach is strongest at developing theory and expectations but is inherently limited in its ability to test general theoretical propositions.

The strength of the survey approach used in this study is that the full array of theoretical ideas about the causes and consequences of segregation can be examined. Although we lose detailed understanding of particular jobs and workplaces, we gain a sense of the fundamental forces that operate across most jobs and workplaces. Previous survey approaches (England et al. 1988; Glass 1990; Jacobs 1989a, 1989b; Rosenfeld 1983; Sorenson 1989a, 1989b) have made great gains in laying out more generalizable knowledge about segregation processes. These studies were, however, hampered by their reliance on aggregate national occupational estimates as proxies for the sex and racial composition of jobs. Although almost all the relevant theory is about segregation at the job level and invokes explanations about household and organizational processes focused on jobs, the available survey data on sex and racial segregation have focused on national aggregate occupational segregation.[1]

William Bielby and James Baron's work stands out as the only series of studies that used job-level segregation data (for sex only) for a diverse sample of jobs. Unfortunately, their data lacked measures of individual characteristics and of job earnings. The important methodological innovation in the North Carolina Employment and Health Survey was that it asked respondents to supply information on the sex and racial composition of their jobs. This was done with three questions. The first question asked the respondent how many people in his or her workplace had the same job title he or she had. Following Bielby and Baron (1984, 1986), the question focused on *job title* rather than on general duties or tasks since it is the proliferation of titles that seems to enhance segregation in larger firms. If the respondent did not have a formal job title, the interviewers prompted with a request for the number of people who had his or her general job. This question was asked only of employees. Once we knew how many people held the job, we followed up by asking how many of that total were white and how many were male. The appendix provides a complete description of the measurement procedure and an evaluation of the validity and reliability of these measures. The conclusion in the appendix is that this approach to measuring job segregation is both valid and reliable. There is measurement error, of course, but it is probably lower than it is in the common practice of substituting national occupational segregation measures for job-level measures. In addition, the systematic measurement error introduced when we use national occupational estimates of racial segregation is avoided here. (The appendix includes further discussion of these ideas.)

Many of the analyses that follow are weighted to represent a random sample of jobs. (The exception is the analysis in chapter 3 that examines an individual supply-side model of the labor market.) The North Carolina Employment and Health Survey used a two-stage sampling strategy. In stage one we contacted a random sample of households. Within households, we took a random sample of employed adults and interviewed them about their primary jobs, yielding a random sample of employed adults. This differs from a random sample of jobs in three ways. First, information on jobs held by people younger than eighteen was not included in the data. Second, information on additional jobs held by respondents was not requested and therefore such jobs were not eligible to become units of analysis. Third, and finally, households with several employed members were sampled at the same rate as households with only one employed member.

This last rule seems to be the most problematic. The first two exclusions represent rather small omissions in the sampling frame and in any case involve the least central jobs economically (those of the very young and second jobs). To overcome any sampling bias introduced by the oversampling of one-employee households, each observation in the analyses reported in all chapters except chapter 3 is weighted relative to the number of employed members in the household.[2] The analyses in chapter 3 do not require weighting because the theories tested concern individual labor market motivations, not job or organizational processes.

The North Carolina Employment and Health Survey included 931 currently employed North Carolinians. The analyses in this study are limited to the 836 *employees* in the sample. Effective sample size varies from chapter to chapter depending on the pattern of missing data for variables in the analyses. Chapters 2, 3, and 4 rely on effective sample sizes of about 795 cases. This represents a modest attrition of 5 percent. Chapter 6 relies on an effective sample size of 654 cases, representing an attrition rate due to missing data of 22 percent. The decrease in the sample size occurred because some respondents refused to answer the earnings question. Although this level of refusal for an earnings question is common in telephone surveys, an analysis of potential sample selection bias was carried out. There were no significant differences between present and missing cases for the central variables used in the analyses in that chapter.[3]

MEASURING JOB SEGREGATION AND COMPOSITION

To explore the creation and consequences of job-level segregation, I will focus on two measures of segregation. The first measure will be familiar to many readers and simply focuses on job composition. Later in this chapter and in chapters 3 and 4 I will address the occupational, individual, job, and organizational sources of variation in the *percent female* and *percent black* in our sample jobs. For the analyses of the consequences of segregation for labor process organization and for wages in chapters 5 and 6, I will focus on the effects of *percent female* and *percent black* in the job on job organization and earnings.[4]

Figure 2.1 charts the frequency distribution of the job sex composition for the sample. Figure 2.1 shows that most jobs are either all female or all male in composition. Only a small fraction (14 percent) of jobs are demographically balanced, and slightly fewer are mixed but male-dominated (8 percent) or mixed but female-dominated (9 percent).

Figure 2.2 shows the racial composition of jobs in the sample. All-white jobs are extraordinarily common (51 percent of all jobs). All-black jobs are uncommon (5 percent), reflecting the smaller proportion of blacks in the population. Still, 25 percent of African-Americans work in all-black jobs.

The second measurement approach to segregation focuses on the degree of job-level separation by status distinction. In this chapter we

Figure 2.1. Percentage of female employees in North Carolina jobs, 1989

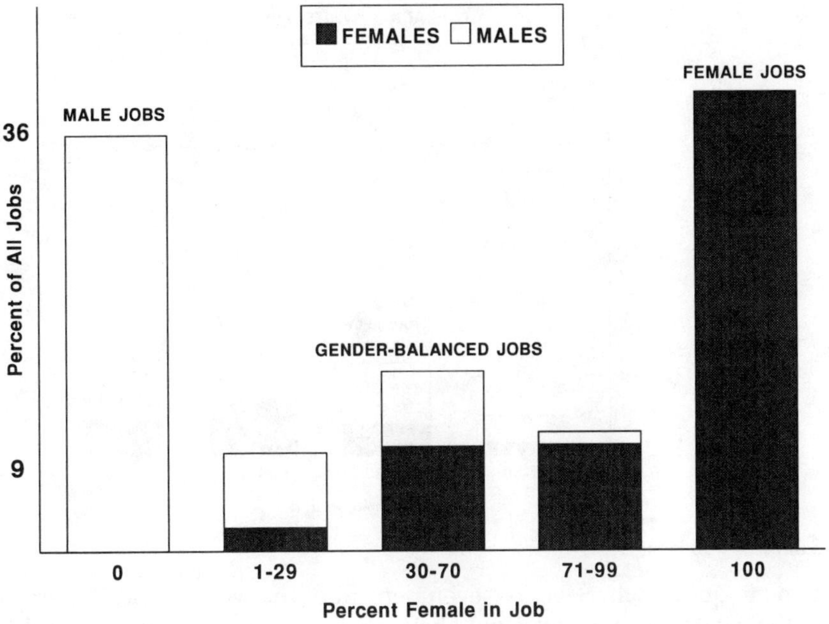

Sample = 815 jobs.

will look at the index of dissimilarity. In later chapters a modified version of this index will be used.

The index of dissimilarity can be interpreted as the proportion in either group who would have to change jobs to achieve an equal distribution across the employment structure. Equality is defined as the actual distribution of men and women and whites and blacks in the labor force. In this study I focus on employees only. Fifty-two percent of employees in North Carolina are women, 22 percent are black. When there is complete equality, the index of dissimilarity is zero. On the one hand, if 52 percent of the incumbents in all jobs were female and 22 percent were black, there would be no sex or racial segregation. On the other hand, if all jobs were perfectly homogeneous with respect to race and sex, then the indexes of dissimilarity for sex and racial segregation would both be 100. The index of dissimilarity is the standard segregation index in studies of occupational sex segregation (e.g., Beller 1984; Bielby and Baron 1984, 1986; Jabobs 1989a, 1989b; Rytina and Bianchi 1984). Table 2.1 reports the index of dissimilarity for sex- and race-based job segregation for the sample used for this study. Sex and racial segrega-

Figure 2.2.   Percentage of minority employees in North Carolina jobs, 1989

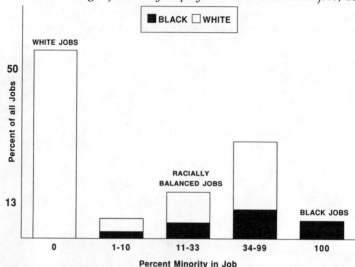

Sample = 796 jobs.

tion are quite high. Seventy-seven percent of the women and 55 percent
✳ of the African-Americans would have to change jobs to achieve complete
integration.

Although I am not aware of comparable racial segregation figures, the
sex segregation levels here are quite a bit lower than those reported by
Bielby and Baron (1984). Using a nonrandom but diverse sample of
California establishments from the late 1960s and early 1970s, they
report an index of dissimilarity for *job*-level sex segregation of 93.4. The
Bielby and Baron sample is not, strictly speaking, comparable to this
one, in that it was nonrandom, was done two decades ago, and sampled
in California (not North Carolina).

It is striking, however, that the only two general-sample *job*-level sex
segregation measures currently available (Bielby and Baron's and the
North Carolina Employment and Health Survey's) seem to parallel the
observed *occupational* trends toward more sex integration of jobs over
the last two decades (Jacobs 1989a; see also Beller 1984). Jacobs (1989a)
reports a 15.2 percent drop in national *occupational* sex segregation
between 1970 and 1986. The level of sex segregation at the *job* level in
North Carolina, reported in figure 2.3, is 17.8 percent lower than Bielby
and Baron's (California) level for a slightly longer period. Available job
and occupational segregation estimates show roughly parallel declines
over the last twenty years. This finding is reassuring for two reasons.
First, it suggests that sex segregation in employment at the job level

Table 2.1. Index of dissimilarity for sex- and race-based segregation for a random sample of jobs in North Carolina, 1989

	Sex segregation	Racial segregation
All jobs	76.8	54.8
Jobs with two or more incumbents	76.5	54.3

may in fact be declining. The case studies done by Reskin and Patricia Roos (1990) suggested that occupational integration was accompanied by job segregation within occupations. If we treat seriously the trend line drawn between the Baron and Bielby (1984) estimate and the one from this project, it may be that there has been some significant progress in sex integration in workplaces over the last twenty years. Second, this finding validates further the measure of sex-based (and race-based) job composition in that it shows that job-level segregation is much higher than occupational segregation, a pattern well established in the literature.

The much higher level of segregation found among jobs suggests that there is much job segregation within occupations. Francine Blau (1975) provided a striking example of such job segregation within a single firm. She reported on a shoe manufacturing company with two plants separated by only about thirty miles. In the first plant, *all* of the assembly workers were men and unionized, and they received relatively high wages. In the second plant, *all* of the assembly workers were women and unorganized, and they received much lower wages. Shoe assembly, in this example, was *occupationally* integrated but *job*-segregated. Bielby and Baron (1986) similarly emphasized the near-total job-level sex segregation in their sample, even when there was considerable occupational integration. Reskin and Roos (1990), in a recent study of occupations that appeared to be sex integrating, reported that job segregation within occupations tended to remain quite high. Although many occupational groups are nearly gender-balanced, the degree of segregation is much higher at the job level.

To examine the organizational theories discussed in chapter 4, we need a job-level sex segregation index as well. The index of dissimilarity is a population measure and so cannot generate segregation scores for each observation (i.e., job). Bielby and Baron (1984), the only other researchers with job-level sex composition data, got around this problem by computing *organizational* rather than job sex segregation indexes. This requires sex composition information on *all* jobs in the organization. I did not have information on all jobs in respondents' establishments and so the organizational segregation route was not available.[5]

Figure 2.3. Trends in job and occupational sex segregation

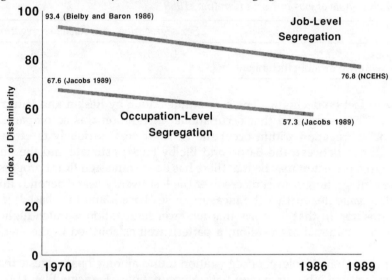

100 = complete sex segregation; 0 = complete sex integration.

The approach used in this study was to compute an index of relative segregation with properties similar to those of the index of dissimilarity; that is, it is 0 with complete integration and approaches 100 under conditions of complete segregation, where segregation is defined as the marginal distributions for the *entire population* (rather than for individual organizations). In this case, the population is defined as the entire North Carolina economy. In North Carolina, 52.6 percent of employees are female.[6] A job has a sex segregation value of 0 when it is 52.6 percent female. Similarly, 21.6 percent of employees are nonwhite, so a job is perfectly integrated when it is 21.6 percent nonwhite. The index has desirable properties of asymmetry and metric change. The utility of the asymmetric nature of the index becomes apparent when we think about racial segregation. In a population that is only 21.6 percent nonwhite, it is substantially easier to create a job that is all white (race segregation = 64) than one that is all black (race segregation = 231). The sex segregation index has the same asymmetric properties, but since the sizes of the relative groups of men and women are similar, the index seems more nearly symmetric. A job that is 100 percent female has a sex segregation index of 95. A job that is 0 percent female has a sex segregation index of 105. Since the proportion black in the labor force is so much smaller, the asymmetry is more pronounced in the relative racial segregation measure used in this study.[7]

The relative segregation index measures the relative deviation of a job from absolute integration, where integration is defined as the actual employment distribution in the economy of women and men and blacks and whites. This formal measure of job segregation is particularly helpful in exploring theories about the organizational sources of job segregation.

The formal index of relative segregation is, however, only a statistical tool for summarizing the degree of sex and racial segregation. Less statistically abstract representations will be used wherever possible. In chapters 3 and 4, multivariate results will be summarized by focusing on simple descriptions of whether a job is relatively segregated or integrated. These descriptions for sex segregation will include *all male, all female, integrated,* and *demographically balanced.* A *sex-integrated* job will be defined as any job that is between 1 and 99 percent female (or male). A demographically sex-*balanced* job, paralleling our formal definition of integration in the index of segregation described above, will be any job that is between 30 and 70 percent female (or male). Thus, this grouping includes those relatively rare jobs in which men and women are nearly equally represented. *Demographically balanced* jobs are also *integrated* jobs, but most *integrated* jobs are not *demographically balanced.*

The same groupings will be used to describe racial segregation. *Racially integrated* jobs are between 1 and 99 percent black. Demographically *racially balanced* jobs are between 11 and 33 percent black. This again mirrors our segregation index, which defined integration as the proportion of the labor force that is black (22 percent). The range is smaller for racial integration than it is for sex integration because African-Americans, unlike women, represent a relatively small group. If the wide range used to define demographically balanced sex-integrated jobs were used for race, then jobs that were only 2 percent black would be defined as racially balanced, clearly an unsatisfying approach.

One consequence of employing a strict demographic definition of balance is that jobs that are filled equally by blacks and whites (50 percent black) are understood to be integrated but not balanced. The approach here is similar to Peter Blau's (1977) random interaction model. In a society where race is not a salient status attribute and where blacks are a relatively small proportion of the work force (as they are in North Carolina), we would expect that the average job would reflect population distributions (i.e., be 78 percent white and 22 percent black). Thus, when a job is 50 percent black, it reflects a fairly dramatic level of racially based sorting. The level of race-based segregation, although not as extreme as sex-based segregation, is quite high. In fact, the average white is in a job that is only 14 percent black, quite a bit lower than the

22 percent one would expect if race were not an important status characteristic for job sorting. The average black is in a job that is 54 percent black, twice what a race-blind job-sorting model would lead us to expect.

One way to make clear the measurement distinctions between the composition of jobs and the two measures of segregation is to use them to examine the distribution of men and women and whites and blacks across major occupational groups.

SEX SEGREGATION IN MAJOR OCCUPATIONAL GROUPS

Table 2.2 reports the sex composition, two segregation measures, and segregation indexes for ten major occupational groups (farmers and members of the armed forces are excluded because there were insufficient cases). The first column lists the sex composition of the occupations. Clerical jobs are clearly dominated by women (81.8 percent female) and craft jobs by men (10.6 percent female). What is most striking about the other eight occupational categories is the nearly equal proportions of men and women in each. All of the other occupational groups are between 40 and 60 percent female. From information on just the sex composition of major occupational groups, one might conclude that integration was the norm and that clerical and craft work were anomalous in their homogeneity.

Nonetheless, the degree of sex segregation within major occupational groups is quite dramatic. The first measure of segregation, reported under the heading *internal segregation index*, is the index of dissimilarity (D) for the occupational groups. The index of dissimilarity takes as its equality baseline the average distribution of men and women within the occupation and then measures how segregated men and women are from each other within the occupation. All occupations have high levels of internal segregation. The lowest level is found among sales workers (D = 44) and the highest among supervisors (D = 91). Sales workers are nearly equally likely to be male or female (53.7 percent female), are often found in mixed-sex jobs (41.0 percent), and have a relatively high probability of being in demographically balanced jobs (20.9 percent). Even given this relatively integrated profile, 44 percent of women (or men) would have to change jobs within sales to achieve demographic balance. By contrast, supervisors, in addition to being slightly disproportionately male (44.6 percent), are extremely unlikely to be in sex-mixed-jobs (13.5 percent) and are almost never in sex-balanced jobs (6.3 percent). Ninety-one percent of male (or female) supervisors would have to change jobs to achieve an equal sex distribution. Clericals have a relatively low index of dissimilarity (D = 58). Although there are very

Table 2.2. Sex composition and job segregation of ten major occupational groups

Occupational groups	Percent female	Internal segregation index (D)[a]	Percent all male	Percent all female	Percent sex-integrated[b]	Percent sex-balanced[c]	Relative segregation index (R)[d]
Managers	41.3	60	52.6	32.1	15.4	10.3	91
Professionals	59.2	66	20.8	29.5	49.7	21.1	75
Technicians	50.5	59	25.4	35.6	39.0	20.3	78
Supervisors	44.6	91	49.0	37.5	13.5	6.3	92
Sales workers	53.7	44	26.9	32.1	41.0	20.9	77
Clericals	81.8	58	11.3	69.8	19.0	5.2	89
Craft workers	10.6	70	72.5	3.4	24.2	5.4	96
Operatives	53.6	83	33.9	39.6	26.4	11.0	87
Laborers	53.5	73	33.3	38.3	28.3	18.3	83
Service workers	51.3	72	25.4	26.2	48.4	29.4	69
All jobs	52.6	76.8	33.3	36.7	30.0	13.6	84

[a]See note 7, chap. 2.
[b]Between 1 and 99 percent female.
[c]Between 30 and 70 percent female.
[d]Modified index of dissimilarity. See note 7, chap. 2.

few male clericals, many of them are in sex-mixed jobs. There do not seem to be any general sex segregation patterns across the remaining occupational groups. Sex segregation within occupations is high everywhere and is not strongly tied to occupational status or authority or even to the sex composition of the occupation.

For all ten occupational groups, the majority of jobs are completely segregated by sex. The percentages in the professional and service occupations are a slim majority, but for most occupations more than 60 percent of the jobs are all female or all male. Jobs with supervisory tasks are least likely to be sex-*integrated*. Clerical and craft jobs, reflecting both their occupational sex composition and internal segregation, are hardly ever relatively *balanced* in their sex composition.

If one were to think of the ratio of sex-*integrated* to sex-*balanced* jobs as a measure of tokenism versus real equality of access to jobs, then tokenism is most common in craft and clerical work, followed by professional and operative occupations. Service workers, managers, and laborers all have high proportions of sex-*integrated* jobs that are also sex-*balanced*. Although managers are rarely in sex-*integrated* jobs (15.4 percent), two-thirds of those jobs are sex-*balanced* (10.3%). By contrast, service workers are relatively likely to be in sex-*integrated* jobs (48.4 percent), and almost two-thirds of those jobs are sex-*balanced* (29.4 percent) as well. Only about a quarter of the sex-*integrated* craft and clerical jobs are sex-*balanced*.

The internal segregation index takes as a given the segregation that is present within the occupation's current labor force. This can be misleading, particularly in the case of clerical and craft work, since they are so strongly sex typed to begin with. The relative segregation index (R) in the last column of table 2.2 is the modified index of dissimilarity discussed in the last section. It takes as its equality baseline the distribution of men and women in the whole labor force, rather than within the particular occupation.

The relative segregation indexes show extraordinarily high levels of segregation across the ten occupational groups. The only exception is service jobs, which are not only relatively balanced in occupational composition (51.3 percent female) but almost 30 percent (29.4 percent) are between 30 and 60 percent female.

Two conclusions can be drawn from this analysis. First, segregation is widespread throughout the occupational structure. As figure 2.4 demonstrates, sex segregation is not associated with high-status or low-status, skilled or unskilled occupations. Most occupational groups have relatively balanced levels of male and female employment (the exceptions being clerical and craft work) but high levels of job segregation.

Figure 2.4. Occupational sex composition by relative job sex segregation within occupations

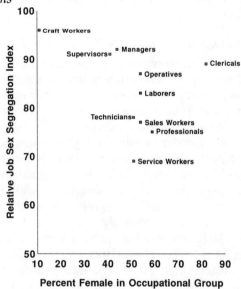

Source: Table 2.2.

This suggests that the sources of sex segregation are unlikely to be in the preferences or backgrounds of labor market entrants. Men and women are almost equally likely to be managers, professionals, technicians, supervisors, sales workers, operatives, laborers, or service workers. The are quite unlikely, however, to work with people of the opposite sex. We will return to this issue in the next chapter.

Second, *integrated* jobs are not necessarily *sex-balanced* jobs. Although 30 percent of all jobs are *sex-integrated*, only 13 percent are *sex-balanced*. Again, the pattern of token integration is not strongly tied to occupational groups in any obvious pattern. On the one hand, people in both high-status (managers) and low-status (laborers and service workers) occupations report relatively high rates of *sex-balanced* jobs given the levels of *sex-integrated* jobs in their occupations. On the other hand, both high-status (professional and craft) and low-status (clerical and operatives) occupations have many more integrated jobs than balanced ones.

Sex segregation is widespread, and although it does vary across occupational groups, no simple explanations based on labor supply, occupational status, or occupational skills seem to fit the patterns depicted in figure 2.4. We shall see in chapters 3 and 4 that analyses at the job, rather than the occupational, level produce more powerful explanations of the processes that lead to sex composition and segregation at the job level.

RACIAL SEGREGATION IN MAJOR OCCUPATIONAL GROUPS

Table 2.3 lists the racial composition, two segregation measures, and segregation indexes for the ten occupational groups. The black population in all jobs is 22 percent. It ranges across occupations from a low of 8 percent among supervisors to a high of 36 percent among service workers. African-Americans are much less likely than their white co-workers to be in white-collar jobs and in higher-skilled jobs.

The degree of intraoccupational segregation is much lower by race than it is by sex. The only exceptions are among managers, where the degree of racial segregation is extraordinarily high (D = 89), and clericals, where both racial and sex segregation are the same (D = 58). Managers and clericals have relatively low levels of within-occupation sex segregation. The lowest levels of intraoccupational racial segregation are among sales workers (D = 40), laborers (D = 43), service workers (D = 43), and professionals (D = 44). Interestingly, sales is also the occupation with the lowest level of within-occupation sex segregation. Service workers and professionals are in-between in their level of sex segregation. The highest level of intraoccupational segregation by far is among managers, followed by supervisors (D = 59), clericals (D = 58), and operatives (D = 58).

Racially *integrated* jobs (44.3 percent) are more common than sex-*integrated* ones (30.0 percent). The probability of finding a racially *integrated* job, however, varies widely across the occupational groups. It is more than 60 percent among operatives and laborers and less than 15 percent among managers and supervisors. White-collar jobs, with the strong exception of managers and supervisors, seem to be somewhat more likely to be both racially *integrated* and racially *balanced* in composition.

Service, laborer, and operative jobs stand out as having very high incidences of racial *integration* but fairly low incidences of racial *balance*. There are no racially *balanced* managerial jobs in the sample. Relative segregation (R) is highest among service, operative, laborer, and manager occupations and lowest in sales and professional occupations. The very high level of relative segregation among service workers reflects the low incidence of racially balanced jobs and the extraordinarily high proportion of all-black service jobs (14.4 percent). This figure is three times as high as the proportion of all-black jobs in the population.

When the racial composition and segregation of occupations are

Table 2.3. Racial composition and job segregation of ten major occupational groups

Occupational Group	Percent black	Internal segregation index (D)[a]	Percent all white	Percent all black	Percent racially integrated[b]	Percent racially balanced[c]	Relative segregation index (R)[d]
Managers	10.7	89	84.6	5.1	10.3	0	77
Professionals	17.4	44	47.4	1.2	51.5	20.5	61
Technicians	20.6	50	49.2	3.4	47.5	15.3	65
Supervisors	8.0	59	83.3	3.1	13.5	5.2	67
Sales workers	17.3	40	52.2	2.2	45.5	25.4	59
Clericals	16.6	58	58.5	6.5	35.1	16.9	68
Craft workers	21.2	53	46.6	4.7	48.6	15.5	68
Operatives	31.9	58	32.6	3.2	64.3	13.1	83
Laborers	30.9	43	35.0	5.0	60.0	11.7	79
Service workers	36.0	43	40.0	14.4	45.6	7.2	96
All jobs	21.6	54.8	50.9	4.8	44.3	14.5	72.0

[a]See note 7, chap. 2.
[b]Between 1 and 99 percent black.
[c]Between 11 and 33 percent black.
[d]See note 7, chap. 2.

Figure 2.5.   Occupational racial composition by relative job racial segregation within occupations

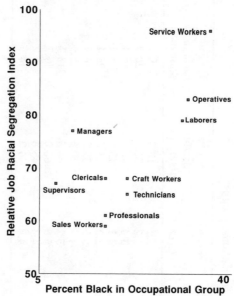

Source: Table 2.2.

examined, some weak patterns emerge that were not apparent for sex composition and segregation. Percent black tends to decline in higher skilled occupations and in occupations with authority over other workers. Intraoccupational racial segregation seems to be more pervasive in occupations with authority. The level of relative segregation, however, shows no obvious patterns regarding skill or authority. This reflects the diverse paths to segregation within occupational groups. Managerial segregation is primarily the result of the exclusion of blacks, secondarily of the existence of all-black management jobs. Although blacks are not excluded from service jobs, there are a disproportionate number of all-black jobs (14.4 percent). In a demographic sense, excluding blacks from a particular job is not difficult since blacks represent only 22 percent of the labor force. The creation of all-black jobs, however, requires fairly extreme organizational practices given the supply of black labor.

Although there are some discernible patterns of racial segregation across these ten occupations, the patterns are weak at best (fig. 2.5). The general conclusions for sex segregation hold here as well. First, although racial segregation is generally less extreme than sex segregation, it is still quite high and present in all occupations. Second, racial segregation is not a function primarily of occupational supply. Except for supervisors and service workers, all *occupations* are roughly racially balanced in their composition. Only in the sales and professional groups are even 20 percent of the jobs racially balanced. Finally, the incidence of racial *integration* is much higher than the incidence of racially *balanced* jobs.

In the next chapter we will examine who is most likely to end up in segregated and integrated jobs. Theories of labor supply that purport to explain the creation of employment structures that further segregation will be examined as well. In chapter 4, theories that attempt to explain the organizational and job processes that lead to or erode segregation will be examined.

CHAPTER 3
DO PEOPLE CHOOSE
SEGREGATED JOBS?

THE THESIS OF THIS BOOK is that segregation is primarily a product of job and organizational processes of status closure. This chapter, however, examines an alternative thesis. Do people choose segregated jobs? Do the supply-side motivations produced by household responsibilities and individual preferences lead to the patterns of sex and racial segregation discussed in the last chapter?

Supply and demand approaches are not inherently contradictory, although much academic discussion is written as if they are. Supply-side explanations focus on the motives of individual labor market entrants, while the demand-side organizational processes discussed in the next chapter focus on jobs and their attributes. It is possible for both sets of processes to be complementary. As we shall see, however, supply-side explanations teach us very little about segregation processes. There are two general theories that provide supply-side explanations of sex and race segregation: human capital theory from economics and socialization theory from sociology.

NEOCLASSICAL ECONOMIC APPROACHES

Many economists assume that sex and racial segregation reflect, at least in part, the preferences and rational choices of labor market entrants. This argument is best developed and most intuitively appealing in reference to sex segregation. The argument is that women expect to devote much of their adult time to children and household work, which leads them to underinvest in human capital. When women enter the labor market, because of current and anticipated household responsibilities, they have less labor force commitment, make lower human capital investments, and self-select into a few female-dominated occupations. Compared with male-dominated occupations, female-dominated occupations, it is argued, have higher starting wages and lower wage growth but a lower depreciation of wages for discontinuous employment and are less demanding of effort both in hours and exertion. In short, the argument goes, women choose women's work, even at some earnings cost, because they want work that is compatible with their actual or anticipated domestic responsibilities (Marini and Brinton 1984; Polachek 1979). Sex segregation, then, reflects women's preferences, which are formed by their rationally weighing their labor market investments against their actual and possible domestic responsibilities.

Thomas Daymont and Anne Stratham summarize the argument (1983:63):

> A potential explanation for occupational segregation is that because women typically bear the major share of nonmarket family responsibilities, they have more constraints than men on the time and energy they can give to the labor market. Having less time to develop labor market skills, they may choose different types of jobs than men.

If women choose occupations that simplify their domestic responsibilities, then why do men not also choose these jobs to simplify their domestic responsibilities? The answer is that men as family members specialize in market work to complement their wives' specialization in domestic work (Becker 1981). Thus, men make the human capital investments and have the labor market commitment that enables them to get the better jobs. Male jobs are better paying because they require more skills. They are male jobs because women have voluntarily segregated themselves into more flexible, less human capital–enhancing, and less well-paying jobs.

This economic model tends to assume that the division of household labor is determined outside the market, generally by historical and biological differences in male and female family responsibility. There is obviously some merit to this assumption; women traditionally do most of the domestic work, and only women can bear and nurse babies. Yet it is only in relatively modern times in industrial labor markets that household work and production work have been carried out in separate spheres (Laslett and Brenner 1989), and there is good historical evidence that the contribution of men to what we would now call housework declined tremendously in the modern period (Cowan 1983). The historical literature suggests that to the extent that men and women specialize in domestic and market work it is not because of biology or ancient history but because members of households are responding to current labor market opportunities. Thus, households supply more male market labor than female market labor when there are children to take care of because males are paid more for possessing characteristics equivalent to those of females. Similarly, husbands may use power derived from their labor market advantage to lessen their domestic work responsibility (Tomaskovic-Devey 1992).

Thus, the human capital argument leads to the expectation that all women, but particularly women with household responsibilities, will choose sex-segregated, preponderantly female jobs. All men, but particularly men with families to support, will choose sex-segregated, preponderantly male jobs. In addition, as human capital investments and labor market commitment rise, both men and women will be more likely to choose jobs that are predominantly male.

The extension of the supply-side model to the creation of racial segregation requires us to drop the assumption that rational choices lead blacks and whites to specialize in different occupations. That would be a potentially racist assumption. The extension to racial segregation requires an a priori admission that historical discrimination is important. In the past blacks as a group had less access to education than did whites, and the education that was available was often of lower qulaity (Farley and Allen 1987: Jaynes and Williams 1989). In addition, since prior labor market discrimination led to low or no returns to education for many African-Americans, some black communities may have developed lower expectations regarding the efficacy of investments in education (Ogbu 1978: Farley and Allen 1987; Jaynes and Williams 1989). Once we admit that past discrimination may be a major motivator of labor force behavior, then a supply-side model can be constructed for race. The rapid convergence in educational achievement by blacks and whites in the post–civil rights era suggests, however, that racial differences in the perceived value of education are not very great, if they exist at all.

Based on the supply-side model, one would expect black men and women with low levels of education to end up in jobs with other people with low levels of education, many of whom would be black. This would lead to an expectation that racial segregation will be the outcome of racial differences in average education but also that racial segregation should be much lower than sex segregation since the process is governed by skill levels rather than by preferences for race-segregated work. According to this model both whites and blacks of low skill should be in predominantly black jobs.

The propositions developed for sex segregation should apply, however, to racial segregation as well. Thus, as family responsibility, labor force commitment, and human capital investments increase, the individual's utility for better jobs should increase and the degree of racial segregation should decline for both blacks and whites. Under these conditions, both blacks and whites have more to gain from the better-paying, higher-skilled jobs that are typically but not exclusively filled by whites. That is, both blacks and whites who have high labor force commitment and investment should seek out more skilled, higher-paying work.

All of those references to choice may be unsettling to some sociologists. In general, neoclassical economic theory paints a much more voluntaristic picture of occupational attainment than does sociological theory. Most sociologists would find plausible the theoretical predictions from human capital theory but would also expect, at least under most circumstances, that they would be empirically trivial. Choice matters when opportunities are abundant. Since the level of sex-segregated employment offered by firms is so high, supply-side explanations are unlikely to be powerful predictors of sex segregation. Since the absolute level of racial segregation is lower and blacks are a smaller fraction of the employed population, choice mechanisms may be stronger in matters of racial segregation in general and for African-Americans in particular.

SOCIALIZATION THEORY

Socialization theory does not assume that rational, income-maximizing motivations lead to sex- or race-based differences in behavior. Socialization theory argues that early childhood experiences teach children gender- (or race-) appropriate behavior. Like human capital theory, socialization theory develops more plausible explanations for gender differences than for racial differences. Socialization theory suggests that women are socialized primarily for adult roles as family caretakers. Encouraging young girls to play with dolls and engage in make-believe domestic chores and keeping them close to home for their play are often cited as examples of this socialization pattern. Boys, by contrast, engage in more career-oriented, independent activities farther from home. Play, as well as many other childhood experiences, foreshadows sex-segregated adult roles. Thus, traditional socialization is seen as leading to female family and male market specialization, as well as to the segregation of adult roles within both realms (Marini 1989; Subich et al. 1989).

Much liberal feminist thought has argued that establishing new socialization patterns is the only, or at least the primary, way to change gender inequality. The socialization perspective suggests that, as we have cohort replacement and younger, less traditionally socialized men and women form families and enter the labor market, gender inequality in the family and the workplace will decline. Although this project can examine only the cohort replacement component of socialization theory, I will return in the conclusion of this chapter to a review of other research that suggests the limitations of this approach.

The socialization perspective predicts that younger workers will be more likely to supply their labor into sex-integrated jobs. This should be true for both men and women since traditional socialization is presumably being eroded for all children, not just young girls.

The translation of the sex role socialization perspective to race is fairly direct, at least in the U.S. South, although the historical period is different. Traditional U.S. race relations, particularly in the South, can be described as a caste system built around occupational, educational, and neighborhood segregation. The civil rights movement has a long history of fighting that segregation and creating an African-American consciousness that is assertive rather than submissive. If it is reasonable to think that traditional sex role socialization was beginning to be eroded in the late 1960s, the caste-based socialization of young African-Americans was seriously challenged at least ten years, but more likely twenty years, earlier. In most places, the caste-based socialization of young whites has probably been seriously challenged only since the late 1960s.

Again, the socialization perspective suggests that since bigotry by whites and submissiveness by blacks should be declining because of the erosion of traditional socialization practices, younger cohorts of blacks and whites should be in more integrated jobs. The change should be most noticeable among whites in the youngest cohorts and among middle-aged blacks. Since entry-level jobs tend to be less segregated (this is discussed in chapter 4), we might be tempted to explain away any cohort integration finding as merely the result of the placement of young people in low-skilled, entry-level jobs. Although there may be some merit to this observation, the absence of historical data on job-level segregation makes it difficult to construct a causal priority. Have young people always been less segregated, or is the historical trend toward decreasing segregation among the young, or both? Jacobs (1989a) suggests that the answer is both. Bielby and Baron (1986) found that sex segregation was lower in entry-level jobs. It is difficult to sort out, however, whether young labor market entrants are more liberal in their attitudes, the jobs are more deskilled, or employer practices have changed. If we find that cohort effects do not hold up in the analyses to follow, then a focus on job and employer attributes may be more reasonable.

We can examine directly the distribution of men and women into sex-integrated jobs. The two qualitative measures of integration, described in the last chapter, are used in the following analysis to examine this supply-side model. The first measure is nominal *integration*, which refers to any job that is not entirely male or white or entirely female or black. The second more restrictive notion of integration refers to any job that is demographically *balanced*. These jobs are between 30 and 70 percent female and between 11 and 33 percent black. First we examine the distribution of men and women into *sex-integrated* jobs based on household constraints. The expectation is that married women, especially those with children, will be more highly represented in sex-segregated jobs. The reverse expectation holds for men.

WHO IS IN SEX-INTEGRATED JOBS?

Table 3.1 shows the percentage of all women and men in the sample who are in integrated jobs, using both the nominal and demographically balanced definitions of integration.[1] Single women are more likely than married women to be in both nominally integrated and balanced jobs. The differences in placement are not great, however; single women are only 2.7 percent more likely to be in gender-balanced jobs and 8.9 percent more likely to be in jobs in which there are some males. Neither of these differences is statistically significant.

More damning for the labor supply explanation of sex segregation is that the presence of children is not associated with significantly more self-selection into female-dominated work. This is even true when we restrict the observations to very young children. In fact, women with children are slightly *more* likely to be in gender-balanced jobs.

If there have been changes in socialization, away from more traditional notions of women's and men's roles, then we would expect sex segregation to decline in younger cohorts. Human capital theory would interpret this socialization perspective in terms of its effects on human capital investments and the formation of preferences. Human capital theory, like socialization theory, sees the formation of preferences as fairly stable over the life course. Thus, in contrast to the labor supply decisions that were made in an earlier era, when women's roles in the labor force were more tightly circumscribed and domestic expectations were higher, one would expect a higher percentage of younger women to be in sex-integrated jobs. Although Jacobs (1989a) found slow decreases in occupational sex segregation across all age groups between 1970 and 1980, change was greatest in the youngest age group. Similarly, Andrea Beller's research (1984) shows greater declines in occupational sex segregation among younger workers.

Table 3.1 reports a clear and statistically significant pattern for both measures of integration. Younger women are in more integrated jobs. The pattern is quite weak for gender-balanced jobs but stronger for

Table 3.1. Family constraints, demographic characteristics, and the percentage of women and men in sex-integrated jobs

	Females		Males	
	Any men	*Gender-balanced*	*Any women*	*Gender-balanced*
Total Population	33.6	15.5	26.5	11.5
Family Constraints				
Married	30.9	14.5	27.4	10.5
Single	38.0	17.2	24.6	13.5
Children	33.0	16.6	25.4	13.7
No children	34.3	14.6	27.4	9.0
Child under 6	31.0	16.0[a]	22.7	11.5[a]
No young child	34.3	13.8	27.6	11.4
Demographics				
Age				
≤25	38.7[b]	**19.4**[b]	15.1	8.1
26–35	34.2	**18.3**	32.0	14.6
36–50	34.6	**13.6**	27.0	9.2
≥51	27.2	**12.3**	30.4	16.1
Race				
White	32.9	**17.1**	26.2	11.1
Black	36.7	**8.9**	27.5	13.0

[a]The young child variable is collinear with any child variable so it is not included in the multivariate model.
[b]The simple bivariate association is significant at the .05 probability level or below. Bold signifies that the association is significant at the .05 probability level or below in the multivariate models that control for other supply-side explanatory variables. See table A3.1 for full models.

nominally integrated jobs, defined as having at least some men. In multivariate models, containing all of the supply-side variables examined in this chapter (except young children and labor force experience, which are too highly correlated with child present and age to include in the models), only the age–gender-balanced relationship is statistically significant.

There are no statistically significant racial differences at the bivariate level in women's placement into integrated jobs. Once family, age, and human capital characteristics are statistically controlled, however, white women do seem to be somewhat more likely than black women to be in demographically gender-balanced jobs. A supply-side explanation might suggest that changes in the socialization patterns among whites away from traditional female employment roles has been more rapid than the changes among African-Americans. This is an implausible explanation since black women have always had much higher labor force participation rates than white women. It seems likely that socialization for paid work has always been stronger in black households than in white households. A more compelling explanation is that there are nested status subordinations here. Where segregation declines, we find traditionally white female work (e.g., secretarial jobs) opening up to black women and traditionally male jobs (e.g., accounting) opening up to white women.

Table 3.1 also provides data on the consequences of family responsibility, age, and race for the placement of males in sex-integrated jobs. Family constraints are unrelated to the probability that men will end up in sex-integrated jobs of either definition. Nor are there discernable age patterns related to the likelihood that men will be in integrated jobs. Black men seem to be slightly more likely to be in nominally integrated jobs, but the difference is not large enough to be statistically significant. Neither socialization nor human capital explanations seem to account for male selection into sex-integrated jobs.

Table 3.2 summarizes the effects of labor market investments and commitment on placement in sex-integrated jobs. The predictions from human capital theory are that as labor force commitment and human capital investments rise women should eschew sex-segregated work and self-select into more integrated settings. Based on my data, however, there are no human capital attributes significantly related to sex composition. We see that gender-balanced integration is higher at the lowest (two or fewer years) and highest (twelve or more years) levels of employer tenure. A similar pattern exists between employer tenure levels and nominal sex integration, but it is even weaker. The results regarding education also are nonsignificant; integration (both measures) is higher among women with low and high levels of education. Most tellingly, part-time work is not associated with higher segregation. About 15 percent of both part-time and full-time jobs are gender-balanced.

What about men? Do men's human capital investments steer them away from sharing jobs with women? There is a negative association reported in table 3.2 between employer tenure and the proportion of men in gender-balanced jobs, and it is statistically significant at the bivariate level. This is the first bivariate association that supports human capital predictions about self-selection into segregated and integrated jobs. In the multivariate models, however, this effect becomes nonsignificant. As their educational levels rise, men are more likely to be in sex-integrated jobs whether integration is defined as demographically balanced or not entirely male. Thus, males who make higher investments in general skills (i.e., education) are more likely to choose jobs

Table 3.2.   Labor market investments and the percentage of women and men in sex-integrated jobs

	Females		Males	
	Any men	Gender-balanced	Any women	Gender-balanced
Total Population	33.6	15.5	26.5	11.5
Education				
Less than H.S.	36.0	21.3	**20.0**[a]	**7.3**[a]
H.S. degree	31.3	15.2	**24.3**	**10.5**
Some college	29.2	7.7	**21.6**	**9.8**
Four year degree	41.3	17.5	**36.2**	**17.2**
Post B.A. degree	47.1	21.1	**41.4**	**17.2**
Experience				
≤ 7 years	40.6	20.3[b]	20.5	13.7[b]
7–13 years	35.0	17.5	33.7	14.0
≥ 14 years	31.5	13.8	25.7	9.8
Employer Tenure				
≤ 2 years	38.5	19.3	25.9	16.4[a]
3–5 years	25.8	10.1	19.4	10.4
6–11 years	32.5	10.8	35.3	11.8
≥ 12 years	34.7	18.6	25.0	6.3
Commitment				
Full time	33.8	15.6	26.1	11.5
Part time	32.9	15.3	32.0	12.0

[a]The simple bivariate association is significant at the .05 probability level or below. Bold signifies that the association is significant at the .05 probability level or below in the multivariate models that control for other supply-side explanatory variables. See table A3.1 for full models.
[b]The experience variable is collinear with the age variable so it is not included in the multivariate model.

that also employ women. This finding is directly contrary to predictions derived from human capital theory. Labor force experience and labor market commitment (i.e., part-time versus full-time status) are unrelated to the sex composition of the job.

It is difficult to find any support for human capital explanations of how men and women self-select into sex-segregated jobs. Out of twenty-eight bivariate comparisons between family constraints, labor force commitment, and human capital investments and the two measures of sex-integrated jobs, only one relationship was statistically signficant for the human capital argument about the creation of sex-segregated jobs at the bivariate level. This one relationship, between employer tenure and gender-balanced jobs, disappears, however, in a multivariate statistical model (see table A3.1 in the appendix to the chapter). Although human capital theory builds a plausible argument about the tradeoffs between family and market work, it is not consistent with the actual distribution of sex-segregated work. The argument must therefore be wrong.

Although my measure of socialization is indirect (age), the data indicate that young women but not young men are more likely to be in demographically balanced jobs. Although the pattern is not a strong one, it is the only supply-side hypothesis from either human capital theory or socialization theory that is statistically significant in multivariate models.

WHO IS IN RACIALLY INTEGRATED JOBS?

To the extent that jobs held by whites are superior to jobs held only or largely by blacks, human capital theory would lead us to expect that as labor market motivation and human capital investments increase everyone will tend to self-select into jobs that are more dominated by whites. For blacks, this movement would be into more integrated jobs; for whites, it would be into all-white jobs. This does not necessarily imply that there is racism, only that workers want to protect their human capital investments. At the same time, if racial segregation reflects employer and organizational practices as well as some general societal-level status closure, then we would not expect human capital predictions to be strongly associated with racial integration.

Table 3.3 focuses on the relationship between family constraints, age, and gender and the probability that whites and blacks will be in integrated jobs. The data indicate that both older whites and older blacks are more likely to be in completely racially segregated jobs. This age effect is statistically significant in the multivariate models, however, only among whites. The age pattern for racially balanced jobs is much more mixed and not statistically significant. The patterns are consistent with predictions based on an expectation that traditional racial socialization practices are declining. Also consistent with the historical argument outlined above, the age pattern is different for the black and white populations. Blacks in the oldest cohort are much less likely to be in integrated jobs than blacks in the younger cohorts. Among whites, the decline in integration occurs among workers age thirty-five and older.

There are no statistically significant family or gender differences in the probability that whites will be in race-integrated jobs. Among blacks, however, the presence of children is associated with a 10 percent higher nominal integration rate, and this relationship is statistically significant in the multivariate model. Among blacks but not whites, being married and *not* having children is associated in the multivariate models with

Table 3.3. Family constraints, demographic characteristics, and the percentage of whites and African-Americans in racially integrated jobs

	Whites		African-Americans	
	Any blacks	*Racially balanced*	*Any whites*	*Racially balanced*
Total population	37.0	12.3	71.4	19.7
Family constraints				
Married	36.0	12.1	74.0	**24.7**
Single	39.0	12.7	68.9	**14.9**
Children	37.1	9.9	**67.4**	**15.1**
No children	36.8	14.3	**77.0**	**26.2**
Child under 6	38.5[a]	10.4[a]	71.8[a]	12.8[a]
No young child	36.5	12.8	71.3	22.2
Demographics				
Age				
≤ 25	**38.8**[b]	11.7	**80.0**[b]	26.6
26–35	**41.5**	11.1	70.6	15.7
36–50	**35.2**	13.7	70.5	25.0
≥ 51	**31.9**	11.5	63.6	9.1
Gender				
Male	27.8	11.0	72.5	23.2
Female	33.9	13.4	67.3	16.7

[a]The young child variable is collinear with any child variable so it is not included in multivariate model.
[b]The simple bivariate association is significant at the .05 probability level or below. Bold signifies that the association is significant at the .05 probability level or below in the multivariate models that control for other supply-side explanatory variables. See table A3.1 for full models.

significantly higher probabilities of being in racially balanced jobs. That being married would lead to more self-selection into racially balanced jobs is consistent with an expectation that marriage encourages more income-maximizing labor market behavior. The finding that the presence of children produces the opposite effect calls that interpretation into question.

Table 3.4 provides data on the relationship between human capital variables and the placement of whites in racially integrated jobs. There are no statistically significant relationships for white workers or any discernable patterns consistent with human capital theory.

Table 3.4 also provides data relevant to human capital predictions for the black population and racial segregation. As their educational levels rise, blacks are more likely to accept jobs in racially balanced settings. This education-integration finding might support a human capital expla-

Table 3.4. Labor force investments and the precentage of whites and African-Americans in racially integrated jobs

	Whites		African-Americans	
	Any blacks	*Racially balanced*	*Any whites*	*Racially balanced*
Total population	37.0	12.3	71.4	19.7
Education				
Less than H.S.	36.5	11.8	75.0	7.1[a]
H.S. degree	40.6	12.4	72.5	**18.8**
Some college	26.6	11.7	61.9	**28.6**
Four-year degree	38.7	13.2	78.6	**35.7**
Post B.A. degree	29.5	11.4	50.0	**25.0**
Experience				
≤ 7 years	39.3[b]	11.6[b]	79.3[b]	31.0[b]
7–13 years	40.8	11.2	79.9	15.4
≥ 14 years	35.0	12.8	64.6	17.7
Employer Tenure				
≤ 2 years	34.7	10.7	**79.2**	22.6
3–5 years	35.1	16.4	**58.1**	16.1
6–11 years	40.3	9.4	**85.2**	25.9
≥ years	38.3	13.1	**61.1**	13.9
Labor force commitment				
Full time	37.2	12.1	73.8	20.6
Part time	35.2	13.6	57.1	14.3

[a]The simple bivariate association is significant at the .05 probability level or below. Bold signifies that the association is significant at the .05 probability level or below in the multivarite models that control for other supply-side explanatory variables. See table A3.2 for full models.
[b]The young child variable is collinear with any child variable so it is not included in multivariate model.

nation; education is strongly linked to age, however, and a final conclusion must await the multivariate analysis. In the multivariate analyses, education in fact is associated with being in racially balanced jobs. Controlling for other individual characteristics, particularly age, I found that the odds of being in a racially balanced job are significantly higher for blacks with some college education, although the advantages decline for those with more than a bachelor's degree.

Blacks with more experience are less likely to be in nominally integrated jobs, a pattern consistent with age and socialization theory. Blacks who work in full-time jobs are much more likely to be in integrated jobs, consistent with human capital theory. There is also a significant association between employer tenure and segregation, but the pattern is distinctly nonlinear. New employees and those who have been with their current employers for six to eleven years are in jobs with much higher integration levels than workers with tenures of three to five and twelve or more years. In a multivariate framework (see chapter appendix), we see that integration rises until about eight years of tenure and then declines dramatically. Consistent with the findings for education, this suggests that there is a glass ceiling above which integrated jobs are quite rare.

HUMAN CAPITAL FINDINGS

The patterns of sex and racial segregation in employment reported in this chapter are not consistent with human capital explanations of labor supply decision making. Human capital explanations are most developed and most plausible when they describe how men and women in families come to make decisions to sex-segregate domestic and market work. It is striking that neither being married and having young children nor working part time affects whether women or men choose sex-segregated employment.

Family constraints are the building blocks from which the whole human capital, new home economics explanation of sex segregation and the male-female earnings gap is built. If family constraints are not associated with the sex composition of jobs, the foundation of the whole theoretical edifice is undermined. Although this study is the first to examine family constraints and job-level measures of sex typicality, other researchers who have looked at occupational sex atypicality have had similar results. Daymont and Stratham (1983) found in a sample of middle-aged women that both marital status and the number and ages of their children were unrelated to whether they worked in sex-atypical occupations. In a more dynamic analysis of women and men of all age groups, Jacobs (1989a) also found that being married and having children were unrelated to the probability of moving into sex-atypical occupations. Rachel Rosenfeld (1983) found the same pattern for women but found that married men were less likely to move from sex-typical to sex-atypical occupations. Bielby (1978), looking at a sample of women who graduated from college in the early 1960s, found that being married was associated with being in sex-typical jobs. Finally, Patricia Brito and Carol Jusenius (1978) found that women who did not have children were more likely to aspire to being in sex-atypical occupations. Although Bielby and Brito and Jusenius found some evidence consistent with the human capital interpretation of women's domestic-occupation tradeoff, the models were quite weak and the findings limited to a pre–women's movement cohort and aspirations rather than actual work.

The former studies are consistent with the findings in this chapter.

Family responsibilities do not seem to govern labor supply in such a way as to create the high levels of sex segregation present in the labor force. Most strikingly, proponents of human capital theory do not even seem to notice when their own models demonstrate that marital status and the presence of children explain none of the male-female wage gap (e.g., Daymont and Andrisani 1984).

It might be argued that all or most women anticipate having family responsibilities whether or not they are currently married or currently have young children and so choose typically female careers. This would account for both the high levels of sex segregation and the absence of variation in segregation among women of different marital and parental statuses. If this more general social role explanation were correct, we would expect sex segregation to decline precipitously among women who have finished their childbearing and child-rearing responsibilities. The age patterns reported in this chapter and in the literature, of course, contradict this expectation directly. Older women and men are most likely to be in sex-segregated jobs.

The research that has already been done on this domestic-market work tradeoff although it is incomplete does lead to fairly strong conclusions. Findings to date do not support the wage depreciation aspects of the thesis (Corcoran, Duncan, and Ponza 1984; England 1982; England et al. 1988; Marini 1989). Women are not selecting typically female jobs to trade higher starting wages for lower wage depreciation when they leave the labor force to have and care for children. Women are just paid less.

The compensating differential argument (Barry 1985; Smith 1979; Filer 1989) has recently been examined by Jennifer Glass (1990) and by Jacobs and Steinberg (1990). The prediction that women will sacrifice upward mobility, wages, and autonomy for sex-typical jobs that offer ease of work and flexibility consistent with their domestic responsibilities gets no support in either study. Glass (1990) finds that as the percentage of females in an occupation rises jobs have less flexibility, fewer unsupervised breaks, and are harder to perform. All these findings are directly contrary to theories that there are compensating differentials in female sex-segregated jobs. These findings are, however, quite consistent with the notion of status composition effects discussed and reported on in chapter 5. Not surprisingly, Paula England and her colleagues (1988), using an extraordinarily restrictive statistical approach, found that the compensating differentials argument does not explain the wage gap between men and women.

Nor are family constraints strongly associated among whites with racial segregation. This is less surprising than the results for sex segregation since family constraints are not directly implicated in a human capital explanation of racial segregation. Rather, would we expect, given the human capital framework, that education and perhaps to a lesser extent age and employer tenure would create the observed segregation patterns, that is, that segregation would be the result of blacks being crowded in lower-skilled jobs. There is no evidence among whites to support this view. Education and tenure among whites are unrelated to a job's racial composition. Among African-Americans, there is more support for this view. As education increases, African-Americans are more likely to be in integrated settings, even racially balanced ones. Thirty-six percent of African-Americans with degrees from four-year colleges are in demographically balanced jobs.

In multivariate models I found that among African-Americans education, tenure, marriage, and being a parent were all predictors of the racial composition of jobs. These patterns were not consistent, however, with any single explanation. Being married and having gone to college were associated with being in more racially balanced jobs, whereas having children was associated with being in all-black jobs. Can it be that childless, college-educated black couples are the most likely to be in integrated settings? Is this a distinct lifestyle?

As tenure with current employer rises, the probability of being in an integrated job also rises, until about eight years of service, after which it falls rapidly. Black employees with twenty years of service are unlikely to be in integrated jobs.

It may be that human capital market models are more applicable to racial segregation than they are to sex segregation. This would be consistent with the finding in the next chapter that market models of statistical discrimination are more powerful in explaining the organizational creation of racial segregation than they are in explaining the sex composition of jobs. This would be surprising, however, insofar as human capital models do not lead to plausible expectations about the family-based sources of segregation that are present in the data and do not predict the curvilinear patterns for job tenure. The finding that higher-educated blacks are in more racially balanced settings is the only finding that is truly consistent with a human capital discussion of the sources of segregation.

SOCIALIZATION FINDINGS

Sex integration was highest among the very youngest women. For both blacks and whites, racial integration was also highest among younger respondents. The cohort patterns were somewhat different for blacks and whites in that segregation among whites was lowest among workers younger than thirty-five and lowest for blacks younger than fifty-one. These patterns are consistent with socialization explanations that lead one to expect that new cohorts with less traditional sex- and race-based expectations will aspire to jobs that are more balanced in their racial and sex composition. The age effects are not strong, however, and only among women and whites are they statistically significant in multivariate models.

The patterns are also consistent with the timing of relevant social movements. Blacks are more likely to be in integrated jobs at older ages than whites. This may be because the civil rights movement raised black consciousness first and affected white consciousness only after public successes. The movement of women into sex-integrated jobs is strongest in the youngest cohort, although there is some movement in the middle-age group (26–50), reflecting the more recent successes of the women's movement. Men's ages and the sex integration of their jobs are not associated, suggesting that if the socialization explanation is correct for these age-integration patterns that changes in male socialization have not yet occurred. Of course, socialization may not be the reason men avoid sex-integrated jobs. As we shall see in chapter 6, there are quite dramatic earnings penalties for males (relative to other males) who are in sex-integrated jobs.

The evidence presented in this chapter is consistent with a historically informed explanation of socialization that sees the erosion of traditional race and sex roles as a result of the civil rights and women's movements. It is important to remember, however, that the patterns are weak. Jacobs (1989a) also found that declines in occupational sex segregation were greatest among the youngest cohort of workers. Although a socialization argument is plausible, it is clearly incomplete. Jacobs (1989a) found that there were declines in sex segregation within all age cohorts between 1970 and 1980. If socialization produces stable personality traits and role expectations, then older cohorts should not exhibit declining segregation levels. In the language of many economists, if preferences are stable across the life cycle and labor market entrants choose to supply their labor to jobs with certain sex or racial compositions, then the primary way for sex or racial segregation to decline is by cohort replacement. Given the great changes in women's labor market behavior in the last thirty years, notions of stable socialization are implausible (Bianco 1992). Socialization and labor supply models cannot explain the decline in segregation within cohorts; nor can they explain the strong findings reported in the next chapter about the importance of organizational processes in the creation of race- and sex-segregated employment.

Jacobs (1989b) provides a thorough empirical critique of the socialization–stable preference labor supply explanations of occupational sex segregation (see also England 1992). He shows that for both men and women preferences for sex-typical work are not stable across the early career. Women's aspirations for sex-typical occupations decrease as they age. Males are much less likely to aspire to typically female occupations but show less of a decrease in these aspirations as they age. According to Jacobs, over a twelve-year period, 60 percent of women aspire to male-dominated occupations at least once. Tellingly for the labor supply perspective, the association between aspirations for a male- or female-dominated occupation and actual occupation is only .21 among all women and a meager .06 among women who have ever changed jobs. Jacobs reports similar fluidity in the sex typicality of college majors and a remarkably weak association between intentions and behavior in choosing college majors.

Irene Padavic (1991) in a study of clerical women invited by their employer to transfer into traditionally male factory jobs found that sex role socialization did not affect whether or not the women chose to move into the "male" jobs. Instead, peer reactions, financial need, and prior mechanical experience, especially in childhood, were important.

Judith S. McIlwee and J. Gregg Robinson (1992) report that an early cohort of female engineers entered the field because they were good in math and someone in high school or early in college advised them that it was an available career option. Nontraditional socialization was not important.

This chapter leaves us without a supply-side explanation of the process that leads people to apply for racially and sex-segregated jobs. Padavic's (1991) work suggests that peer pressure may be important. McIlwee and Robinson (1992) emphasize career information. Jacobs (1989b) suggests that there is a lifelong pattern of social control that rewards gender-appropriate occupational segregation. Susan Hanson and Geraldine Pratt (1991) suggest that the use of personal networks to collect job information might be a potent source of self-segregating behavior. Hanson and Pratt found that women in male-dominated occupations were more likely to have gotten their information about the job from family members than from other sources. Job segregation by race may be particularly tied to the source of job information since racial residential segregation (and so one would assume personal networks) is quite high (Farley and Allen 1987; Massey 1990).

Labor supply explanations of sex and racial segregation, whether based on socialization or human capital theory, are very weak. There is almost no empirical support in my research or in the literature for the human capital explanation of how jobs come to be sex-segregated. There is support in this chapter and in the literature, particularly in England

(1992) and Jacobs (1989b), that socialization, as expressed by age and pre–labor market preferences, may play some role in creating sex- and racially segregated employment structures. That role is a weak one, however, in that labor supply decisions are not the primary source of segregation at the job level. Networks of job information and informal social control by peers probably warrant further examination. Job-level segregation, as we shall see in the next chapter, is primarily a result of organizational processes that either erode or exacerbate societal tendencies toward discrimination and social closure based on race and sex.

Appendix to Chapter 3

The following pages contain the complete regression models on which the conclusions and the tables in the chapter are based. *Percent female* and *percent black* models were not discussed in the text but are presented here. For a coefficient to be statistically significant at the .05 level, it should have a t-statistic higher than 2. R²s for the logistic regressions are taken from comparable ordinary least-square regression equations.

Table A3.1. Regression (percent female) and logistic regression (integrated and balanced jobs) of sex composition on supply-side characteristics (unstandardized coefficients and t-statistics [in parentheses])

	Males			Females		
	Percent female[a]	Integrated jobs[b]	Balanced jobs[b]	Percent female[a]	Integrated jobs[b]	Balanced jobs[b]
Married	−.05 (−.21)	.13 (.42)	−.12 (−.29)	.36 (1.72)	−.27 (−1.22)	−.29 (−.97)
Child	−.07 (−.34)	−.18 (−.67)	−.42 (−1.05)	.11 (.51)	−.10 (−.43)	−.10 (−.36)
Minority	.15 (.60)	.18 (.61)	.32 (.79)	−.02 (−.06)	.14 (.51)	−.96 (−2.16)
Age	.01 (.56)	.00 (.12)	.02 (1.14)	.01 (.06)	−.00 (−.71)	−.03 (−2.38)
Education						
Less than H.S.	−.20 (−.67)	−.30 (−.75)	−.40 (−.64)	−.37 (−1.22)	.29 (.90)	.57 (1.45)
Some college	.04 (.16)	−.11 (−.36)	.33 (.76)	.09 (.36)	.01 (.04)	−.53 (−1.38)
B.A./B.S.	.49 (1.68)	.54 (1.54)	.83 (1.74)	−.25 (−.85)	.44 (1.43)	−.04 (−.12)
Graduate degree	.72 (1.89)	.74 (1.69)	.84 (1.37)	−.48 (−1.00)	.54 (1.08)	.34 (.57)
Tenure	−.03 (−.93)	−.01 (−.21)	−.06 (−.99)	−.02 (−.55)	.01 (.41)	.00 (.02)
Tenure^2	.00 (1.05)	.00 (.51)	.00 (.19)	.00 (.58)	−.00 (−.56)	.00 (.75)
Part time	.14 (.37)	.38 (.82)	−.18 (−.28)	.02 (.09)	−.00 (−.56)	.00 (.75)
Model R^2	.027	.029	.032	.021	.017	.040
N		373			425	

[a] Ordinary least-squares regression, percent female is measured as the logit of percent female.
[b] Logistic regression model.

Table A3.2. Regression (percent black) and logistic regression (integrated and balanced jobs) of racial composition on supply-side characteristics (unstandardized coefficients and t-statistics [in parentheses])

	Whites			Blacks		
	Percent black[a]	Integrated jobs[b]	Balanced jobs[b]	Percent black[a]	Integrated jobs[b]	Balanced jobs[b]
Married	−.13 (−.71)	−.10 (−.50)	.14 (.50)	−.87 (−1.71)	.65 (1.44)	1.29 (2.35)
Child	.04 (.24)	−.01 (−.07)	−.50 (−1.80)	.89 (1.71)	−1.21 (−2.38)	−1.41 (−2.64)
Female	.21 (1.29)	.17 (1.04)	.22 (.92)	−.51 (−1.07)	.61 (1.39)	−.04 (−.10)
Age	−.02 (−1.95)	−.02 (−2.17)	−.00 (−.39)	−.00 (−.15)	−.02 (−1.04)	−.01 (−.38)
Education						
Less than H.S.	−.07 (−.27)	−.09 (−.34)	.12 (.32)	−.44 (−.66)	.76 (1.13)	−.91 (−1.03)
Some College	−.31 (−1.52)	−.15 (−1.45)	.34 (1.11)	.55 (.99)	−.70 (−1.50)	1.00 (1.89)
B.A./B.S.	−.37 (−1.52)	−.10 (−.43)	.14 (.79)	.20 (.24)	.16 (1.62)	1.02 (1.44)
Graduate degree	−.65 (−1.91)	−.37 (−1.02)	.18 (.36)	1.29 (.89)	−1.02 (−.84)	.90 (.70)
Tenure	.03 (1.15)	.02 (.83)	.00 (.00)	−.11 (−1.38)	.16 (1.62)	.07 (.61)
Tenure²	−.00 (−.27)	.00 (.04)	.00 (.19)	.01 (2.36)	−.01 (−1.99)	−.00 (−.96)
Part Time	−.06 (−.23)	−.04 (−.19)	.10 (.27)	.36 (.55)	−.82 (−1.50)	−.20 (−.29)
Model R²	.024	.018	.008	.106	.161	.048
N	643			147		

[a]Ordinary least-squares regression, percent black is measured as the logit of percent black.
[b]Logistic regression model.

CHAPTER 4
WORKPLACE SOURCES OF JOB-LEVEL SEX AND RACIAL SEGREGATION

THIS CHAPTER FOCUSES ON the demand side of the labor market—the organizational production of sex- and racially segregated jobs. We learned in the last chapter that supply-side approaches to segregation provide only weak explanations of the sources of segregation. In this chapter we turn to the behavior of employers and co-workers. Organizational processes are conceptualized to have a logic relatively independent of that of households and socialized individuals.

The two generic explanations that will help to organize our discussion about the creation of segregated employment are statistical discrimination and social closure processes. Both see the exclusion of minorities and women from desirable jobs as the outcome of processes of discrimination at the workplace. They differ in their proposed source of the discrimination (employers versus employers in collusion with advantaged workers) and the scope of discrimination (job-training costs versus all attractive job attributes).

STATISTICAL DISCRIMINATION

The theory of statistical discrimination is associated with human capital and search theories in economics. From human capital theory, it gets the argument that segregation might represent rational reactions of employers to different average productivity and career patterns between groups (Becker 1957). This argument suggests that when firms employ workers with high levels of firm-specific skills, they will prefer more stable labor forces (Williamson 1981).

Search theory explains why employers might translate a preference for more productive workers into discrimination against whole classes of potential employees. Employers, who have limited reliable information at the individual level as to future productivity, use statistical averages, real or perceived, for groups to discriminate between job candidates. Since women and blacks, on average, are perceived to have less stable career patterns, it is economically rational for employers to reserve jobs with high on-the-job training costs for white males (see Arrow 1973a, 1973b; Thurow 1975; and especially the discussion in Bielby and Baron 1986).

This economically rational but discriminatory process leads to the segregation of the work force into jobs of unequally valued skills, which in turn leads to observed inequalities in pay. The general argument for women is that since family responsibilities tend to lead to interrupted career patterns, women are more likely to be concentrated in jobs with low levels of firm-specific skills and on-the-job training (Polachek 1979, 1985). Since African-Americans, on average, are perceived to have lower-quality educational backgrounds and more interrupted careers (leading to less general human capital–enhancing experience), they should be concentrated in lower-skilled jobs (Arrow 1973b). Oliver Williamson (1981) goes beyond a simple productivity notion when he suggests that as organizations increase the formalization of their procedures, the extra training time required to learn the rules of the organization lead employers to prefer white male (i.e., more stable) workers.

The general prediction of the efficiency-based statistical discrimination model is that where there are small differences in productivity between groups, they may become manifest in higher levels of observed segregation. Since the statistical discrimination theory is an efficiency-based theory, however, it predicts as well that over the long term small differences in productivity when linked via segregation to large differences in wages should be eroded by the substitution of cheaper for more expensive labor.

There is not much in the way of direct evidence that white males are actually more productive workers. Many economists infer that they must be more productive since they are paid more, a clearly unsatisfying methodology. Direct evidence is at best anecdotal. There is some evidence that women work harder than men (Bielby and Bielby 1988) and that productivity is *higher* in industries in which high proportions of the labor force are African-American (Galle, Wiswell, and Burr 1985; Tomaskovic-Devey (1988). If there are no real differences in the average productivity rates of women and men or whites and blacks at the aggregate level, then one can no longer claim the statistical discrimination theory is describing a rational, efficiency-based process. Under these conditions, statistical discrimination is reduced to a narrow form of status closure linked to skill and exclusion from on-the-job training.

Just because we reject the *assumption* that there are no differences in group productivity rates does not mean we should reject the notion that *perceptions* of group differences are not widespread. They are. If employers *assume* that white males are more productive, and particularly more stable and easier to train, then we would expect patterns of discrimination in hiring that would be strongly associated with the skills and training time required.

SOCIAL CLOSURE, PATRIARCHY, AND RACISM

The notion of social closure can be traced to Max Weber (1968) but has its fullest contemporary treatments in Frank Parkin (1979) and Raymond Murphy (1988). In general, a status group creates and preserves its identity and advantages by reserving certain opportunities for members of the group. Exclusionary policies ensure that the best positions and most desirable opportunities are reserved for members of more powerful status groups. Discrimination is not merely a matter of prejudice or belief systems but of creating and preserving advantage.

In the sex segregation literature, this idea of social closure is most clearly embodied in the general concept of patriarchy (Hartmann 1976; Reskin 1988; Walby 1986). Patriarchy is the system by which male advantage is preserved. In workplaces, patriarchal practices include excluding women from good jobs and defining whatever work is done by women as less valuable or of lower status. Reskin (1988) argues forcefully that the basic goal in patriarchal workplaces is the preservation of male advantage. Sex segregation is merely a current rule by which male advantage is insured. Sylvia Walby (1986) suggests that segregation has supplanted total exclusion as the primary method for disadvantaging women in the labor force.

Since the patriarchy account is primarily about male privilege, according to this theory, it is male employees as well as male employers who subordinate women. Heidi I. Hartmann (1976), Walby (1986), and Ruth Milkman (1980) have documented a number of instances in which male unions consciously strove to exclude women from desirable jobs. Walby (1986) describes the two main strategies men use to create patriarchy at work: excluding women from paid employment and confining women to jobs that are graded lower than those of men. She notes that these strategies are historically embodied in both trade union and state policies and that employers often go along for the ride.

Cockburn (1988) has developed a more sociologically sensitive account that, while acknowledging the role of male craft unions and professional associations in formally excluding women from some jobs, extends the analysis to the gendered nature of jobs. In her account both people and jobs are gendered, producing powerful social expectations within organizations that encourage gender-appropriate sex-job matches. Mismatches are stressful (see also Kanter 1977) and must be explained. Samuel Cohn (1985), studying a sex-integrating occupation, clerical workers in Great Britain at the turn of the century, describes the organization-specific ideologies that develop to legitimate sex segregation. He also shows that even where unions are not strong enough to force employers to sex-segregate jobs, males as individuals always protest integration. Finally, Cockburn (1991), in a case study of four firms, shows that active male resistance to sex integration and gender equality is commonplace.

The general notion, then, is that males actively strive to ensure their advantage in workplaces. Social closure theory suggests that practices that exclude women from jobs and foster segregation should increase as the desirability of the job increases. Dominants do not strive to monopolize all jobs; they reserve the best jobs for themselves. Competing for desirable jobs is particularly threatening to male advantage and is typically avoided through the creation of segregated employment opportunities. Reskin and Roos (1990), in a study of traditionally male occupations with recent female inroads, find that men tend to leave these occupations because they are no longer attractive or there are better opportunities in other jobs for men at their skill level. Women move in as men move out (see also Cockburn 1988).

According to this explanation, employers can be understood to be forming coalitions with white male workers to exclude women and minorities from desirable jobs (Hartmann 1976; Cockburn 1988; Walby 1986; Wilson 1977). To quote Reskin and Roos (1990:310): "In downgrading women, then, employers take the path of least resistance by following standard procedures, while perhaps appeasing male workers who could make hiring women costly and indulging a shared sex bias."

One reason white male workers' desires for exclusion is widespread may be that the level at which hiring is done is generally close to the job-operation level. Thus, when white women, black women, or black men apply for jobs, they are seen as potential threats to the status not only of the white men at that level but also to those at the next highest level, at which the hiring decision is being made (Hartmann 1976; Reskin and Roos 1990).

Racism can play a similar role in creating and reinforcing white workers' labor force advantage. Ray Marshall (1974) characterizes the general process of racial segregation in the workplace as a desire among whites for social distance from blacks. The main motive for racial segregation is to preserve white status and authority over African-

Americans. Wilson (1978) makes a similar argument to the one proposed by the patriarchy theorists discussed above. His explanation of black subordination in both the South and the North is that it is an attempt by working-class whites to exclude blacks from desirable jobs.

Stanley Lieberson (1980) has shown that the pressure to exclude African-Americans from specific occupations increases with their relative size in the population (see also Blalock 1967). This racial competition hypothesis has been supported in numerous studies (see the review in Fosset, Galle, and Burr 1989). In general, the argument is that the motivation of whites to exclude blacks from desirable jobs is a function of the threat that the minority is perceived to pose to the whites' privileged position (Lieberson 1980; Bonacich 1972, 1976). The racial competition hypothesis also suggests that status closure processes may be somewhat different for segregation by race than by sex. Racially based exclusionary practices should be stronger where African-Americans are a large proportion of the population. Unlike patriarchy, which is ultimately based in households and reinforced in workplaces, racism is created in workplaces and communities and so flourishes in those contexts where competition is greatest.

Since African-Americans are a distinct minority in most places and generally have lower rates of completion of higher education, they are only a limited direct threat to white workers in jobs that require higher levels of education. Thus, racial competition and status closure processes are hypothesized to be strongest for working-class positions. This leads us to expect that as the quality of jobs increases, African-Americans should be more discriminated against. Pressures to segregate white and black workers at comparable job levels should be strongest, however, in working-class jobs.

Research suggests as well that the competition between working-class blacks and whites has been exacerbated by employers, particularly in the American South (Reich 1981; Bloom 1987; Wilson 1978). Race-based social closure processes may be weaker in labor markets with small black populations and for jobs where there are few qualified black applicants. Because women are more numerous and spatially evenly distributed and have educational qualifications similar to men's, they represent a status threat throughout the job hierarchy.

Many authors have argued that sex or racial segregation can be understood to be a process of segregation by rank in which higher-skill, opportunity, or authority positions are reserved for men (Bielby and Baron 1985; Cockburn 1988; Walby 1986; Halaby 1979; Malkiel and Malkiel 1973; Roos and Reskin 1984; Wolf and Fligstein 1979b) and/or whites (Doeringer and Piore 1971; Kaufman 1986; Lieberson 1980). This literature emphasizes that the importance of status closure increases as the general attractiveness of jobs increases. In jobs with low levels of skill, power, or opportunities for promotion, we expect to find more blacks and women but also less segregation. As skill, power, or opportunities for promotion rise, we expect the tendencies toward social closure to increase and that there will be fewer blacks and women *and* more segregation. Thus, the women and blacks in high-skill, high-authority positions will tend to be in positions with other women or blacks (e.g., nursing supervisors or clergy in black denominations) or in idiosyncratic jobs (e.g., affirmative action officers). As mentioned earlier, the historical literature on U.S. race relations makes the opposite prediction—racial competition and so segregation are expected to be greatest in low-skill jobs. The fragmentation of tasks, creating a few specialized integrative jobs and a larger number of fragmented, repetitive, and standardized jobs, makes the creation of segregation by rank possible as well. We also expect jobs with many incumbents, because they are more likely to be fragmented and routinized in nature, to have increased subordinate status as well as less segregation.

The patriarchy and racism analyses of sex and racial segregation focus on specific instances of the more general status process of social closure. Thus, a social closure understanding of sex and racial segregation leads us to expect segregation anywhere there are general societal distinctions by status that create patriarchal or racist environments. Unlike statistical discrimination theory, which is narrowly focused on training costs and employer motivations, social closure theory predicts that status-based attempts to preserve male and white privilege will be widespread. Reverse discrimination charges notwithstanding, race-based exclusionary practices may be weaker in jobs requiring the highest educational credentials, where African-Americans are demographically scarce and therefore unlikely to be a serious threat to white privilege.

SOCIAL CLOSURE STRATEGIES

Social closure is an active strategy of superordinates—not a foregone conclusion.[1] That is, segregation should vary as a function of the motivation and capacity of males or whites to enforce segregation. If there are organizational locations where we would expect patriarchal and racist practices to be weaker, then there should be lower levels of exclusion and segregation. Where there are cultural or organizational structures that enhance or retard the operation of patriarchal and racist goals, segregation should vary accordingly.

CULTURAL VARIATION

Places vary in their cultural expectations of sex- or race-based social closure. There is evidence that the degree of occupational segregation by race in the United States is highest in the South (Fosset, Galle, and Burr 1989; Semyonov, Hoyt, and Scott 1984) and that sex segregation in jobs (Rogers and Gudy 1981) and voluntary organizations (McPherson and Smith-Lovin 1986) is higher in smaller towns and rural areas. The interpretation in both cases is that there are cultural and regional differences in the degree to which both status distinctions and therefore status-based segregation are normative.

The sources of this cultural variation can be complex. Two important sources are likely to be economic competition and political power processes. Where the civil rights or women's movement has been strong, for example, we might expect a general erosion of both beliefs and institutional practices that support differentiation based on sex and race. The economic threat hypothesis, which contends that economic competition and perceived threat by the white population rises with the percentage of blacks in the population, is probably also a fundamental source of cultural variation across regions and over time. Jack Bloom (1987) has argued that elites in the U.S. South have fought to maintain the racial caste system longer and stronger in rural areas. This is because the legacy of the antebellum slave-based plantation and postbellum free-black sharecropping systems in these areas is a political economy based on cheap black labor.

COMPETING MARKET PRINCIPLES

Neoclassical economic theory has identified a competing principle to sex- and race-based social closure, namely, capitalist competition and profit goals. According to this argument, in general, sex- and race-based exclusion from good jobs should be undermined by economically rational capitalists hiring cheaper female and black labor. Over time, competitive market pressure should erode segregation and eventually race- and sex-based inequalities (Becker 1957). This argument leads to the prediction that only firms that are isolated from market pressure (i.e., that operate in oligopolistic or otherwise protected markets) will have the resources to indulge their "tastes for discrimination" for very long.

Although not proceeding from neoclassical economic assumptions, Cohn (1985) views what he calls "buffering from labor costs" as an important source of the growth of female employment in clerical jobs. He argues that as labor costs rise as a proportion of all production costs—that is, in labor-intensive firms and numerically large occupations within firms—the pressure to substitute low-cost (female) for high-cost (male) labor rises. Thus, we can expect that tastes for discrimination should be eroded when there is money to be made or at least when the cost of not hiring the cheaper low-status labor becomes prohibitive.

There is, in fact, good evidence that as total labor costs rise employers hire more female and minority workers. Henry Jay Becker (1980) found that the percentage of blacks tended to increase in numerically large occupations within firms and when occupations represented a high proportion of total firm employment. Bielby and Baron (1986) had a similar finding for women. Following the neoclassical logic, this should be true as well when general pressures for profitability are created through market competition. On the one hand, Michael Wallace and Arne Kalleberg (1981) and William Bridges (1980, 1982) found that the percentage of females is highest in labor-intensive industries with firms of larger than average size (interpreted as those with higher labor demand). On the other hand, Robert Kaufman (1986) and I (1988) both found that the likelihood of a firm hiring African-Americans was positively related to the average profitability of the industry in which the firm operated. This finding is inconsistent with cost-pressure accounts, although if minority hiring were used to lower labor costs it could conceivably have the effect of increasing profitability.[2]

ORGANIZATIONAL STRUCTURE

The observation that there are social tendencies toward sex- and race-based social closure practices does not imply that the opportunity to segregate is a constant. One argument is that the fragmentation of tasks implied by bureaucratization leads both to opportunities to segregate and to an enhanced motive to engage in strong social closure practices (Cockburn 1988). The motive increases with bureaucratization because there is increased differentiation by rank, skill specialization for relatively unique jobs, and deskilling and fragmentation of mass-production jobs. Bielby and Baron (1986) argue similarly that as task differentiation increases, the degree of segregation increases as well because it becomes more practical to proliferate job titles and thereby socially isolate women and men in different jobs.[3]

Bielby and Baron (1984) found that smaller and larger firms had higher levels of sex segregation than medium-sized firms. They interpreted this finding as evidence that there are constant societal tastes for discrimination, which they said produce firm-level segregation in small firms since there is little task differentiation, and segregation at the job level in large firms through the proliferation of sex-segregated job titles. Medium-sized firms (20–100 employees) become more integrated by default—they are too large to indulge their tastes for discrimination and too small to have an effective bureaucratic process of differentiation. Segregation in large firms requires a certain administrative capacity to link social distinctions to job titles and so we expect an inverted U pattern for the relationship between firm size and segregation.

The discussion of firm size leads to discussions of the role of bureaucracies in the creation of segregated jobs. Bielby and Baron's (1984) interpretation of their nonlinear firm size–sex segregation pattern is that bureaucratization enhances an organization's ability to conform to societal or white male employees' pressures or employer tastes for discrimination. One might speculate, however, that one aspect of bureaucratization—formalization of the employment relationship—might help reduce segregation if it made job-bidding processes more open to public scrutiny and insofar as more formalized employment relationships are characterized by clear job definitions and procedures for hiring and promotion that act as external logical alternatives to the sex and race of job applicants when hiring decisions are made. Robert Szafran (1982), after reviewing a largely case study literature, concludes that job segregation declines as formalization of the employer-employee relationship increases.

SUMMARY OF EXPECTATIONS

Statistical discrimination theory argues that as required skills and training costs increase, firms make efficiency-based hiring decisions to exclude members of suspect status groups. Unlike the more sociologically informed theories, statistical discrimination theory sees employment segregation as the outcome of generally rational, if exaggerated, attempts by employers to reduce the costs of employee screening under conditions of imperfect information. Statistical discrimination theory makes no specific predictions about job segregation.

The skill requirements of a job are measured using three variables: credentials required for the job, measured in educational degrees (Required Credentials); prior experience requirements for the job (Prior Experience); and training time required to learn to do the job well (Training Time). In addition, there is a variable for the presence of a company training program for the job (Firm Training). The appendix to the book gives the means and standard deviations for all these measures.

The social closure hypothesis states that pressures for social closure increase as the relative value of a job goes up. Women and blacks, it is predicted, will be more likely to be excluded from jobs that are not fragmented and routinized or that have more organizational power, more internal labor market opportunity, or higher levels of job skill. The level of segregation, as distinct from the sex or racial composition of the job, should rise as well with job desirability. There is an alternative prediction that racial segregation will be highest in jobs with low-skill levels. This is based on the historical literature, which suggests that the working-class racial competition fostered by white elites leads to pressures by whites for segregated jobs.

The statistical discrimination and social closure approaches can be differentiated in that statistical discrimination theories focus only on a firm's training costs whereas the social closure hypothesis refers to all dimensions of job ranking—skill, power, internal labor market opportunity, and fragmentation. In addition, according to the social closure hypothesis, pressures for *exclusion* will increase with the quality of the job and levels of *segregation* will rise at higher ranks as well, irrespective of the sex or racial character of the job. Statistical discrimination theory makes no such prediction. In addition to job skill (measured as required education and training time), social closure pressures should be tied to supervisory power, opportunity for promotion, and the fragmentation of jobs through detailed divisions of labor.

Organizational rank and authority (power) is measured with a seven-item summated scale.[4] The items include formal supervisory authority, supervising someone else who also has supervisory authority, responsibility for deciding subordinates' pace of work, independent authority to hire a subordinate, budget authority, and ability to change products, programs, or services significantly.[5]

Opportunity for promotion is measured using a three-item summated scale. The items tap the degree to which the respondent's job can be interpreted to be on a job ladder. The questions ask whether anyone in a similar job has been promoted in the last year, whether the respondent thinks he or she may be promoted in the next year, and whether the respondent agrees with a statement that suggests that one works hard to get a raise or promotion.

Job fragmentation is measured by the number of people in the job title. This is the same measurement strategy pursued by Bielby and Baron (1984). Job titles with fewer people associated with them are easier to segregate.[6] Thus, as the number of people in a job increases, segregation should decrease. At the same time, jobs with many people in them are likely to be the most fragmented and routinized within a firm's division of labor.

Employees can be expected to vary in their capacity and motivation to exclude and segregate women and minorities. Countries, regions, and communities may vary in their cultural expectations of race- and sex-based social closure. Specifically, the literature leads us to expect that more traditional belief systems are stronger in rural areas and in the U.S. South. Since the data employed in this analysis are for North Carolina only, only urban-rural differences will be examined empirically. Urban location (Urban) is measured as the size of the place where the respondent lives. It is coded as follows: (1) rural/open country, (2) small town, (3) large town/small city, and (4) large city.[7]

Although some aspects of bureaucratization may enhance segregation, we might expect the formalization of the employment relationship to increase the hiring of minorities and women and to reduce segregation by making explicit and accountable the hiring and promotion decision-making process. The formalization (Formalization) of organizational employment relations is based on four questions. The questions ask whether the respondent received a formal letter of appointment, a written job description, or a contract and whether there is an employee handbook. The items were selected from the Aston formalization scale (Pugh et al. 1968).

Neoclassical economic theory suggests that market competition, by creating pressures for profitability, will force firms to substitute lower-cost female and black labor for white male labor and over the long term eliminate segregation. Profit pressures may thus undermine costly tastes for discrimination among employers. It is particularly plausible that jobs that represent large proportions of the total labor costs in firms with high profit pressures will be most likely to be filled by lower-cost females or blacks. Overall segregation may be unaffected, however, if other more specialized jobs are reserved for superordinate employees.[8]

Profit pressures are measured by characterizing the industry as in the competitive sector, the oligopolistic sector, or the government and nonprofit sector.[9] Given neoclassical economic logic, we would expect segregation to be highest in the state sector, followed by the oligopolistic sector, and lowest in the competitive sector, where profit pressures are highest.

Jobs that create profit pressures will be measured as the total number of people with the reference job title divided by establishment size (Relative Number). As the number of people with a job title increases as a proportion of total labor costs, it represents an increased internal source of profit pressure.[10]

The final theorized source of variation in the sex and racial composition of jobs focuses on the capacity of organizations to exclude women and minorities and, once they are hired, to segregate them. As organizations increase in size, excluding minorities and women from the labor force becomes impractical. The sheer problem of finding sufficient workers mitigates against complete segregation. The pressures of labor costs, and thus the attractiveness of lower-cost female and minority labor, can be expected to rise with establishment size for similar reasons. The capacity to segregate may decline at intermediate sizes, however. It is only after organizations get large enough to proliferate formal job titles, institute technical divisions of labor, and the like that they are able to resegregate.

Establishment size, again following Bielby and Baron (1984), is measured using three size categories. All organizations with fewer than twenty employees are Small Size. All establishments with one hundred or more employees are Large Size. The comparison category is Medium Size, where we expect higher levels of integration.

We will focus on three job status composition measures each for sex and race. The first is percent female and percent nonwhite in the job.[11] The second measure is the relative segregation index, discussed in chapter 2.[12] It measures the degree of job-level separation by status distinction. The segregation index is a measure of the relative deviation of the job from balanced integration, where integration is defined as the average employment distribution in the economy for the status attribute. Thus, it does not matter if the job is filled by males or females or whites or blacks but the degree to which the rate represents a deviation from complete demographic balance between whites and blacks and men and women. The third measure captures whether or not the job is sex- or race-balanced. Status composition tells us about exclusion from desirable jobs. Segregation tells us if tendencies toward status separation increase for better jobs. Status balance helps us understand whether the general processes that create job status composition and segregation also explain the relatively rare occurrence of demographic balance. Descriptive statistics on all these measures can be found in chapters 2 and 3.

To test the utility of statistical discrimination and social closure strategies, a series of multivariate regression models were estimated.[13] As in the last chapter, the multivariate models will be the bases of substantive conclusions, but tables and figures within the chapter will present simple descriptive statistics. The tables also indicate whether the relationships between Percent Female, Percent Black, Sex Segregation, Race Segregation, Sex-Balanced Job, Race-Balanced Job, and the organizational and job explanatory variables are statistically significant.[14] It is the presence or absence of statistical significance in multivariate models (indicated with bold numbers in the tables) that is used to reach conclusions about the adequacy of theoretical predictions. As in the last chapter, full statistical models can be found in the appendix to the chapter.

SEX AND RACIAL COMPOSITION

Tables 4.1 and 4.2 report the results for the analysis of both percent female and percent black in the jobs. I will focus first on organizational capacity to discriminate.

On average, both the competitive (51 percent) and oligopolistic (50 percent) sectors have lower proportions of females in their jobs than does the state sector (59 percent). This is the opposite of predictions based on neoclassical market models. The difference between the oligopolistic sector and the competitive sector is trivial and not statistically significant. Further, once job characteristics are statistically controlled, none of the differences is significant, suggesting that differences in how the work is organized between sectors has created the significant differences in sex composition.[15]

As expected, as establishment size rises so do the proportions of women in jobs. Place size is not significantly related to percent female in the job, but percent female in the job rises significantly with the level of formalization. Informal jobs average 48 percent female, but jobs with high formalization average 55 percent female.

I turn now to issues of job quality. Women are much less likely to be in jobs with high levels of power over other people, opportunity for promotion, or long training periods. Women are quite likely to be in (nominal) supervisory jobs without any power. These results strongly support the social closure hypothesis. The interpretation of training time that it represents rational statistical discrimination by employers can be ruled out since the direct measure of a training program is not statistically significant in this model and is only marginally significant at the zero-order correlation level. More important, proportion female in a job tends to *increase* with required educational credentials. Fragmentation is the only measure of job desirability not significantly associated with percent female in the job.

Neoclassical and statistical discrimination predictions do not seem to account for the sex composition of jobs. The overall demand for labor (establishment size) and the skill, power, and mobility potential of jobs seem to be the primary determinants of sex composition. These results fit a pattern whereby employers use female labor because it is cheaper but do not allow most women access to the better jobs in the firm.

Tables 4.1 and 4.2 also report the results for the analysis of percent black. We see as predicted that percent black in jobs rises with establish-

Table 4.1.   Percent female and percent black in jobs and organizational characteristics (N = 764–770)

Organizational characteristics	% female	% black
Sector		
Competitive	**50.8**[a]	**17.3**[b]
Oligopolistic	**49.9**	22.2
State	**58.7**	27.7
Establishment size		
Small (≤20)	**48.2**[b]	**16.1**[b]
Medium (21–100)	**55.4**	20.5
Large (≥101)	**53.6**	26.2
Place size		
Rural/open country	51.7	**17.7**[b]
Small town	52.7	25.3
Large town/small city	51.4	19.8
Large city	56.1	26.1
Formalization		
None	48.2	**14.6**[b]
Low	52.6	22.3
Medium	53.9	22.9
High	55.2	27.7

[a]**Bold** indicates a significant association at the .05 probability level. Regressions are reported in the chapter appendix.
[b]Significantly associated at the .05 probability level with percent female or percent black at the bivariate level.

ment size. African-Americans represent 16 percent of the employees of small firms, compared with 26 percent of the large firms.

Percent black in the job is lowest in the competitive sector (17 percent), followed by the oligopolistic sector (22 percent), and highest in the state sector (28 percent), directly the opposite of neoclassical predictions. Percent black in the job is also higher in more urban areas. Although not reported in table 4.1 (see table A4.1), the interaction of jobs with relatively large numbers of incumbents and sector is statistically significant. As jobs grow as a proportion of total establishment size, they have *higher* proportions of blacks in the state sector but *lower* proportions in the oligopolistic and competitive sectors. Again, this is the opposite of competitive market predictions. As we saw for gender, organizations with more formalized employee relations also tend to have higher percentages of blacks.

Turning to job characteristics, we see that the percentage of blacks rises dramatically with increased job fragmentation and drops with higher required credentials. It also drops with higher employer-pro-

Table 4.2. Percent female and percent black in jobs and job characteristics (N = 764–770)

Job characteristics	% female	% black
Power		
None	**56.9**[a]	24.7[b]
Nominal supervisor	**65.0**	28.0
True supervisor	**50.2**	15.8
Nominal manager	**45.5**	16.1
True manager	**19.2**	9.9
Job size (fragmentation)		
1 incumbent	51.8	**12.6**[b]
2–10 incumbents	51.0	**20.8**
11–30 incumbents	54.8	**30.2**
31–70 incumbents	67.2	**35.2**
≥ 71 incumbents	48.5	**35.9**
Promotion opportunity		
0 (no mobility)	**65.9**[b]	19.8[b]
1	**52.3**	19.5
2	**49.6**	23.9
3 (high mobility)	**40.6**	25.3
Training time		
0–1 week	**70.0**[b]	32.5[b]
2–5 weeks	**62.5**	29.1
6–26 weeks	**62.7**	25.1
27–52 weeks	**53.5**	21.9
≥ 53 weeks	**36.5**	13.3
Required credentials		
Less than high school	**54.9**	32.7[b]
High school	**51.7**	24.6
High school plus	**49.6**	12.3
Two-year college	**58.8**	12.5
Four-year college	**53.6**	19.6
Professional/graduate	**35.1**	4.2
Firm training		
None	53.7	20.2[b]
Some	47.8	27.5
Prior experience required		
No	**61.2**[b]	24.7[b]
Yes	**48.5**	20.0
Relatively large job (percent of establishment employment)		
1–20%	52.1	**20.9**[c]
21–40%	53.5	**20.3**
41–67%	52.1	**23.5**
68–100%	51.3	**22.0**

[a]**Bold** indicates a significant association at the .05 probability level. Regressions are reported in the chapter appendix.
[b]Significantly associated at the .05 probability level with percent female or percent black at the bivariate level.
[c]Relatively large has a significant interaction with sector.

vided training time. Of the three variables, fragmentation (absolute job size) is the strongest determinant of racial composition in these analyses.

It seems that fragmented and deskilled jobs are more likely to be filled by minorities and jobs that require high levels of education are less likely. The measure of relative labor cost (Relatively Large) is not associated with racial composition. Interestingly, neither power nor opportunity for promotion is associated with racial composition once we have controlled for job size and skill.

SEX AND RACIAL SEGREGATION

Tables 4.3 and 4.4 focus on the processes that lead to the level of sex and racial segregation in jobs. Sex segregation is lower in the state (80) and competitive (84) sectors than it is in the oligopolistic sector (88). Table A4.1 reports significant interactions between relative job size (Relatively Large) and sector. Here we find that in the state sector jobs become more integrated as they become a larger proportion of total employment. In the two private sectors, jobs become less integrated under the same conditions. This is, again, the direct opposite of neoclassical competitive market model predictions.

Consistent with local and organizational culture predictions, sex segregation is lower in more urban areas and more formalized firms. Sex segregation also declines with establishment size rather than following the expected pattern of falling in medium-sized firms and rising in larger ones. This effect of establishment size is created through job fragmentation, which has a very strong relationship to the level of sex segregation. This means that large firms create more specialized divisions of labor, including standardized jobs with many incumbents. It is these jobs that are more sex-integrated.

Both increased on-the-job training time and a job requirement of prior experience are associated with higher levels of sex segregation. Required credentials show a strong curvilinear relationship with sex segregation in which it first rises and then falls. In general, sex segregation is most influenced by organizational and opportunity constraints, although it does seem to increase in jobs with higher skill requirements and in less fragmented jobs. Table A4.2 in the appendix to the chapter reports the interaction of fragmented (absolutely large) jobs with required credentials for sex segregation. Here we see that although jobs with many incumbents are *less* segregated (Fragmentation) and jobs with high required educational credentials are *more* segregated, segregation is highest when jobs with high credentials are absolutely large in terms of numbers of incumbents. These latter jobs would most likely be semipro-

Table 4.3. Sex segregation and racial segregation of jobs and organizational characteristics (N = 764–770)

Organizational characteristics	Sex segregation	Racial segregation
Sector		
Competitive	**83.9**[a]	**68.4**
Oligopolistic	**88.4**	**74.4**
State	80.3	**74.8**
Establishment size		
Small (≤20)	89.6[b]	**74.6**
Medium (21–100)	82.4	67.5
Large (≥101)	82.2	73.3
Place size		
Rural/open country	85.6[b]	65.4
Small town	88.3	81.8
Large town/small city	83.5	66.7
Large city	75.8	76.5
Formalization		
None	87.7[b]	73.6[b]
Low	87.3	71.6
Medium	82.8	70.6
High	76.6	77.6

[a]**Bold** indicates a significant association at the .05 probability level. Regressions reported in the chapter appendix.
[b]Significantly associated at the .05 probability level with sex segragation or racial segregation at the bivariate level.

fessional, such as computer programming, nursing, and teaching in primary and secondary schools. Overall fragmentation is the strongest cause of segregation in the analysis.

Tables 4.3 and 4.4 also report the results of analyses for the racial segregation of jobs. The competitive sector has significantly less racial segregation than the oligopolistic sector, which in turn has marginally less than the state sector. Size has a significant relationship to racial segregation, and it displays the curvilinear pattern found by Bielby and Baron (1984) for sex segregation in their sample of California firms. Racial segregation is higher in large and small firms than it is in medium-sized firms. Community size and formalization are not related to the degree of racial segregation.

Fragmented jobs are less racially segregated. Jobs that require more advanced credentials are also less segregated, but the effect is curviliear; the curve first declines as education rises and then increases at the highest education levels. As training time needed to master a job increases, racial segregation declines. Conversely, when there are firm-

Table 4.4. *Sex segregation and racial segregation of jobs and job characteristics*
(N = 764–770)

Job characteristics	Sex segregation	Racial segregation
Power		
None	83.5[a,b]	74.4
Nominal supervisor	82.8	80.0
True supervisor	86.7	61.6
Nominal manager	82.6	69.7
True manager	93.5	72.1
Job size (fragmentation)		
1 incumbent	99.9[c]	84.9[b]
2–10 incumbents	81.0	66.8
11–30 incumbents	78.5	67.7
31–70 incumbents	63.8	76.2
≥ 71 incumbents	74.8	60.2
Promotion opportunity		
0 (no mobility)	87.1	72.4
1	83.8	69.4
2	84.2	77.1
3 (high mobility)	82.5	70.3
Training time		
0–1 week	89.2[b]	99.9[b]
2–5 weeks	80.2	81.3
6–26 weeks	82.8	72.5
27–52 weeks	85.9	67.3
≥ 53 weeks	87.2	64.6
Required credentials		
Less than high school	77.6[c,d]	86.9[b,d]
High school	85.1	75.3
High school plus	94.5	57.6
Two-year college	88.9	63.7
Four-year college	79.3	68.3
Professional/graduate	82.5	61.7
Firm training		
None	85.3	70.6
Some	80.4	77.9
Prior experience required		
No	79.5[b]	73.0
Yes	86.8	71.5
Relatively large job (percent of establishment employment)		
1–20%	87.8[e]	71.5
21–40%	83.0	72.0
41–67%	83.3	70.5
68–100%	82.9	73.3

[a]**Bold** indicates a significant association at the .05 probability level. Regressions reported in the chapter appendix.
[b]Significantly associated at the .05 probability level with sex segregation or racial segregation at the bivariate level.
[c]Fragmentation has a significant interaction with credentials.
[d]The relationship between credentials and both sex and racial segregation is curvilinear (see fig. 4.1).
[e]Relatively large has a significant interaction with sector.

level formal training programs associated with a job, racial segregation increases significantly.

The curvilinear relationship between required credentials and sex and racial segregation bears further examination. Figure 4.1 charts the relationship between required credentials and sex and racial segregation. Racial segregation decreases with more advanced credentials but at a declining rate. The lowest level of reported racial segregation is at the four-year college degree level. Racial segregation is slightly higher for people with graduate-level degrees. By contrast, sex segregation increases as credentials increase, peaking for those jobs that require post–high school training in a skilled trade. They decline thereafter. The lowest reported levels of sex segregation are associated with jobs that require less than a high school degree.

Sex-Balanced and Racially Balanced Jobs

The final set of analyses focuses only on those jobs that are demographically balanced. Race-Balanced and Sex-Balanced are dichotomous dependent variables and are regressed in logistic analyses on the variables we have been examining (see table A4.3). A job is defined as sex-integrated if it is between 30 and 70 percent female. A job is defined as racially integrated if it is between 11 and 33 percent minority.[16] Tables 4.5 and 4.6 report the results of the analysis. Only 13 percent of the jobs are sex-balanced by this definition. Fourteen percent are racially balanced.

The state (15 percent) and competitive (15 percent) sectors are more likely than the oligopolistic sector (10 percent) to produce truly sex-balanced jobs. Large cities (24 percent) are much more likely to produce sex-balanced jobs than rural areas (12 percent). Formalization and firm size are not significant causes of the creation of sex-balanced jobs.

Fragmented jobs (titles with many incumbents) are also likely to be sex-balanced. Again, sex-balanced jobs have a curvilinear relationship to required credentials. Sex balance is most rare at the apprenticeship/some college but no degree level and most prevalent at the less than high school and postbachelor's levels. Jobs that require prior experience are 8 percent less likely to be sex-integrated than those that do not. Job power, promotion opportunity, and training time are unrelated to the creation of sex-balanced jobs.

As firms get larger they are less likely to create racially balanced positions. There are no significant sector differences. Nor does it matter whether the workers live (and work) in rural or urban areas. Formalization of the employment relationship, however, is an important source of racial balance. Organizations with highly formalized employment

Figure 4.1. Relationship between required educational credentials and sex and racial segregation

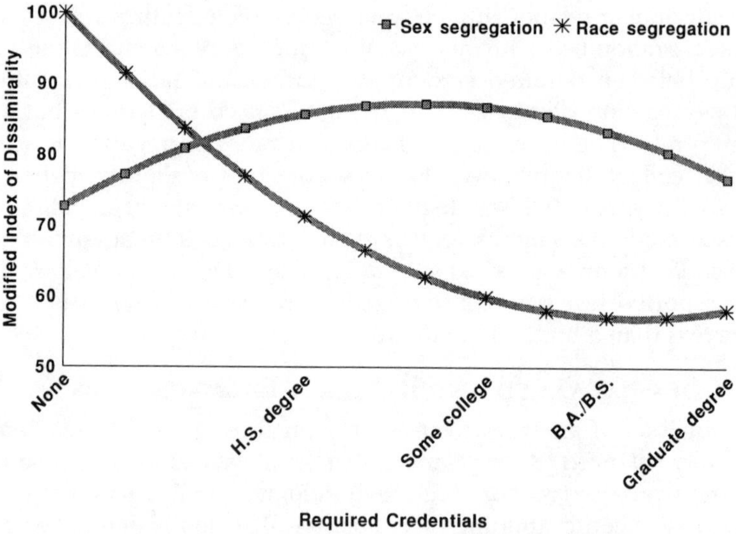

Required Credentials

100 = complete segregation.

relationships are three times more likely to have racially balanced jobs than those that are completely informal.

Again, larger jobs with more incumbents (fragmentation) are more likely to be racially balanced. In fact, one-third of job titles with more than seventy incumbents are racially balanced in composition. There is a weak curvilinear relationship between required credentials and the odds of a job being racially balanced. The degree of balance is at its highest at the post–high school but no college degree level and falls at advanced-degree levels.

This pattern is somewhat different from that in figure 4.1 and merits some comments. It would seem that minimal levels of racial integration are positively (but at a declining rate) associated with requirements for credentials. Complete integration, however, is least likely to occur in jobs with the highest credential requirements, consistent with a pattern of token hiring and with the rarity of black applicants for jobs at this level.

CONCLUSIONS

There is strong evidence that the basic process that determines the sex composition of jobs is best understood as resulting from patriarchal social closure pressures to reserve the best jobs for men. Jobs that are

Table 4.5. *Percentage of sex-balanced and racially balanced jobs and organizational characteristics*

Organizational characteristics	Sex balanced	Racially balanced
Sector		
Competitive	**14.7**[a]	20.1[b]
Oligopolistic	**10.1**	12.0
State	**15.2**	12.9
Establishment size		
Small (≤ 20)	9.8	**8.1**[b]
Medium (21–100)	13.9	**19.1**
Large (≥ 101)	15.5	**15.8**
Place size		
Rural/open country	**12.5**[b]	17.3[b]
Small town	**7.6**	8.9
Large town/small city	**14.6**	15.4
Large city	**24.0**	17.0
Formalization		
None	10.9[b]	**5.6**[b]
Low	10.7	**12.1**
Medium	14.9	**18.5**
High	18.9	**18.9**

[a]**Bold** indicates a significant association at the .05 probability level. Regressions reported in the chapter appendix.
[b]Significantly associated at the .05 probability level with sex balanced or racially balanced at the bivariate level.

associated with firm-learned skills, higher power, and more opportunities for promotion are much more likely to be filled by males. Statistical discrimination theory does not help us understand the process by which the sex composition of jobs is determined. Since the theory is not supported for sex composition, it is logically not a useful explanation for sex segregation either.

There is some evidence that the racial composition of jobs is consistent with statistical discrimination arguments. Racial composition is strongly tied to job-skill level (both required credentials and training time) but not to power or opportunity for promotion (in multivariate models). Racial composition is also strongly tied to job fragmentation.

Gender status distinctions are strongest in jobs with intermediate educational requirements. This conclusion is consistent with evidence produced by Jacobs (1989b), Beller (1984), and Nancy Rytina and Suzanne Bianchi (1984) that occupational sex segregation is marginally lower among new labor market entrants and among professionals and managers. Racial status distinctions are strongest in jobs with limited edu-

Table 4.6. Percentage of sex-balanced and racially balanced jobs and job characteristics

Job characteristics	Sex balanced	Racially balances
Power		
None	13.5	15.0
Nominal supervisor	18.8	15.6
True supervisor	9.4	15.1
Nominal manager	17.6	15.4
True manager	9.5	4.0
Job size (fragmentation)		
1 incumbent	**0.0**[a,b]	**0.0**[b]
2-10 incumbents	**17.7**	**15.9**
11-30 incumbents	**14.9**	**23.4**
31-70 incumbents	**29.1**	**30.3**
≥71 incumbents	**20.6**	**34.4**
Promotion opportunity		
0 (no mobility)	9.4[b]	9.6
1	12.2	16.4
2	14.4	13.3
3 (high mobility)	19.6	17.9
Training time		
0-1 week	3.6	0.0
2-5 weeks	18.6	14.9
6-26 weeks	14.4	16.9
27-52 weeks	11.2	13.4
≥53 weeks	11.0	14.4
Required credentials[c]		
Less than high school	**21.8**[b]	**11.4**
High school	**13.0**	**14.5**
High school plus	**2.7**	**18.4**
Two-year college	**8.9**	**12.7**
Four-year college	**16.2**	**16.8**
Professional/graduate	**14.6**	**6.3**
Firm training		
None	12.2[b]	14.1
Some	18.7	16.3
Prior experience required		
No	**18.9**[b]	16.0
Yes	**10.7**	13.7
Relatively large job (percent of establishment employment)		
1-20%	10.5	**11.6**
21-40%	15.6	**15.1**
41-67%	14.5	**16.1**
68-100%	13.6	**15.3**

[a]**Bold** indicates a significant association at the .05 probability level. Regressions reported in the chapter appendix.
[b]Significantly associated at the .05 probability level with sex balanced or racially balanced at the bivariate level.
[c]Relationship between credentials and both sex and racial segregation is curvilinear (see fig. 4.1).

cational requirements, in which low-skilled whites have only one advantage—their race. This is certainly consistent with historical analyses of racial segregation in the U.S. South (Reich 1981; Wilson 1978).

Pressures for social distance and status exclusion are most intense among unskilled, relatively low-paid southern whites, whose only resource is their race. Racial segregation may be a less necessary part of the political formula for whites in jobs at higher skill levels. At these levels racial competition for jobs is less intense and there is less pressure to defend the small historical advantages of being white rather than black working class.[17] The exception is fragmented jobs, in which both racial integration and balance are greatest. The analysis of race-integrated jobs suggests also that demographic balance is quite rare in jobs with requirements for advanced credentials, although nominal integration is relatively frequent. This may reflect a pattern of token hiring for jobs that require at least a college education.[18]

In general, more formalized employee-employer organizational practices reduce sex and racial segregation. Such practices seem to be important in reducing discrimination in hiring and promotion. We shall return to this issue in the final chapter.

Sex segregation is less extreme in urban areas of North Carolina than in rural areas. This pattern is consistent with the previous findings of J. Miller McPherson and Lynn Smith-Lovin (1986) and of David L. Rogers and Willis J. Gudy (1981). Racial segregation, however, is not lower in more urban places. There is good reason to think that regional differences are policy-relevant as well. If there are cultural variations, they must result from something. My guess is that they result from past social movement activity.

There is almost no evidence that market competition undermines traditional sex- and race-based practices of discrimination. The state sector is more likely to employ women and blacks and has less sex segregation than the private sector, all of which runs counter to market efficiency predictions. The racial and sex compositions of the oligopolistic and competitive sectors were quite similar, suggesting that market pressures do not play an important role here either. In fact, in the case of jobs with relatively large numbers of incumbents, the black labor force increased only in jobs in the state sector. Even though market pressures to employ cheaper labor should have been greater, the competitive and oligopolistic sectors had dramatic and very similar declines in minority employment. On balance, there is no evidence to support the argument that competitive markets undermine tastes for discrimination. The measures used here can be criticized for their crudeness, and this issue is certainly not closed, but the weakness of evidence for the market view is striking.[19]

The final set of explanations focuses on the organizational need for labor and the capacity to create segregation. At the firm level, establishment size is positively related to the percentages of females and of blacks. Similarly, having a large number of incumbents in a job is positively related to the percentage of blacks, at least in the state sector. Firms and jobs requiring larger labor forces are less able to exclude women and minorities.

Large firms hire subordinate-status workers. They are also less sex-segregated, largely because of the creation of jobs with large populations. Racial segregation follows the U-shaped pattern predicted by Bielby and Baron (1984) in which small and large establishments are more segregated than medium-sized firms. Presumably, medium-sized firms are not sufficiently large to institute the bureaucratic proliferation of job titles accomplished so easily in large firms. Consistent with their explanation, the curvilinear pattern is mediated by job fragmentation. Unexpectedly, large firms continue to have higher racial segregation than small or medium-sized firms even after controlling for job fragmentation. Perhaps other bureaucratic mechanisms are present in large firms that are not addressed in this study that create this capacity for the largest firms to have the most racial segregation. Why the U-shaped pattern is not also present for sex segregation is unclear.

Social closure processes in the workplace provide strong explanations of the sex composition of jobs. As the desirability of jobs increases, women are more likely to be excluded. This is true for jobs with employer-provided training, promotion opportunities, and supervisory power. Deskilled occupations with numerically large populations are open to female employees.

Sex segregation pressure also tend to increase as the desirability of a job goes up. The few women who end up in high-opportunity, high-power jobs are likely to be in typically female occupations. The exception to this general status closure process is jobs that require the very highest educational credentials, in which sex segregation pressures marginally recede.

Statistical discrimination theory was offered as an alternative organizational theory of the sources of status composition and segregation. In most ways this theory is a more narrowly framed version of social closure theory in that it focuses only on the training costs to employers associated with hiring decisions rather than on the more general status exclusion fostered by both employers and employees. The racial composition of jobs does seem to be more narrowly tied to skill, particularly required educational credentials and employer-provided training time. Racial segregation actually *declines* in jobs at higher skill levels, directly contrary to social closure predictions. The pattern for racial composition and segregation seems to be roughly consistent with a statistical discrimination argument. This may mean that employer prejudice is a more important source of exclusion based on race than the preferences of white employees. The literature on racial competition, particularly in the southern United States, suggests, however, that general race-based social closure processes may be limited to working-class jobs. If this is the case, then the lack of an association between racial composition and power or internal labor market opportunity may merely reflect that all holders of working-class jobs are quite effectively denied these opportunities. This limited social closure theory is consistent with findings that racial segregation declines in jobs with higher educational and training-time requirements. This interpretation should not, however, be understood as an argument that there are working- and middle-class cultural differences that govern the level of racism perpetuated by white employees. Rather, the white working class is in direct competition for jobs with much of the black labor force. The white middle class tends to be protected from this competition by their educational credentials.

APPENDIX TO CHAPTER 4

The conclusions in this chapter are based on the following ordinary least-squares and logistic regression models.

Table A4.1. Logit of percent female in job (N = 770) and logit of percent black in jobs (N = 764) regressed on organizational and job characteristics

	% female equations		% black equations		
	1[a]	2	1[a]	2	3
Organizational characteristics					
Competitive sector[b]	−.52 (−.07)]*	−.15 (−.02)	−.84 (−.16)]***	−1.17 (.22)]***	−.37 (−.07)
Oligopolistic sector[b]	−.63 (−.07)]*	−.22 (−.03)	−.73 (−.13)]***	−.99 (−.17)]***	−.09 (−.02)
Large size[b]	.25 (.03)]*	.53 (.06)]*	.67 (.12)]**	.32 (.06)	.33 (.06)
Small size[b]	−.22 (−.02)]*	−.67 (−.07)]*	−.31 (−.05)]**	.13 (.02)	.17 (.03)
Place size	.05 (.01)	.09 (.03)	.25 (.10)**	.31 (.13)***	.33 (.13)***
Formalization	−.01 (−.00)	.26 (.08)+	.08 (.04)	.21 (.09)*	.19 (.09)*
Job characteristics					
Fragmentation[c]	—	−.21 (−.08)	—	.49 (.27)***	.49 (.27)***
Internal labor market	—	−.63 (−.16)***	—	.17 (.06)+	.17 (.06)+
Supervisor[b]	—	1.46 (.18)*	—	—	

Table A4.1 continued

	% female equations		% black equations		
	1[a]	2	1[a]	2	3
Power	—	−.52 (−.27)***	—	−.02 (−.01)	−.02 (−.01)
Training time	—	−.90 (−.32)***	—	−.25 (−.13)***	−.24 (−.13)***
Required credentials	—	.18 (.12)**	—	−.24 (−.24)***	−.24 (−.25)***
Firm training[b]	—	−.38 (−.04)	—	.37 (.05)	.37 (.05)
Prior experience[b]	—	.06 (.01)	—	.33 (.06)	.32 (.06)
Relatively large (RL)[c]	—	1.33 (.10)+	—	−.30 (−.03)	1.04 (.12) ⎤
RL * oligopolistic	—	—	—	—	−1.99 (−.19)*** ⎬
RL * competitive	—	—	—	—	−1.71 (−.22) ⎦
Adjusted R^2	.006	.133	.055	.220	.227

[a] Ordinary least squares metric coefficients (standardized coefficients).
[b] Dummy variables and reference categories are state sector, medium establishment size, nonsupervisor, no firm training program, and no prior experience required for the job.
[c] Interactions between Relatively Large and Sectors, between Relatively Large and Credentials, and between Absolutely Large jobs and Credentials were explored but did not improve model fit for sex composition. Only Relatively Large by Sector was significant for racial composition.
+ Statistically significant at or below the .1 probability level.
* Statistically significant at or below the .05 probability level.
** Statistically significant at or below the .01 probability level.
*** Statistically significant at or below the .001 probability level.

Table A4.2. Logit of sex segregation[a] in jobs (N = 770) and logit of racial segregation[a] in jobs (N = 764) regressed on organizational and job characteristics

	Sex segregation equations				Racial segregation equations	
	1[b]	2	3	4	1[b]	2
Organizational characteristics						
Competitive sector[c]	.12 (.03)}**	.09 (.02)}**	−.24 (−.05)	.10 (.02)	−.26 (−.07)}	−.38 (−.10)}*
Oligopolistic sector[c]	.61 (.13)}	.60 (.13)}	.09 (.02)	.60 (.13)**	−.08 (−.02)}	−.14 (−.03)}
Large size[c]	−.20 (−.05)}*	.07 (.01)	.08 (.02)	.01 (.00)	.33 (.09)}*	.40 (.10)}*
Small size[c]	.44 (.09)}	−.02 (−.01)	−.05 (−.01)	−.00 (−.00)	.23 (.06)}	−.06 (−.01)}
Place size	−.22 (−.11)**	−.21 (−.10)**	−.22 (−.11)**	−.21 (−.11)**	.06 (.04)	.10 (.05)
Formalization	−.18 (−.10)*	−.17 (−.10)*	−.17 (−.09)*	−.17 (−.10)*	−.10 (−.06)	−.01 (−.01)
Job characteristics						
Fragmentation[d]	—	−.46 (−.31)***	−.46 (−.31)***	−.53 (−.35)***	—	−.21 (−.16)**
Internal labor market	—	.02 (.01)	.02 (.01)	.02 (.01)	—	.02 (.01)
Power	—	−.01 (−.01)	−.01 (−.01)	−.02 (−.02)	—	−.00 (−.01)
Training time	—	.16 (.11)**	.16 (.11)**	.16 (.11)*	—	−.16 (−.12)**

Table A4.2 continued

	Sex segregation equations				Racial segregation equations	
	1[b]	2	3	4	1[b]	2
Required credentials (RC)	—	.29 (.36)*	.30 (.37)*	.27 (.34)*	—	−.30 (−.44)**
RC * RC	—	−.03 (−.41)**	−.03 (−.42)***	−.03 (−.40)**	—	.02 (.27)+
Firm training[c]	—	−.11 (−.02)	−.10 (−.02)	−.09 (−.01)	—	.39 (.08)*
Prior experience[c]	—	.31 (.07)+	.32 (.07)+	.30 (.06)+	—	.18 (.04)
Relatively large[d]	—	.27 (.04)	−.36 (−.05)]*	.12 (.01)	—	.32 (.05)
RL * oligopolistic	—	—	1.12 (.13)]*	—	—	—
RL * competitive	—	—	.73 (.12)	—	—	—
Absolutely large* credentials	—	—	—	.0006 (.09)*	—	—
Adjusted R^2	.047	.144	.145	.147	.003	.053

[a]Sex and racial segregation are measured as the logit of the modified job-level index of dissimilarity. See notes 4 and 14, chap. 4.

[b]Ordinary least squares metric coefficients (standardized coefficients).

[c]Dummy variables, reference categories are state sector, medium establishment size, no firm training program, and no prior experience required for the job.

[d]The interaction between relatively large jobs and required credentials was explored but was not statistically significant for sex segregation. No interaction was significant for racial segregation.

+Statistically significant at or below the .1 probability level.

*Statistically significant at or below the .05 probability level.

**Statistically significant at or below the .01 probability level.

***Statistically significant at or below the .001 probability level.

Table A4.3. Logistic regression of sex-balanced and racially balanced jobs on organizational and job characteristics[a]

	Sex-balanced[b]		Racially balanced	
Organizational characteristics				
Competitive sector[c]	.06	(1.06) }*	−.01	(0.99)
Oligopolistic sector[c]	−.58	(0.56) }*	−.34	(0.71)
Large size[c]	−.23	(0.80)	−.86	(0.42) }***
Small size[c]	.10	(1.10)	1.00	(2.73) }***
Place size	.31	(1.36)***	−.02	(0.97)
Formalization	.16	(1.17)	.25	(1.28)*
Job characteristics				
Fragmentation	.38	(1.46)***	.99	(2.71)***
Internal labor market	.21	(1.24)+	.04	(1.04)
Power	.03	(1.03)	.06	(1.06)
Training time	.01	(1.01)	.09	(1.09)
Required credentials	−.52	(0.60)***	.32	(1.38)
RC * RC	.04	(1.04)***	−.03	(0.97)*
Firm training[c]	.34	(1.41)	−.06	(0.95)
Prior experience[c]	−.66	(0.51)**	−.19	(0.83)
Relatively large	−.78	(0.46)	−2.80	(0.06)***
N	766		758	

[a]A sex-balanced job is between 30 and 70 percent female. A racially balanced job is between 11 and 33 percent black.
[b]Metric logit coefficient (odds ratio).
[c]Dummy variables and reference categories are state sector, medium establishment size, no firm training program, and no prior experience required for the job.
+Statistically significant at or below the .1 probability level.
* Statistically significant at or below the .05 probability level.
** Statistically significant at or below the .01 probability level.
*** Statistically significant at or below the .001 probability level.

CHAPTER 5
LABOR PROCESS INEQUALITY AND THE SEX AND RACIAL COMPOSITIONS OF JOBS

THIS CHAPTER EXPLORES the labor processes that lead to sex and racial inequalities in the workplace. Most studies of sex and racial inequalities focus on wage inequality. We shall explore that topic in the next chapter. For now, we shall try to understand why women and men and blacks and whites tend to have different experiences at work. Wages matter, of course, but so do creativity, autonomy, power, and opportunity. These are the intrinsic aspects of work that condition day-to-day, on-the-job experiences. Alienation, job satisfaction, and even mental health are all linked to the actual labor process under which people work. In addition, jobs high on these attributes tend to reap higher earnings because the holders of these jobs are compensated for the value of their skills or the extent of their power.

This chapter asks and answers several empirical questions: Are blacks and whites and men and women sorted into jobs that are organized differently? That is, do white males tend to have the better jobs—those with more creativity, autonomy, power, and opportunities for promotion? Do human capital differences explain these sex and racial differences in the quality of jobs? Or are there exclusionary *social closure* processes that ensure that the best jobs are reserved for white males? Finally, is there an emergent *status composition* effect whereby the racial or sex composition of a job has an independent effect on the organization of the labor process? It is the last question that is the most important.

From past research we know that there are profound racial and gender inequalities in access to intrinsically interesting and powerful jobs. We also know that discrimination in hiring that is linked to race and gender is widespread. If we find that the sex and racial compositions of jobs have an effect on how work is organized that is independent of the sex or race of individual workers, we will have strong evidence that gender and race are important in how organizations create their practices, structures, and rewards.

LABOR PROCESS

The labor process is conceived broadly here as the social attributes of a work organization that directly affect workers' activities and motivations on the job. These attributes are not social psychological but concrete aspects of the tasks and control structures of the workplace. These attributes, in addition to wages and benefits, are the major rewards associated with employment. The desirability of jobs is often expressed by workers in terms of their creativity, autonomy, authority, decision-making power, and opportunities for promotion. It is these aspects of work that I examine. Employers often evaluate these dimensions of the labor process, as well as education and experience, either informally or formally, in determining wages. The experience of work, the rewards, and the frustrations are also intimately linked to how the labor process at the workplace is organized.

Five different dimensions of the labor process are explored in this chapter. Past research has shown that in addition to earnings they directly affect job satisfaction, self-esteem, and even mental health. I will briefly describe each dimension and its measurement.[1]

Closeness of supervision refers to the degree to which a worker's tasks are closely supervised. This dimension is based on four questions. The questions asked whether the respondent decides how to do the work and how fast, whether there is a lot of freedom on the job, and whether the boss keeps a close eye on the worker. High scores indicate close supervision; low scores indicate substantial workplace autonomy.

Task complexity refers to the variety of task experiences on the job. It is also based on four questions. The questions asked whether the work is basically the same day to day, whether there are standard rules and operating procedures, whether there is variety on the job, and whether the job requires the worker to learn new things. High scores indicate complex and challenging jobs; low scores indicate routinized activity.

The degree of internal labor market opportunity measures the placement of the job on a scale that ranges from completely vulnerable to the external labor market to substantial opportunities for promotion within a job ladder. The scale was composed by simply adding whether or not someone in a job similar to that of the respondent had been fired (reverse coded), laid off (reverse coded), or promoted in the last year; whether the respondent thought she or he might be promoted in the next year; and whether or not the respondent had ever changed jobs or been promoted within the current firm. High scores signify high-opportunity internal labor markets; low scores signify exposure to external labor markets.[2]

Managerial authority refers to the ability to make decisions to change the organization's products or services or about the firm's budgets or major purchases. It was calculated by summing two questions. The first asked the respondent whether he or she has final decision-making authority to change organizational practices significantly. The second asked the respondent whether he or she can make major budgetary decisions. Eighty-three percent of the respondents said their jobs had no managerial authority.

Supervisory responsibility refers to the degree to which a worker has direct control over other workers' labor. It was calculated as the sum of five variables. The respondent was asked whether he or she supervises, whether any of his or her subordinates also supervise, and whether he or she can assign tasks, set the pace of work, or fire subordinates. Sixty-five percent of the respondents said they had no supervisory responsibility.[3]

THEORETICAL EXPLANATIONS

Human capital, social closure, and status composition theories all provide explanations of gender and racial inequalities in the labor process. Human capital explanations suggest that differences in job placement based on gender and race arise from individual differences in productivity acquired through education, labor force experience, and job tenure (Becker 1957). The assumption is that there is a relatively efficient labor market that sorts individuals into jobs that are commensurate with human capital characteristics, such as education and labor force experience. Although human capital theory did not prove compelling in explaining the sources of job segregation discussed in chapter 3, it has a long history of providing useful, if not total, insights into the job-allocation process. It is hard to argue that education, training, and experience are not linked to job requirements. Particularly in the case of racial inequality, it is likely that differences in human capital acquisition, which reflect historical discrimination and current class advantages or handicaps, provide at least a partial explanation of black-white inequality in the labor process.

Another theoretical explanation focuses on exclusionary social closure processes. The social closure arguments developed in the last chapter suggest that women and minorities are likely to be excluded from desirable jobs simply because of their sex or race. Labor market segmentation theory, although it does not typically use explicit social closure language, is an example of exclusionary social closure logic. Here the argument is that institutionalized discrimination—that is, traditional patterns of hiring fostered by employers and white male employees—*sorts* women and blacks into less advantageous organizations and within organizations into less advantageous jobs.

The organizational closure argument is associated with dual economy theory (O'Connor 1973; Edwards 1979) as well as with discussions of tastes for discrimination in neoclassical economic theory (Becker 1957). In general, the argument is that high-resource organizations (i.e., large firms in oligopolistic sectors of the economy) can afford to employ higher-paid white males.

The job closure argument is that more highly skilled and otherwise advantaged jobs are reserved for white males (Bonacich 1972; Cockburn 1988; Edwards 1979; Halaby 1979; Marshall 1974; Walby 1986). The general argument is that employers discriminate in hiring, often with the support of white male employees, thereby allocating women and minorities to lower-skilled jobs than they might be able to perform.

Sex differences in access to desirable jobs in the United States are well documented. Controlling for human capital attributes, women have been found to hold jobs with less task complexity (Baron and Bielby 1982; Kalleberg and Leicht 1986), more routinized, controlled work (Baron and Bielby 1982), and less supervisory authority (Wolf and Fligstein 1979a, 1979b; Wright 1979) and are less likely to be in internal labor markets (Kanter 1977) and more likely to be controlled thorugh external mechanisms, such as technology or direct interaction by the employer (Form and McMillen 1983).

Research on racial differences in the labor process reveals similar patterns. Arne Kalleberg and Kevin Leicht (1986) and Baron and Bielby (1982) found that African-Americans held jobs with significantly lower levels of task complexity than whites even after statistically accounting for human capital differences. Baron and Bielby (1982) found these differences to be entirely a function of the organizational characteristics of the firms the African-Americans worked for, while Kalleberg and Leicht (1986) found racial differences persisted after accounting for organizational and even job-skill characteristics. Erik Olin Wright (1978), among many others, has found that African-Americans are much less likely than whites with comparable education and work experience to be in supervisory and managerial jobs.

The research that has found sex and racial differences in access to desirable job characteristics has tended to be framed in terms of human capital versus segmentation (i.e., social closure) explanations. There is substantial evidence in this research that human capital approaches provide weak explanations for gender inequality in job attributes and stronger but still incomplete explanations of racial inequality. All of the research cited strongly suggests that there are status closure processes, generally labeled organizational and job segmentation, that powerfully influence gender and racial inequalities as they affect access to intrinsically rewarding and powerful jobs. This argument about individual access to jobs parallels the discussion in the last chapter about the social closure determinants of the sex and racial compositions of jobs.

Yet another explanation of why women and men and blacks and whites have different work tasks and opportunities is that there is a status-based structuring of organizational activity. We call this the *status composition* hypothesis. Here the argument is that jobs that are dominated disproportionately by females or blacks become stereotyped and the work process itself begins to reflect the devalued master status of typical incumbents (see Caplow 1954:230–47; Acker and Van Houten 1974; Bielby and Baron 1985; Treiman and Hartmann 1981). This argument does not focus on discrimination against individuals but toward jobs. Jobs and organizational structures may be fundamentally determined by race and gender (Acker 1990; Cockburn 1988; Walby 1986).

We already have learned that organizational processes are important determinants of the observed sex and racial segregation of the labor force at the job level. Now we explore the potential impact of this segregation on the intrinsic characteristics of jobs—or how the labor process in which individual job holders work is influenced by the status composition of the job itself.

The case study evidence that the labor process reflects the typical sex of workers is fairly convincing. Female-dominated jobs have historically been associated with deskilling, loss of autonomy, and increased routinization of the work process (see, for example, Reskin and Roos 1990; Cohn 1985; Cockburn 1988; Walby 1986). The problem with the case study literature is that processes of social closure (i.e., job segmentation) are difficult to distinguish from status composition effects. Glass (1990), in one of the only general survey approaches to this issue, found that controlling for incumbents' sex, the higher the percentage of females in the occupation, the less flexible the work and the less chance for promotion.

The remainder of this chapter explores five general questions: (1) Are there significant racial and sex inequalities in access to intrinsically rewarding work? (2) Do racial and sex differences in human capital characteristics account for some of these inequalities in labor process opportunity? (3) Do social closure processes at the organizational level account for some of the racial and sex inequalities in job quality? (4) Does social closure at the job level account for some of the observed sex and racial labor process inequalities? (5) As the percentages of blacks or of females in jobs increase, does the labor process become less advantageous to incumbents regardless of their individual sex or race?

Although none of these questions is mutually exclusive, each can be ranked by the degree of institutionalized discrimination it represents. The human capital argument (question 2) suggests that historical, individual, and familial constraints on the acquisition of individual human capital, rather than direct discrimination, account for current inequalities in the organization of the labor process. The organizational closure hypothesis (question 3) suggests that organizations have different tastes for discrimination. More specifically, the argument is that more advantaged organizations (large firms in the oligopolistic sector of the economy, or conglomerates) have the resources to construct higher-quality jobs and to hire more white and male workers. From this point of view, small, competitive-sector firms might hire African-Americans and women because that is all they can afford. The job closure hypothesis (question 4) suggests that firms reserve their more skilled jobs for white males. This hypothesis is particularly consistent with the research evidence, which shows very high levels of sex and racial segregation at the job level within firms (Bielby and Baron 1985, 1986; chaps. 2, 3, and 4). Questions 3 and 4 both assume that underlying exclusionary *social closure* processes based on race and sex create organizational and job segmentation.[4] The *status composition* hypothesis (question 5) suggests that sex and racial discrimination is more than a matter of historical and contemporary group differences in opportunities but extends to the organizational constuction of the labor process itself.

For questions 2 through 5, sex and racial differences in the five labor process domains will be examined by controlling statistically for a set of explanatory variables. The general procedure will be to build a series of statistical models and examine the size, direction, and statistical significance of sex and racial differences in the labor process after controlling statistically for the human capital (Q2), organizational characteristics (Q3), and skill levels of jobs (Q4).[5] Any remaining effects of sex and race after these statistical controls have been introduced will be provisionally interpreted as unique *status composition* effects on the labor process.[6] That assumption is tested further by substituting the *sex and racial composition* of jobs for the sex and race of incumbents. In these analyses, we can see whether the percentage of blacks or females in a job influences the within-race and within-sex distribution of labor process opportunities. To the extent that whites or males are affected by the

racial and gender compositions of their jobs, we have strong evidence
for a *status composition* effect on the labor process that is independent of
the status characteristics of the incumbents in the job.

   *Question 1: Are there significant racial and sex inequalities in access to
   intrinsically rewarding work?*

   Table 5.1 presents race and sex comparisons for the labor process
variables. We see that both race and sex are strongly associated with the
organization of the labor process. Blacks are more closely supervised
than whites and have less complex jobs, less managerial authority, and
less supervisory rseponsibility. There are no racial differences in the
degree of internal labor market opportunity.

   Women, on average, have less complex jobs than men. They also have
less access to internal labor markets, managerial authority, and supervisory responsibility. The answer to question 1 is strongly affirmative.
There are pervasive sex and racial inequalities in the organization of the
labor process.

   *Question 2: Do racial and sex differences in human capital characteristics
   account for some of the inequalities in labor process opportunity?*

   To answer question 2 we need to control statistically for the effects of
individual human capital differences in the sorting of African-Americans and women into jobs. If African-Americans and women are less
qualified on average than whites and males, it would not be surprising
to find them in less complex or more supervised jobs.[7]

   Table 5.2 shows the estimates of sex and racial differences before
(columns 1R and 1S) and after (columns 2R and 2S) statistically controlling for the human capital characteristics of individuals.[8] Columns 1S
and 1R list baseline estimates of the sex and racial inequalities in the
organization of the labor process. Columns 2S and 2R list those inequalities controlling for the human capital attributes of individuals—education, experience, experience squared, and job tenure. By comparing the
R estimates in columns 1 and 2, one sees, for example, that blacks are
.53 more closely supervised than whites. This inequality drops to .41
after one controls for differences in human capital characteristics between whites and blacks. Thus, we can say that about a fifth (.12/.53) of
the black-white inequality in the degree of supervision is a function of
human capital differences.

   From the table, we can see that adding human capital characteristics
tends to reduce observed racial differences in labor process organization. For the four labor process variables that demonstrate significant
racial inequality, the human capital deficits of average African-Americans (relative to whites) account for about a quarter of the disadvantage
blacks experience. After controlling statistically for human capital char-

Table 5.1. *Mean scores (and standard deviations) for labor process variables for a random sample of North Carolina jobs*

Labor process	All (N = 836)		White (N = 678)		Black (N = 158)		Significant racial inequality?	Male (N = 378)		Female (N = 458)		Significant gender inequality?
Closeness of supervision	5.97	(1.78)	5.87	(1.76)	6.39	(1.82)	Yes	5.88	(1.71)	6.04	(1.83)	No
Task complexity	8.05	(1.70)	8.18	(1.67)	7.50	(1.71)	Yes	8.21	(1.63)	7.92	(1.74)	Yes
Internal labor market opportunity	3.74	(1.20)	3.76	(1.22)	3.67	(1.13)	No	3.83	(1.24)	3.67	(1.17)	Yes
Managerial authority	0.24	(.57)	0.27	(.59)	0.12	(.42)	Yes	0.30	(.63)	0.19	(.49)	Yes
Supervisory responsibility	1.30	(2.00)	1.40	(2.07)	0.84	(1.59)	Yes	1.60	(2.23)	1.05	(1.76)	Yes

Table 5.2. *Absolute inequalities between blacks and whites and women and men for labor process variables, controlling for human capital, organizational, and job-skill characteristics*

Labor process	Racial inequality				Gender inequality			
	1R	2R	3R	4R	1S	2S	3S	4S
Closeness of supervision	.53	.41	.37	.32	.18	.13	.15	.07
Task complexity	-.69	-.51	-.52	-.33	-.31	-.27	-.28	-.06
Internal labor market opportunity	-.09	-.05	-.06	-.03	-.17	-.21	-.22	-.18
Managerial authority	-.15	-.11	-.09	-.05	-.12	-.11	-.10	-.04
Supervisory responsibility	-.59	-.43	-.36	-.18	-.57	-.54	-.50	-.25

Note: Numbers are the average absolute difference between black and white and female and male scores on the labor process variables. **Bold** indicates a statistically significant sex or racial difference below the .05 probability level. All differences are estimated from multiple regression models in which race and sex are entered as dummy variables.
Columns 1 contain only the sex and race variables.
Columns 2 control for human capital characteristics (years of education, educational credentials, firm tenure, firm tenure squared, labor force experience, and labor force experience squared).
Columns 3, in addition to human capital, control for industrial sector, establishment size, urban location, out-of-state ownership, subsidiary status, and multiestablishment status.
Columns 4, in addition to human capital and organizational characteristics, control for job-skill segmentation with measures of required educational credentials, prior experience requirements, and weeks needed to master the job.

acteristics, however, African-Americans are still more closely supervised and are found in jobs with less task complexity, managerial authority, and supervisory responsibility than whites with similar levels of education, experience, and firm tenure. Thus, in similar jobs the average African-American is better qualified based on education and experience than the average white. This strongly suggests that some level of race-based discrimination is operating; it remains to be seen what form that discrimination takes.

Table 5.2 also provides data on sex differences in the labor process before (column 1S) and after (column 2S) controlling for human capital characteristics. Human capital characteristics account, on average, for none of the labor process disadvantage experienced by women. In one case, internal labor market opportunity, controlling for human capital actually increases women's disadvantage relative to men. In all cases women's disadvantage remains relatively large and statistically significant. Sex-based differences in labor process outcomes are much less consistent with human capital explanations than are racial differences. Again, this implies that for a given level of job quality women tend to be more qualified on average than men in comparable jobs.

Question 3: Do social closure processes at the organizational level account for some of the racial and sex inequalities in job quality?

To examine question 3 we need to control statistically for the differential hiring by race and sex into organizations that are stratified in their resources, technology, and other factors that might influence the labor process. Industrial sector, firm size, and organizational structure are the three variables most often discussed in the literature as having decisive effects on the quality of jobs and the organization of the labor process (Averitt 1968; Baron 1984; Doeringer and Piore 1971; Edwards 1979; Sorensen 1983). In these models industrial sectors (extractive, construction, manufacturing, transportation-utilities, wholesale trade, retail trade, business services, public administration, and social services) are included to control for the effects of the product market on a firm's resources.[9] Employment size of the establishment is used to control for economy-of-scale effects on labor process organization and for resource differentials within industrial sectors. Three variables tap whether or not the firm is part of a conglomerate (out-of-state ownership, subsidiary status, part of a multiestablishment firm). To the extent that the labor process becomes more tightly controlled and hierarchical in conglomerates (Chandler 1962; Braverman 1973; Clawson 1980) and these firms are more likely to hire women and blacks (Hodson 1983), we can expect that some of the sex and racial differences in labor process inequality would be a function of organizational structure. Finally, since we suspect that racial and sex segregation and discrimination are higher in the rural South than in more urban areas (Rogers and Gudy 1981), a final variable that controls for rural workplaces is included as well.

Table 5.2 presents the results of controlling for organizational characteristics on sex and racial differences in labor process variables. Comparing columns 2R with 3R, it is apparent that organizational segregation accounts for virtually none of the racial differences in labor process organization. The reported coefficients barely change after controlling for organizational characteristics.

For sex differences, there are surprising results associated with statistically controlling for organizational characteristics. In three cases, controlling for organizational characteristics *increases* the absolute gender inequality in labor process experience. This suggests that women tend, on average, to be hired into firms with less close supervision, more complex tasks, and more internal labor market opportunity than men. This location in more favorable firms masks a marginally larger sex differential in labor process experience. This also suggests that, on average, there is more gender-based labor process inequality *within* firms than there is *between* firms.

On balance, the organizational closure hypothesis receives no support. Although four of the racial differences are eroded by controlling for organizational characteristics, the differences are so small that they could as easily be attributable to sampling errors as to true differences. The organizational segmentation hypothesis is also rejected as an explanation of gender differences. In fact, controlling for organizational characteristics amplifies gender inequality in the labor process. The weak effects of human capital variables, and essentially the absence of any effect of organizational variables, strongly suggest that most labor process inequality is created at the job level.

Question 4: Does social closure at the job level account for some of the observed sex and racial inequalities?

If employers allocate African-Americans and women into less skilled jobs than they do comparably skilled white male employees, it may be that a within-organization sorting process is at work. If this were true, in general, blacks and women would be more likely to be assigned to low-skill, low labor market–power jobs within firms, and this low-skill, low-power level would determine their other labor process disadvantages. To test this argument requires job-specific skill measures that are independent of the status composition of the job itself. Since we suspect that employers tend to undervalue the work performed by women and minorities, employer-based skill assessments are unlikely to be helpful. Thus, the strategy I pursued was to use as measures of job skill self-reports by workers on the educational and prior experience requirements of their jobs and the number of weeks that it generally takes to learn to do these jobs well. These are the same job-skill measures used in the analysis discussed in the last chapter.[10]

These measures of the skill level of jobs seem to be relatively objective and should be reliable measur,s independent of the sex composition of the jobs. This is not to say that these skill levels are unambiguously interpreted as *organizationally constructed* in the workplace independent of the sex and racial compositions of jobs. It seems reasonable to assume that both the skill levels of jobs lead to race- and sex-based sorting into positions and that the sex and racial compositions of jobs affect the social construction of skill requirements at the workplace. Some of the covariance in these job-skill equations (table 5.2, columns 4R and 4S) that is captured as a "skill" effect is likely to represent as yet unmeasured sex and racial composition effects on skill levels. Thus, adding these skill variables to the labor process models (table 5.2, columns 4R and 4S) represents a quite liberal test of *job closure* and a conservative approach to the *status composition* explanations of sex-linked and race-linked labor process inequalities.

The results in table 5.2 suggest that about half the race-linked disparities in labor process organization may be attributed to required educational credentials and experience and the time it takes to learn to do the job. African-Americans' lower degrees of managerial and supervisory authority are cut roughly in half and are statistically nonsignificant once job skill has been controlled. Closeness of supervision, however, is still significantly higher for blacks than for whites once job-skill, organizational, and human capital requirements have been statistically controlled. Similarly, task complexity is lower for black employees than it is for white employees even with comparable human capital, organizational, and job-skill requirements. Job-skill controls reduce race differences by about a third.

The job closure hypothesis, which argues that social closure pressures operate primarily at the job level, receives strong support. All of the race-linked differences in labor process organization are at least partially explained by variations in formal job-skill requirements. In fact, two out of the four racial inequalities become nonsignificant once job skill is statistically controlled. The status composition hypothesis also receives some provisional support. Once individual human capital, organizational closure, and job closure are controlled, significant racial inequalities in task complexity and closeness of supervision remain.

The results for sex differences (table 5.2, column 4S) are similar.

Women's task complexity and managerial authority disadvantages are no longer statistically significant once job-skill measures are introduced. Women continue to have significantly lower internal labor market opportunity and less supervisory responsibility than men. The supervisory responsibility disadvantage, however, is cut in half once job-skill requirements are controlled. Three of the four labor process disadvantages experienced by women are at least partially explained by job-skill closure by sex. Significant gender inequality remains, however, in access to supervisory positions and internal labor market opportunity.

The results reported in table 5.2 strongly support the job-skill closure hypothesis and cause one to reject the human capital and organizational closure accounts. They also leave open the possibility that there is a status composition process at work here.

Question 5: As the percentages of blacks or of females in jobs increase, does the labor process become less advantageous to incumbents regardless of their individual sex or race?

At this point we have evidence that suggests that some sex-linked and race-linked inequality in the labor process cannot be interpreted in terms of job closure, organizational closure, or individual human capital differences. Can the remaining inequality be interpreted as a *status composition* effect on the labor process itself? Table 5.2 reflects measurement assumptions that exaggerate the effects of the job-skill variables since it essentially does not account for the realistic proposition that sex or racial composition leads to job-skill expectations. On the one hand, even though sex or racial differences are not statistically significant in some final models reported in table 5.2, the very large differences in average on-the-job training time by sex (thirty-seven weeks) and race (twenty-five weeks) suggest that it would be premature to reject the status composition hypothesis (H5). On the other hand, the unexplained gender and racial inequalities in the labor process reported in table 5.2 might be attributable to unmeasured *job closure* or direct individual discrimination rather than to a *status composition* effect on the labor process.

To address this somewhat sticky conundrum, it becomes necessary to look for a status composition effect that is independent of any individual-level race- or sex-based sorting into low-skill, low-power jobs. This is done in the following analysis by estimating labor process models separately for blacks and whites and men and women and by examining the effects of the racial and sex compositions of the job on the five labor process variables. The sex and racial compositions of the job are measured as percent black and percent female in the job.

Table 5.3 presents equations similar to those reported in table 5.2 first

Table 5.3. *Standardized partial correlations between percent black in job and labor process variables, controlling for human capital and organizational characteristics, and the skill level of the job*

Labor process	All jobs (N = 836)			Jobs with white incumbents (N = 678)			Jobs with black incumbents (N = 156)		
	1A	2A	3A	1W	2W	3W	1B	2B	3B
Closeness of supervision	**.13**	**.10**	.08	**.11**	**.09**	.06	.02	.03	.06
Task complexity	**−.20**	**−.28**	**−.11**	**−.18**	**−.15**	**−.10**	−.06	−.09	−.06
Internal labor market opportunity	−.01	−.03	−.12	**−.16**	**−.13**	**−.08**	.06	.02	.05
Managerial authority	**−.11**	**−.06**	−.01	**−.11**	**−.07**	−.03	**.18**	**.17**	**.18**
Supervisory responsibility	**−.16**	**−.12**	**−.07**	**−.16**	**−.13**	**−.08**	.06	.02	.05

Note: Standardized multiple regression coefficients reported. **Bold** indicates a statistically significant relationship below the .05 probability level.
Columns 1 report uncontrolled relationships.
Columns 2 report correlations, controlling for all human capital and organizational characteristics.
Columns 3 report correlations, controlling for all human capital and organizational characteristics, and job-skill levels.

for all jobs (1A, 2A, 3A), then for jobs held only by white employees (1W, 2W, 3W), and finally for jobs held only by black employees (1B, 2B, 3B).[11] Columns 1A–3A show that the results are nearly identical to those in table 5.2. After controlling for skill levels, as the percentage of blacks in the job rises, task complexity falls and the closeness of supervision rises. Racial composition, like individual race, is linked to all the labor process variables except internal labor market opportunity. It continues to be significant for task complexity and supervisory responsibility after statistically controlling for human capital, organizational closure, and job-skill closure.

Strong evidence for a racial composition effect on the labor process would require the racial composition effect to be present within racial groups. If a racial composition effect is present across groups (columns 1A–3A) but not within groups, then the evidence suggests some unmeasured process of racial sorting into different jobs consistent with the organizational and job closure hypotheses. If the effect occurs within one or both groups, then it very strongly suggests a *status composition* effect on the labor process itself.[12]

In columns 1W–2W we see that, indeed, *among jobs with white incumbents* the percentage of blacks is associated with closer supervision, less task complexity, less internal labor market opportunity, less management authority, and less supervisory responsibility. This continues to be the case for all variables except closeness of supervision after human capital characteristics have been statistically controlled. Even when controlling for job skill, the percentage of blacks remains significantly and negatively correlated with task complexity, internal labor market opportunity, and supervisory responsibility. These findings strongly suggest that as the percentage of blacks in a job rises the labor process becomes disadvantaged, that some of this disadvantage is worked out through a general process of deskilling in the workplace definition of the job, and that the process is linked to the racial composition of the job, *not the race of the job holders.* Because these effects are for white job holders only, we can effectively rule out that the findings are a result of some unmeasured *race-based* sorting process.

The results in columns 1B–3B are for jobs with black incumbents only and are surprising in that there are no significant correlations in the expected direction. The only significant correlation suggests that as the percentage of blacks increases in jobs held by blacks so does the level of managerial authority. This effect is quite robust and even remains once skill levels have been controlled. This suggests that blacks in largely black jobs get managerial authority; otherwise, they are crowded out from these positions by whites. Although plausible (and consistent with

Rosabeth Kanter's [1977] theory of status proportions), this result is directly contrary to the status composition hypothesis.[13] The result is consistent with Charles W. Mueller, Toby L. Parcel, and Kazako Tanaka (1989), who found that blacks tend to advance to managerial positions only in settings where they supervise other blacks. Overall, there is no conclusive evidence that blacks are negatively affected by the racial composition of their jobs. I strongly suspect, however, that such racial composition effects would be present in larger samples.

Table 5.2 reported significant racial differences in task complexity and closeness of supervision after controlling for organizational and job-skill conditions. In table 5.3 we find that racial composition does not condition blacks' experience of the labor process. This suggests that the significant racial differences reported in the last column of table 5.2 may reflect some level of direct face-to-face discrimination *within jobs* in the organization of the labor process.

Table 5.4 presents a parallel analysis for the relationship between the percentage of females in a job and labor process variables for all jobs (1A–3A), for jobs with only male incumbents (1M–3M), and for jobs with only female incumbents (1F–3F). The results for columns 1A–3A are, again, very similar to those in table 5.2. If anything, they suggest stronger sex composition effects since the negative correlations between the percentage of females and managerial authority remains statistically significant even after controlling for job-skill levels. The nonsignificant sex differences in table 5.2 for this variable underestimated the sex composition effect since males as well as females lose access to managerial authority as the percentage of females rises. This becomes more clear when we look at within-sex comparisons. Managerial authority and supervisory responsibility decline for both men and women as the percentage of females rises.[14] Percent female seems to have a stronger negative effect on the degree of male internal labor market opportunity, no doubt reflecting the much higher opportunity levels in disproportionately male jobs.

As the percentage of females rises, task complexity falls for women but not for men. Since table 5.2 suggested that men and women were sorted into jobs of different complexity, the result is not surprising. It is important, however, that there remains, for women at least, a sex composition effect over and above that attributed to their being sorted into less complex jobs.

Racial Inequality

This chapter has revealed that there are clear and pervasive race-based differences in the organization of the labor process. Black employ-

Table 5.4. Standardized partial correlations between percent female in job and labor process variables, controlling for human capital and organizational characteristics, and the skill level of the job

Labor process	All jobs (N = 836)			Jobs with male incumbents (N = 378)			Jobs with female incumbents (N = 458)		
	1A	2A	3A	1M	2M	3M	1F	2F	3F
Closeness of supervision	.03	.03	.01	**−.09**	−.06	−.08	.05	.05	.05
Task complexity	**−.11**	**−.11**	**−.06**	.01	.00	.00	**−.12**	**−.11**	**−.12**
Internal labor market opportunity	**−.09**	**−.12**	**−.11**	−.06	**−.11**	−.07	−.04	−.04	−.03
Managerial authority	**−.13**	**−.13**	**−.08**	−.08	**−.09**	−.08	**−.12**	**−.12**	**−.12**
Supervisory responsibility	**−.18**	**−.18**	**−.13**	**−.10**	**−.10**	**−.10**	**−.14**	**−.12**	**−.13**

Note: Standardized multiple regression coefficients reported. **Bold** indicates a statistically significant relationship below the .05 probability level.
Columns 1 report uncontrolled relationships.
Columns 2 report correlations, controlling for all human capital and organizational characteristics.
Columns 3 report correlations, controlling for all human capital, organizational characteristics, and job-skill levels.

ees are more closely supervised and have less complex tasks, less managerial authority, and less supervisory responsibility.

The hypothesis that race-based differences in labor process organization are partially caused by individual-level differences in human capital characteristics was supported for all labor process characteristics. About 25 percent of observed racial inequality can be plausibly accounted for by the historical racism that created differences in educational attainment, firm tenure, and labor force experience.

The hypothesis that remaining racial differences reflect exclusionary organizational closure of the labor force along racial lines is soundly rejected. Not only is there little organizational segregation, but it has no apparent effect on race-based differences in the labor process. This is consistent with findings reported in the last chapter that all but the smallest organizations hire both African-American and female labor but do so into low-skill, low-power, and fragmented jobs.

The hypothesis that job-level exclusionary closure would account for some of the remaining race-based labor process inequality is strongly supported. Up to half of the observed racial difference in labor process organization is associated with job-skill levels. Substantial race-based inequalities in the labor process remain, however, after job-skill levels have been accounted for. Blacks are more closely supervised, have less task complexity, and are less likely to be in jobs that are self-controlled than whites even after controlling for human capital, organizational, and job-skill characteristics. This finding mirrors the results reported in the last chapter. Processes of skill-based discrimination are important sources of racial inequality. Employers seem to discount black candidates' human capital characteristics when allocating them into jobs; thus, black employees end up in lower-skilled jobs that are more tightly controlled and more routine and less complex, and they have less authority than comparable white employees.

The processes by which the racial composition of a job affects the labor process may be race-specific. That is, whites experience declines in their task complexity and supervisory authority as the percentages of blacks in their jobs rise. Whites also experience declines in managerial authority and a rise in the closeness of supervision as the percentage of blacks rises. These latter effects are linked to the skill level of jobs as well.

By contrast, labor process opportunities for blacks do not seem to be tied to the racial composition of their jobs. Blacks are, however, absolutely disadvantaged in the task complexity and closeness of supervision of their jobs. This suggests a much more direct subordination of African-Americans at work that is independent of other labor process characteristics, including the racial composition of the job, but that this subordination affects whites only when they are in jobs that have high proportions of minority incumbents.[15]

There is also a racial composition effect that tends to benefit blacks in jobs with high proportions of blacks. It is in these jobs that blacks find access to managerial authority.

Overall, the status composition hypothesis is not supported for racially mixed jobs with black incumbents but is strongly confirmed for racially mixed jobs held by whites. Whites suffer relative to other whites when they are in jobs held disproportionately by blacks, even controlling for human capital, organizational characteristics, and job skill. Blacks, by contrast, are not advantaged relative to other blacks when they are in jobs generally held by whites. In fact, blacks lose access to managerial authority as jobs get increasingly dominated by whites. These negative results bring us full circle. African-Americans are disadvantaged relative to whites in the labor process. Although some of this disadvantage reflects differences in human capital characteristics and much reflects race-based sorting into lower-skilled jobs, as much as half of the racial differences in closeness of supervision and task complexity may result from some level of direct *individual-level discrimination in the organization of the labor process.*

Race-based effects on the labor process that are conditioned by the sex of the job incumbent were examined as well. There were significant differences between men and women for both race and the association between percent black and the closeness of supervision and task complexity. These models suggest that racial composition effects on the closeness of supervision and task complexity are stronger among women than among men. Further, racial composition effects are important only among whites; thus, as the percentage of blacks rises, white females are more likely than white males to be more closely supervised and to have less complex jobs. Overall, black women are at the most extreme labor process disadvantage because they experience the double disadvantage of both race and sex.

GENDER INEQUALITY

There are also clear differences by sex in the organization of the labor process, but the mechanisms are different than for race. Women's jobs have less complex tasks, less internal labor market opportunity, less managerial authority, and less supervisory responsibility.

The human capital hypothesis can be rejected as an explanation of differences by sex in the organization of the labor process. Human capital differences account for practically none of the observed inequality.

The organizational closure hypothesis can also be rejected. Not only do organizational characteristics not account for gender inequality in the labor process but to some extent they hide the true extent of females' disadvantage in the organization of work.

By contrast, the job closure hypothesis is strongly upheld. Social closure processes in access to desirable jobs are important sources of male-female labor process inequality. The sorting of women into jobs requiring lower skill than those held by men accounts for more than half of the observed gender inequality in labor process organization. It is important that there are few sex-based human capital differences but very large sex-based job-skill differentials (particularly for weeks needed to master the job).

Most important, the status composition hypothesis is strongly supported. The degree of internal labor market opportunity, task complexity, managerial authority, and supervisory responsibility are all depressed as the percentage of women in jobs increases. This is true both across all jobs, and for jobs with men or women only, suggesting a relatively strong status composition effect.[16] The clear presence of this effect for these four variables is consistent with observations that women's jobs provide less access to job ladders, particularly those with managerial and supervisory rungs (Halaby 1979). This result is also consistent with studies that show that for both males and females there is a negative association between the percentage of females in a job and earnings (e.g., Michael, Hartmann, and O'Farrell 1989; England et al. 1988; chap. 6). Female-dominated jobs, whether filled by males or females, provide less access to high-opportunity, high-pay positions within organizations.

Sex and sex composition effects on the labor process that are conditioned by the race of the job incumbent were examined as well. There were no significant differences between blacks and whites for sex effects. For sex composition, the results are more complex. As the percentage of females rises, task complexity falls for blacks but not for whites. Since this relationship was confined to females, sex composition is particularly salient for black females' task complexity. This finding parallels the percent black by sex interaction reported above.

The only other significant percent female by race interaction effect was for internal labor market opportunity. Black males experience significantly lower internal labor market opportunity (relative to white males) as the percentage of females in a job increases. Again, this is a consequence of having double status disadvantages.

CONCLUSIONS

Clearly there are pervasive sex and racial inequalities in the organization of the labor process. For blacks but not for women, some of this inequality can be accounted for by differences in human capital. Race- and sex-linked organizational closure accounts for essentially none of the observed inequality in labor process opportunity. Both blacks and women are more likely to be sorted by employer and general labor market forces into lower-skilled jobs than white males. This job-level closure into low-skill, low-power jobs accounts for much of the observed racial and sex inequalities in access to desirable job characteristics. Finally, there are racial and sex composition effects on the labor process. Whites are disadvantaged in their closeness of supervision, task complexity, managerial authority, and supervisory responsibility when they are in jobs that are held largely by African-Americans. Men and women are disadvantaged in their internal labor market opportunity, managerial authority, and supervisory responsibility in jobs that are held largely by females.

Although blacks are disadvantaged in the labor process over and above their human capital and job-skill characteristics, this disadvantage is not associated with the racial composition of their jobs. This suggests the presence of pervasive *individual-level* direct racial discrimination in the labor process. Since the predominant discrimination patterns used to explain racial inequality in the organization of the labor process were social closure or statistical discrimination processes (as they were in the last chapter as well), it is not surprising that we find evidence pointing to the presence of direct discrimination against black Americans. The statistical discrimination argument is that employers discriminate against black job applicants based on perceived racial differences in average productivity. It does not matter whether these differences are real; what matters is that employers tend to discount blacks' skills and therefore hire them for jobs requiring fewer skills. Although the theory focuses primarily on initial hiring, if the real issue is that there is a generalized prejudice concerning the productivity of black employees, then the process should reproduce itself in opportunities for promotion, individual supervision, and in general throughout the person-job match. I will return to the argument in the penultimate chapter because it provides a plausible explanation for the much higher rates of dissatisfaction and anger over employment opportunities one finds among African-Americans than among the population of white women.

In the next chapter we turn to the consequences of the sex and racial compositions of jobs on the pay gap between men and women and whites and blacks.

Chapter 6
Sex and Racial Segregation and Pay Gaps

Sex segregation in employment has come to represent the dominant (but certainly not the exclusive) explanation in the sociological literature for the male-female earnings gap (see Marini 1989 for a fairly complete review of competing explanations). It is well established that the earnings of both males and females fall as the percentage of females in an occupation rises (e.g., Baron and Newman 1990; Bridges and Nelson 1989; England et al. 1988; Jacobs and Steinberg, 1990; Parcel 1989; Sorenson 1989a, 1989b).[1] Less is known about racial segregation in employment, but researchers have found that as the percentage of minorities in an occupation rises, earnings tend to decline for minorities and dominants alike (Baron and Newman 1990; Parcel 1989; Semyonov and Lewin-Epstein 1989 [for Israel]; Sorenson 1989a, 1989b).

Although the research is fairly conclusive on the link between sex composition and earnings, interpretations of this conclusion are still being debated. Most sociologists argue that the link reflects the status closure and status composition processes that I have been discussing. Women are allocated into low-quality jobs, and high concentrations of women further depress the value assigned to jobs. In particular, the sociological perspective suggests that sex composition becomes a part of the organizational value of a position. This interpretation is disputed by neoclassically inclined economists such as Randall K. Filer (1989, 1990), who expect that market mechanisms will allocate rewards to individuals. Filer's expectation is that there are compensating differentials that make women's work more desirable and that women are compensated with these nonmonetary but still valued rewards. As has already been discussed, the empirical support for this contention is weak (see England et al. 1988; Glass 1990; Jacobs and Steinberg 1990; chap. 5). Filer (1990) points out, however, that the strongest tests of the sex composition–earnings relationship and the refutation of the compensating differentials argument have focused on state civil service positions (see Baron and Newman 1990; Bridges and Nelson 1989; and especially Jacobs and Steinberg 1990). Filer argues that market mechanisms are unlikely to have strong effects in the state sector in that organizational practices are administered rather than market controlled. This study has a clear advantage in meeting this criticism in that it includes the whole labor market, not a single organization, and it includes the private sector. We have already seen (chap. 4), that in fact market competition is associated with *more* rather than less sex and racial segregation.

DEVELOPING AN EARNINGS MODEL

Two similar approaches to estimating earnings inequality were explored for this chapter. The first approach follows the typical strategy of comparable worth or pay equity models and focuses on the effects of the sex and racial compositions of jobs on earnings, controlling for relevant job characteristics. The second approach is more closely related to the typical human capital or sociological wage determination models in that wage-setting processes are estimated separately for men and women and blacks and whites. The substantive results are similar with both approaches. The discussion will focus on the simpler comparable worth approach.

Comparable worth models are generally developed to ascertain the degree to which organizations create discriminatory job structures. Discrimination here refers to the worth attributed to black-dominated or female-dominated jobs, that is, independent of the real differences in skills required to perform the work. A comparable worth model conceptualizes earnings as a function of the productivity or skill-related characteristics attached to jobs and the percentage of blacks or females in the job. The effect of the percentage of females or blacks in the job is interpreted as a status composition effect on the compensation policies of the firm. It is anticipated that the effect on wages will be negative if firms are creating gendered and racial job structures.[2]

To extend this generic model to a general population of jobs with identifiable incumbents, we need to modify the model to take into account the potential impact of individual-level variations in skills, productivity, and organizational value and extend the model to include interfirm as well as intrafirm wage variations. This expanded model implies that wage variations across jobs are a function of job-related characteristics, firm characteristics, individual skill-related characteristics, the racial and sex compositions of the job, and the race and sex of the individuals in the job.[3] This model is substantively similar to comparable worth models in that it assumes that a single process sets wages for all jobs. It diverges from these models in that it controls for the variation in wages attributable to individual characteristics and differences in a firm's resources.

The approach used here is similar to the approach used in the last chapter to analyze labor process inequality. Here, I examine the degree to which racial and gender inequalities in wages reflect individual human capital, organizational resources, job-skill characteristics, and the status composition of jobs. In the last chapter, I referred to these as human capital, organizational closure, job-skill closure, and status composition processes. In this chapter, the wage gaps will be decomposed into those portions attributable to these four basic processes of inequality.

It is also useful to distinguish between the interpretation of job characteristics in this study and that of the typical comparable worth model. In pay equity and comparable worth models (and their academic counterparts), measures of job characteristics are treated as unambiguously representative of real job differences in skill requirements (e.g., Sorenson 1989a, 1989b; Gerhart and Milkovich 1989; Filer 1989). Many sociologists see jobs as defined not only by their production skills but also as power struggles over control of the organization (e.g., Kalleberg, Wallace, and Althauser 1981; Acker 1987). The job characteristics measured in this chapter (complexity, autonomy, training time, required credentials, required experience, supervisory power) are known to be both the outcome and the playing field for struggles between management and labor and between groups of employees for control of organizational activity. As the last chapter pointed out, complexity, autonomy, internal labor market opportunity, and supervisory power are certainly all influenced by job-status composition. That these characteristics are typically evaluated as embodying varying levels of skill is undeniable. The actual organization of jobs, however, is not the unambiguous product of efficiency considerations but represents the outcome of organizational gender, racial, and class politics in the workplace.

The general pay equity model assumes that the earnings process is the same for racial and gender groups. Many scholars have noted that the earnings process can be quite different across these groups. This implies that it is appropriate to examine the general model separately for males and females and blacks and whites. The earnings process will be examined first for the whole sample and then separately for men and women and whites and blacks.[4]

The model estimated for the whole sample probably represents the best policy model in that there is a normative assumption that the earnings process should be the same for blacks and whites and men and women. Some economists have assumed that earnings models estimated for white males only represent nondiscriminatory labor market operations (e.g., Daymont and Andrisani 1984). This is a naive perspective. To the extent that blacks or women are discriminated against in labor markets, some group must benefit, and that group often includes white male employees. In some situations, it may be that employers pocket all of the profits from discrimination, but overall both the historical accounts and the status closure perspective employed in this study lead to the conclusion that superordinates benefit. If only employers benefited, there would be no material incentive for white male employees to support race and gender status hierarchies. Since white males clearly fare better in the quality of their jobs, they certainly benefit, at least given the current distribution of opportunity.[5]

Models that control for human capital, organizational resources, and job-skill variables and that include both racial and sex composition and dummy variables for gender and race can be interpreted fairly unambiguously. The estimated effects of the racial and sex compositions of jobs on earnings represent the institutionalization of an earnings disadvantage over and beyond any individual or job-related productivity or other valued organizational characteristics. Estimates of the sex and race of individuals represent direct estimates of the amount of discrimination not tied to the job.[6]

The general pay equity model employed in this chapter assumes that all of the measured variables have equal causal status in the earnings determination process. To the extent that this is false and the sex and racial compositions of jobs are important determinants of other job characteristics (a clear finding from chapter 5), models that control for job characteristics will tend to underestimate the impact of sex and racial compositions on earnings (Cain 1986). Thus, the pay equity models will reveal only part of the effects of racial and sex compositions on earnings. They will obscure the indirect effects created through the status composition effect on the labor process. In the last chapter I provided strong evidence that sex and racial composition profoundly influence the organization of work (see also Acker and Van Houten 1974; Glass 1990; Reskin 1988; Walby 1986). I get around this problem by presenting upper (i.e., total effects) and lower (i.e., direct effects) estimates of the contribution of the sex and racial compositions of jobs to earnings.[7] Thus, there will be a range of estimates, including the largest and smallest possible racial and sex composition effects on earnings inequality.

The analyses of earnings in this chapter focus on hourly earnings as the dependent variable. Means and standard deviations for the sample and explanations of the measurements for all variables are reported in the methodological appendix.[8]

Years of education, experience, experience squared, and years of tenure with current employer are the indicators of individual human capital just as they were in the last chapter. Job characteristics include whether the job is directly supervised, the degree of supervisory authority, job complexity, closeness of supervision, union membership, job-required credentials, prior experience requirements, and the weeks necessary to learn to do the job well. This is an unusually broad range of job characteristics that can be expected to influence earnings somewhat independently of the racial and sex compositions of the job.

Characteristics of the firms are used to model possible interfirm variations in wages that might reflect differences in their resources (Kalleberg, Wallace, and Althauser 1981; Hodson 1983; Tomaskovic-Devey 1989). The measures used to model such variations include twelve industrial sectors, establishment size, and whether or not the establishment is a for-profit firm.[9]

FINDINGS

Table 6.1 reports the average hourly wages and pay gaps of male and female and white and black employees in North Carolina in 1989. Female employees earned, on average, $3.46 less per hour than male employees, or 71 percent of the males' wages. Black employees earned $2.30 less per hour than white employees, or 78 percent. The pay gaps are, of course, larger when the self-employed are included in the sample and when monthly earnings rather than hourly wages are compared. Females make only 53 percent of males' monthly earnings, reflecting their lower probability of being self-employed and the fact that, on average, they work substantially fewer hours than males. This gap is very similar to current national male-female hourly wage gaps (Marini 1989). Blacks earn in a month only 64 percent of whites' monthly earnings.

Figure 6.1 is the starting point for our investigation into the degree to which these observed pay gaps can be attributed to the sex and racial compositions of jobs. Figure 6.1 reports the simple regression of earnings on the percent black and percent female in the job for the entire sample. As the percent black in the job rises, earnings fall dramatically. The picture is even more dramatic for percent female.

Table 6.2 reports earnings consequences for five samples and four different models of a rise in percent female and percent black. The numbers in the table represent the earnings loss associated with a 1

Table 6.1.   Male-female and white-black hourly wage inequalities among North Carolina employees, 1989

Panel A	Male	Female	Pay gap	Female as % male
Average hourly wage	11.83	8.37	3.46	70.75
(standard deviation)	(10.93)	(4.11)		

Panel B	White	Black	Pay gap	Black as % white
Average hourly wage	10.33	8.03	2.30	77.73
(standard deviation)	(8.69)	(4.00)		

percent rise in percent female or percent black. The samples represent the whole population of jobs and those subsamples of jobs filled only by males, females, whites, and blacks respectively. The first set of models reports the gross effects of percent black and percent female on earnings controlling for no other variables. The next model controls for individual human capital characteristics. The third model adds to the human capital control variables statistical controls for job and firm characteristics. The final model adds individual variables that reflect sex and race. Sex and racial differences in earnings that are not explained by these models are reported in the final two rows.[10]

For the whole population as well as the sex and race subsamples, we see that as the proportion minority and proportion female in the job rises, hourly earnings fall. There are two exceptions at the level of gross effects. Among the black subsample, the relationship between percent black in the job and earnings is consistently nonsignificant. This may reflect the small size of the sample and limited variation for this variable among blacks. Percent female is not significantly related to earnings among males at the level of gross effects. It is significant, however, once job characteristics are controlled, reflecting that sex-integrated jobs are somewhat more common when the educational requirements are higher.

Once we control for individual human capital characteristics, the effect of percent black is reduced substantially for all models, suggesting that variations in human capital between whites and blacks as well as between white-dominated and black-dominated jobs account for some of the observed association between racial composition and earnings. Controlling for human capital differences does not substantially influence the relationship between percent female and earnings. Both findings are consistent with the labor process analyses in chapter 5. Con-

Figure 6.1. Percent female and percent black and hourly wages of North Carolina jobs, 1989

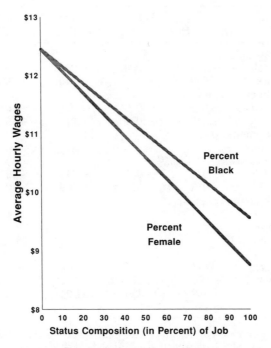

trolling for job and firm characteristics reduces the size of the effect of both percent female and percent black in the model that contains the whole population. The percent black relationship with earnings is quite weak at this point. The percent female coefficient is now strongly statistically significant for the male subsample. Overall, percent female is associated significantly with lower wages for all subsamples, even when human capital, firm resources, and an extensive set of job skill and power characteristics are statistically controlled. The effect of percent black is weaker, and although it is significant for the whole population and for the male and female subsamples, it is not significant within the race subsamples when control variables are included.

The final set of models adds (where appropriate) individual race and gender variables.[11] For the whole-population model, percent female remains significantly negatively associated with the earnings net of human capital, firm resources, job characteristics, and even the individuals' sex. Sex is not significantly associated with earnings in this model. Neither the individuals' race nor the racial composition of the job is significantly associated with the earnings net of human capital, job, and

Table 6.2. Effects of racial and sex compositions on hourly wages of employed North Carolinians for various models, 1989

	All (N = 654)	Males (N = 294)	Females (N = 360)	Whites (N = 539)	Blacks (N = 115)
Gross effect					
Percent female	− .027	.008	− .020	− .040	− .023
Percent black	− .029	− .041	− .020	− .026	.006
Effect net of human capital					
Percent female	− .036	− .020	− .016	− .038	− .024
Percent black	− .018	− .021	− .013	− .016	− .001
Effect net of human capital, job characteristics, and firm characteristics					
Percent female	− .024	− .063	− .013	− .027	− .016
Percent black	− .012	− .028	− .009	− .018	.003
Effect net of human capital, job characteristics, firm characteristics, and individual gender and/or race					
Percent female	− .023	− .063	− .012	− .036	.006
Percent black	− .009	− .027	− .002	− .018	.003
Minority	− .459	− .126	−1.24	–	–
Female	− .120	–	–	.968	−2.48

Note: Metric regression coefficients reported. **Bold** indicates statistically significant at or below the .10 probability level, although almost all **bold** coefficients are significant below the .05 probability level. All tests of statistical significance are one-tailed tests. Models including human capital, job characteristics, and firm characteristics can be found in tables A6.1 and A6.2

firm characteristics. The results from this model are consistent with previous findings that the percent female influences the earnings net of job and human capital controls but that percent black does not. When race dummies are not included in the model, however, the relationship between percent black and earnings is significant for the whole population as well as for the male and female subsamples.

The results across the subsamples are consistent for percent female. Males and females experience declining real wages as percent female rises. In fact, the earnings penalty for males associated with a rise in percent female is much higher than the penalty for females. For every 10 percent increase in percent female in their jobs, males' wages decline by $.63; for the same increase, females' wages decline by only $.13. Percent female becomes nonsignificant in the model for the black subsample once the female dummy variable is entered. Black females, however, do have significantly lower wages ($2.48) than black males even after controlling for human capital, job, and firm characteristics.

Racial composition is consistently nonsignificant in the final models, although black women seem to face a direct earnings disadvantage not tied to any job characteristic.

Table 6.3 uses the results of the pay equity model (all sample) to estimate the effects of racial and sex compositions on the pay gap between whites and blacks and males and females. In pay equity studies, all job characteristics are seen as legitimate sources of pay variation, while the effects of percent female and percent black are the indicators of institutionalized discrimination to be remedied. Since these studies make the unreasonable assumption that job characteristics are not themselves the result of the sex and racial compositions of jobs, they undoubtedly underestimate the contribution of sex and racial segregation to earnings inequality at the job level.[12]

The gross effect of percent female on earnings (reported in table 6.3) suggests that 86 percent of the pay gap between males and females is associated with the gender composition of jobs. Once individual human capital is controlled, fully 83 percent of the pay gap remains associated with the sex composition of jobs. This number can be interpreted as an upper-bound estimate. If all job and firm characteristics that affect earnings and that are associated with sex were the product of sex composition, a clearly improbable assumption, then we could attribute 83 percent of the sex gap in earnings among employees in North Carolina in 1989 to the sex composition of jobs. The effect of the sex composition net of human capital, job, and firm characteristics accounts for $1.92 or 56 percent of the original pay gap between male and female employees. Racial composition has only a trivial relationship to this gap.

The gross effect of percent black on earnings, reported in table 6.3, suggests that 50 percent of the pay gap between blacks and whites is associated with the racial composition of jobs. Once individual human capital is controlled, only 31 percent of the gap remains associated with the racial composition of jobs. This number can also be interpreted as an upper-bound estimate. If all job and firm characteristics that affect earnings and that are associated with race were the product of racial composition, again an improbable assumption, then we could attribute 31 percent of the gap in earnings between white and black employees in North Carolina in 1989 to the racial composition of their jobs. The effect of the racial composition net of human capital, job, and firm characteristics accounts for $.48 or 21 percent of the original pay gap between

Table 6.3. *Proportion of pay gap associated with percent black and percent female, based on pooled pay equity–type model, among employed North Carolinians, 1989*

	Gender		Race	
	Dollar value	% of gap	Dollar value	% of gap
Gross effect[a]				
Percent female	2.96	86	−.20	−9
Percent black	.03	1	1.16	50
Effect net of human capital[b]				
Percent female	2.88	83	−.20	−9
Percent black	.02	1	.72	31
Effect net of human capital, job characteristics, and firm characteristics[c]				
Percent female	1.92	56	−.13	−6
Percent black	.01	0	.48	21

[a]Corresponds to equation 1 in table A6.1.
[b]Corresponds to equation 2 in table A6.1.
[c]Corresponds to equation 3 in table A6.1.

white and black employees. Sex composition has a small relationship to this gap, slightly favoring African-Americans.

Table 6.4 decomposes the pay gap into its constituent parts for the pay equity model. This is accomplished in the same manner as in table 6.3 except that it is done for all variables in the model and the contribution to the pay gap that results from sex- and race-specific average levels of the variables are summed within the three categories of human capital variables, firm variables, and job characteristics.[13] Notice that the reported levels for percent female and percent black are identical to those in the bottom rows of table 6.3.

The $3.46 male-female pay gap is almost totally explained (all but $.02) by this model. Fifty-six percent of this gap is associated with the sex composition of jobs even after extensive controls for human capital, job characteristics, and firm characteristics. Job characteristics explain an additional 28 percent. Firm-level segmentation is associated with 13 percent of the gap, and human capital characteristics with 3 percent. Thus, status composition effects explain 56 percent, status closure effects (job + firm characteristics) 41 percent, and human capital only 3 percent of the male-female pay gap.

The pattern for the black-white pay gap is quite different. Black-white differences in their mean levels of job characteristics explain 38 percent

Table 6.4. Proportion of pay gap among employed North Carolinians attributable to racial and sex compositions, human capital, and job and firm characteristics, based on pooled pay equity–type model, 1989

	Male-female dollar pay gap	Proportion of gap	White-black dollar pay gap	Proportion of gap
Total	3.46	100%	2.30	100%
Percent female	1.92	56	−.13	−6
Percent black	.01	0	.48	21
Human capital	.12	3	.70	31
Job characteristics	.95	28	.88	38
Firm characteristics	.44	13	.04	2
Unexplained	.02	1	.33	14

Note: All results are calculated from within sex and race category mean substitution into equation 3 of table A6.1.

of the pay gap, and human capital differences explain an additional 31 percent. Only 21 percent is attributable to the racial composition of jobs. Finally, firm characteristics play a trivial role in creating the black-white pay gap. Thus, status composition effects explain 21 percent, status closure 40 percent, and human capital 31 percent of the black-white pay gap.[14]

CONCLUSIONS

At the very least, 56 percent of the $3.46 hourly earnings gap between men and women employees in North Carolina can be attributed to the sex composition of jobs. This estimate is quite a bit higher than Elaine Sorenson's (1989a, 1989b) estimate, which was 20 percent. In her models, however, fully 39 percent of the white male–white female and 48 percent of the white male–minority female gaps went unexplained. If most of the unexplained portion of the gap was, in fact, attributable to the sex composition of jobs but missed in her models because of the use of aggregate measures of sex composition, then the estimates are not too far apart. The portion of the male-female earnings gap attributable to the sex composition of jobs is somewhat more comparable to the early estimate of Donald Treiman and Heidi Hartmann (1981), which was 48 percent.

Although the effects of racial composition on earnings were weaker than the effects of sex composition, this study did find significant racial composition effects in models that control for human capital, job characteristics, and firms' resources. The models suggest that at the very least 21 percent of the black-white gap in earnings among North Carolina employees in 1989 may have been attributable to racial segregation

Figure 6.2.   Sources of the male-female pay gap among North Carolina employees, 1989

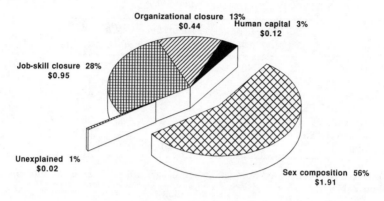

Organizational closure 13%
$0.44   Human capital 3%
$0.12

Job-skill closure 28%
$0.95

Unexplained 1%
$0.02

Sex composition 56%
$1.91

Hourly wage gap = $3.46

at the job level. This is almost four times the effect reported by Sorenson (1989a, 1989b). Although the use of job-level measures of racial composition does seem to have strengthened the observed association with earnings (relative to more aggregate occupational measures), the association is still fairly weak. Job characteristics and human capital differences are more important determinants of racial differences in earnings than is the racial composition of employment. Status closure processes predominate, followed by class inequalities in the creation of racial inequality (see figs. 6.2 and 6.3).[15]

There is ample theoretical reason to expect that gender composition profoundly influences the organization of work (Reskin 1988; Cockburn 1988; Walby 1986; Acker and Van Houten 1974). Recent empirical studies have demonstrated that the sex and racial composition of jobs may profoundly influence the labor process (Glass 1990). In the last chapter we learned that as the percentage of females in a job increases there is a decrease for both men and women in levels of supervisory authority, managerial responsibility, and internal labor market opportunity, controlling for job-skill levels. As the percentage of blacks in a job increases, whites have less autonomy, task complexity, managerial responsibility, and supervisory authority than other whites, again controlling for job skill. Thus, pay equity models with their assumption that job characteristics and racial and sex compositions are equally exogenous to the wage-setting process are most likely wrong and tend to lead us to underestimate the consequences of sex and racial segregation on wage inequality. One can go further and criticize the material in chapter 5 for

Figure 6.3. Sources of the white-black pay gap among North Carolina employees, 1989

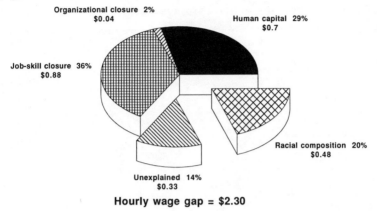

Organizational closure 2%
$0.04

Human capital 29%
$0.7

Job-skill closure 36%
$0.88

Racial composition 20%
$0.48

Unexplained 14%
$0.33

Hourly wage gap = $2.30

treating any job-skill measures as outside the labor process. Reskin (1988) and Cockburn (1988) provide strong theoretical arguments that we should expect that the very definition and evaluation of skill are influenced by the gender of typical job incumbents. It seems reasonable to expect the same, if perhaps a weaker, status effect for race.

All of these findings support the general conclusion that racial composition probably explains somewhat more than 21 percent of the black-white earnings gap in North Carolina but less than the upper-bound estimate of 32 percent (from the model that controls for just human capital). Similarly, the real-world effects of sex composition on the male-female earnings gap is probably greater than 56 percent, but less than the 83 percent upper-bound estimate when only human capital characteristics are controlled.

There are also substantively different processes by which the black-white and male-female wage gaps are generated. The male-female wage gap is not the result of sex differences in human capital, whereas black-white differences in human capital are extremely important sources of black-white differences in earnings. Exclusionary status closure processes are important sources of both race-based and sex-based wage inequalities. Both earnings gaps are substantially linked to segregation in the skills and power invested in jobs. It is quite likely that some of this skill and power segregation reflects status processes whereby the sex and racial compositions of jobs influence the social organization of the work. Most of this skill and power segregation, however, probably reflects discrimination in hiring.[16] The characteristics of firms seem to explain more of the male-female gap than the black-white gap in earnings.[17] Finally, although both the sex and racial compositions of jobs influence their respective earnings gaps, the effect of gender is much more powerful.

Appendix to Chapter 6

Not all multiple regression equations are reported in this appendix since that would add many pages to the book without adding much in clarity. The primary equations on which the pay gap decompositions are based are presented in table A6.1. In addition, a representative set of incremental models for the whole sample is reproduced in table A6.2. The means, standard deviations, and measurement definitions for all variables are presented in the methodological appendix to the volume.

Table A6.1.   Pooled regressions (all employees) of hourly earnings on the racial and sex compositions of jobs, human capital, and job and firm characteristics (N = 654)

Characteristics	Equation 1[a]		2		3	
Percent female	−.037	(.01)	−.036	(.01)	−.024	(.007)
Percent black	−.029	(.01)	−.018	(.01)	−.012	(.01)
Education	−	−	1.06	(.12)	.59	(.17)
Firm tenure	−	−	.31	(.04)	.23	(.04)
Experience	−	−	.27	(.07)	.18	(.07)
Experience squared	−	−	−.005	(.02)	−.004	(.002)
Autonomous (yes = 1)	−	−	−	−	1.23	(1.13)
Supervisory authority	−	−	−	−	−.07	(.15)
Job complexity	−	−	−	−	.38	(.19)
Closeness of supervision (yes = 1)	−	−	−	−	−.18	(.16)
Union member	−	−	−	−	2.99	(.99)
Job-required credential	−	−	−	−	.12	(.16)
Prior experience (yes = 1)	−	−	−	−	.13	(.63)
Weeks to learn job	−	−	−	−	.02	(.004)
Establishment size	−	−	−	−	.51	(.17)
For-profit firm (yes = 1)	−	−	−	−	2.37	(.99)
Sector						
Extractive	−	−	−	−	.86	(3.26)
Construction	−	−	−	−	−2.11	(1.75)
Manufacturing	−	−	−	−	−1.75	(1.40)
Transport/utility	−	−	−	−	7.27	(1.86)
Wholesale trade	−	−	−	−	−1.48	(1.97)
Retail trade	−	−	−	−	−1.67	(1.45)
Business services	−	−	−	−	.99	(1.50)
Personnel services	−	−	−	−	−.61	(2.21)
Social services	−	−	−	−	−1.07	(1.11)
Constant	12.45	(.53)	−5.25	(1.89)	−6.82	(3.32)
Adjusted R^2	.048		.204		.303	

[a]Regression coefficient (standard error).

Table A6.2. *Regression hourly wage models for sex and racial groups*

Characteristics	Male		Female		White		Black	
Percent female	−.063	(.032)	−.013	(.009)	−.027	(.008)	−.016	(.008)
Percent black	−.028	(.202)	−.009	(.007)	−.018	(.015)	.003	(.010)
Education	.88	(.32)	.19	(.13)	.72	(.21)	.22	(.19)
Firm tenure	.26	(.08)	.13	(.03)	.22	(.05)	.17	(.06)
Experience	.14	(.14)	.06	(.06)	.19	(.08)	.07	(.09)
Experience squared	−.002	(.004)	−.001	(.002)	−.004	(.002)	−.001	(.003)
Autonomous (yes = 1)	2.99	(2.12)	−1.28	(.85)	1.09	(1.25)	1.07	(3.13)
Supervisory authority	−.41	(.30)	.21	(.12)	−.11	(.18)	.30	(.21)
Job complexity	1.12	(.40)	−.08	(.13)	.51	(.23)	−.17	(.26)
Closeness of supervision	−.41	(.33)	−.04	(.10)	−.27	(.19)	.17	(.18)
Union member (yes = 1)	6.76	(1.95)	−.38	(.69)	3.63	(1.21)	1.40	(1.16)
Job-required credential	−.22	(.32)	.51	(.11)	−.01	(.19)	.44	(.19)
Prior experience (yes = 1)	−.19	(1.35)	.38	(.41)	.17	(.76)	−.33	(.66)
Weeks to learn job	.02	(.008)	.007	(.004)	.02	(.005)	.03	(.01)
Establishment size	1.01	(.34)	.15	(.12)	.54	(.20)	.25	(.20)
For-profit firm (yes = 1)	3.30	(2.95)	.89	(.57)	2.77	(1.16)	−.78	(1.23)
Sector								
Extractive	2.13	(5.49)	−3.24	(3.29)	−.38	(3.98)	6.90	(3.57)
Construction	−2.36	(3.71)	−2.31	(1.94)	−2.72	(2.13)	.61	(1.91)
Manufacturing	−2.88	(3.39)	−1.75	(0.99)	−2.06	(1.69)	.36	(1.64)
Transport/utility	6.70	(3.81)	5.80	(1.80)	7.40	(2.26)	4.58	(2.03)
Wholesale trade	−1.08	(4.16)	−3.38	(1.57)	−2.25	(2.35)	2.00	(2.33)
Retail trade	−1.71	(3.64)	−3.08	(1.00)	−2.07	(1.77)	.54	(1.64)
Business services	2.71	(3.82)	−.66	(1.01)	.68	(1.81)	1.26	(1.72)
Personnel services	1.50	(4.52)	−1.76	(1.68)	−.46	(2.73)	−.97	(2.20)
Social services	−2.81	(2.28)	−1.30	(.83)	−1.46	(1.37)	.02	(1.20)
Constant	−16.96	(6.17)	5.34	(2.65)	−7.98	(3.97)	−.32	(4.72)
N	294		360		539		115	
Adjusted R^2	.298		.339		.292		.435	

Note: Regression coefficient (standard error).

CHAPTER 7
THEORETICAL CONCLUSIONS

T HIS BOOK HAS FOCUSED on the sources and consequences of race- and sex-based job segregation. I have examined theories of social- ization, competitive market behavior by employers and employees, status-based processes of social closure, status composition processes, and the cultural and organizational context of both segregation and discrimination. Along the way, we have learned that the racial and sex compositions of jobs are among a limited number of social processes that lead to black-white and male-female workplace inequalities. The sex and racial compositions of jobs are fundamental determinants of both the organization of work and the rate of pay for men and women and blacks and whites. Status closure, particularly the exclusion of women and minorities from desirable jobs, is also an extremely impor- tant source of both labor process and wage inequalities.

This chapter is organized around major theoretical traditions and their utility for understanding processes of both segregation and work- place inequality. The conclusions about these traditions are based on the findings in the preceding chapters and supporting evidence from other studies. This chapter is not a summary of findings or of methods. Such summaries can be found in chapter 1 and elsewhere throughout the text. I begin by examining the utility of market models derived from neoclassical economics.

FAILURE OF NEOCLASSICAL ECONOMIC MODELS

Theoretical economists generally limit the scope of neoclassical theory to a set of hypothetical conditions. These conditions presume utility- (generally lifetime or long-term income) maximizing behavior on the part of individuals and firms; competitive markets for all commodities, including capital, products, and labor; and perfect information among all market participants. Under these ideal conditions, markets are assumed to allocate resources in a maximally efficient manner. One implication of this model is that employees will be rewarded with wages, benefits, and other remuneration consistent with their individual productivity. The expectation is that there are extraordinarily dynamic institutional arrangements whereby the actors are continually changing production processes, employees, capitalization patterns, and competitive strategies in rational attempts to maximize income.

Empirically, most economists recognize that individuals may have competing sources of utility (e.g., leisure, custom, family, as well as earnings), that markets are often less than purely competitive, and that information is imperfect, all of which lead to inefficiencies in labor, capital, and product allocation. Given these empirical deviations from idealistic theory, economists in the neoclassical tradition tend to emphasize the short-term *marginal* effects of competitive market forces and the long-term tendencies for competing utilities (especially in this context traditional discriminatory status hierarchies), market imperfections (segregated labor markets or oligopolistic product markets), and information deficiencies (false prejudices about group productivity) to be eroded by the income-maximizing behavior of firms and individuals.

Thus, racism and sexism are seen as representing historical vestiges of alternative utilities, precapitalist social relations, short-term market imperfections, and informational deficiencies. To the extent that racial and gender inequalities represent anything but actual (and potential) workplace differences in productivity, labor market mechanisms should in the short term marginally erode inequalities and over the long term obliterate them as profit-maximizing employers employ lower-priced black and female labor and in so doing bid up their wage rates. Similarly, income-maximizing minorities and women should seek out nondiscriminating employers and invest in the necessary human capital to compete for the best jobs.

To the extent that racial and gender inequalities are based on actual workplace differences in productivity, labor markets are expected to reflect those differences and in the short term to reproduce those inequalities. In fact, when neoclassical economists are disappointed by the slow pace of change, their theoretical bias is to account for this slow pace by assuming actual (but unmeasured) differences in productivity, sometimes based on different utilities (e.g., Becker 1985). Some neoclassical economists, particularly when confronting enduring and perhaps widening racial inequalities in the United States, have been led to doubt the usefulness of the neoclassical economic model at all for understanding racial and gender inequalities (e.g., Cain 1986).

The strength of neoclassical theory is in its clear predictions that one set of processes may erode racial and gender inequalities. Neoclassical thinking oversteps its potential contribution when it attempts to provide a total and decontextualized explanation of racial and gender inequalities. Market mechanisms, although potentially powerful, must share the stage with cultural, legal, political, familial, and organizational processes, which together shape the labor process of workplaces, the allocation of people to jobs, and the administration of commodity and capital markets. Since there are multiple causal factors, and these factors can interact with one another, often in unanticipated ways, it would be naive, in the extreme, to give theoretical (or policy) priority to the neoclassical model of labor market organization.

A central problem with the neoclassical expectation that discrimination will be eroded by market prices is that the imperative of market competition in determining a firm's survival is an occasional disruption of normal economic life rather than a condition of everyday life. Neoclassical economics makes the same theoretical mistake that functionalist sociology does—it conceptualizes society as tightly integrated around a single organizing principle (competition and functional necessity respectively). Social systems are, however, generally loosely coupled; competition (or dysfunctional practices) are only occasionally threatening to organizational survival. Thus, Reskin and Roos (1990) find that market forces occasionally do compel employers (e.g., insurance adjusters) to substitute cheaper female labor for male labor but that they are the exception to the more general pattern of business as usual.

HUMAN CAPITAL: THE SUPPLY-SIDE NEOCLASSICAL MODEL

The historical legacies of slavery and the American apartheid system that legally existed (at least in the South) until the mid-1960s have produced a clear disadvantage for blacks in the accumulation, and possibly the quality, of their human capital–enhancing education.[1] In addition, to the extent that African-Americans are more likely to be geographically concentrated in labor markets with low on-the-job training costs and intermittent employment opportunities (i.e., central cities and the rural South), they will have fewer opportunities than whites (who are more spatially disbursed and more likely to live in high-opportunity locales). Given a human capital model of labor market organization and the historical and geographical experience of blacks in the United States, the neoclassical model predicts that black Americans as a group will have distinct labor market disadvantages, even in environments that do not discriminate on the basis of race.[2]

In this study human capital differences between blacks and whites account for about a quarter of both the labor process and wage inequalities. It would be a mistake, however, to interpret these differences as nondiscriminatory. Even within the neoclassical framework, for these differences to be nondiscriminatory would require that they be the result of innate differences in *potential* productivity rather than the legacy of historical and contemporary but pre–labor market discrimination (Cain 1986). Human capital–based black-white inequality should be interpreted as discrimination that has its sources in history, homes, and communities rather than in the labor market.[3]

As it should be clear, however, not all human capital disadvantages are tied to individual education and community structures that provide opportunities. African-Americans confront substantial discrimination in hiring, leading to a higher unemployment rate than that of the white majority. The effect is to reduce blacks' labor force experiences and the valuable on-the-job training that they can provide. Even if the current employer is not discriminating on the basis of race, it is quite possible that the last employer did.

Over the long term, and it is here that neoclassical theory is weakest, the prediction is that African-Americans, in efforts to maximize their utility, will invest aggressively in education, avoid race-segregated jobs in the labor market, and move to higher-opportunity labor markets. Employers should be motivated by competitive market processes as well as profit-maximizing goals to hire black labor and over the long term bid up their wages and so close the black-white gap in earnings. This research did not find that African-Americans with higher human capital investments (or more pressing family responsibilities) were more likely to avoid segregated jobs. Nor did it find that firms in more competitive markets were any less likely to have segregated jobs. In fact, segregation tended to be higher in the private sector than in the totally noncompetitive public sector, and there were no consistent differences in the patterns within the private sector that reflected the degree of product market competition.

There is no evidence in this study that income- and profit-maximizing behavior by employees and employers will lead to an erosion of racial segregation. The evidence in other studies suggests that the most important sources of the contemporary convergence of blacks' and whites' earnings has been the civil rights movement and its derivative antisegregation and affirmative action policies in both educational institutions and workplaces (Burstein 1985) and changes in the occupational structure, particularly the erosion of low-wage jobs in southern agriculture and in domestic work, where many black Americans have historically been concentrated (Wilson 1978; Fosset, Galle, and Burr 1989). The near convergence in the late 1970s and early 1980s of blacks' and whites' educational achievements followed by more than a decade the period of the most rapid convergence in earnings, 1967–1974. This reversal of the proposed timing of gains in equality is strong evidence against the long-term prediction of human capital theory. It was, of course, during the earlier period that political, legal, and administrative efforts to end racial discrimination in the United States were at their peak.

The current neoclassical explanation of gender differences in workplace productivity is made in the context of the new home economics, associated most closely with Gary Becker (1981, 1985). The argument is that households, not individuals, maximize their utility by devising a household division of labor in which partners specialize in market or domestic work. In most households, men specialize in market work and women in domestic work for reasons of socialization, custom, and childbearing and because males in contemporary labor markets are generally able to earn higher wages.

Sex segregation and the wage gap between men and women are described as the outcomes of this household decision-making process. Although many wives work, they choose jobs that allow them the flexibility to specialize in their primary household responsibility—domestic work. Thus, they choose part-time jobs or jobs with high starting wages but low wage growth and low penalties for labor force withdrawal. Employers, it is argued, react to these labor supply preferences and create a segregated male and female employment structure that fulfills the needs of wives and mothers for flexible, interruptable work (Polachek 1979, 1985).

In the new home economics, male-female wage inequality is not the result of discrimination but of the rational household allocation of labor. According to this formulation, over the long term the wage gap and segregated occupational structures may endure because they are consistent with the maximization of household (rather than individual) utilities. There are "compensating differentials" in women's work, such as flexibility and the freedom to leave the labor market for periods of full-time domestic work, that balance out the typically low wages paid in female-dominated occupations.

Past research has shown that the predicted relationship between women's starting salaries and the wage depreciation for labor force withdrawal does not exist (England 1982; England et al. 1988; Corcoran and Ponza 1984; Greenberger and Steinberg 1983). In a recent study,

Glass (1990) showed that as the percentage of females in an occupation rises, work organizations actually become less flexible. I found that in those households where one would expect men to be most likely to specialize in market work and women in domestic work (i.e., married men and women with children), there were no particular tendencies for men or women to end up in sex-stereotyped jobs. Since this is a central link in the causal process described by the new home economics, this finding sheds considerable doubt on this explanation. Although it is undeniable that women more often elect, generally for domestic reasons, to work part time and have more labor market interruptions than men, these domestic considerations do not affect the sex composition of the jobs they enter. Since sex composition is so strongly implicated in the earnings gap between men and women, the current neoclassical account tells us mostly about the portion of the wage gap that is attributable to differences in hours worked, but it is largely wrong in describing the processes that create sex-segregated jobs. It is also clearly the case that a neoclassical account is not required to understand, and does not have any theoretical advantages over, a more general sociological theory of the household labor process (England and Farkas 1986).

The rejection of the new home economics leads us back to a more traditional neoclassical account that predicts a long-term erosion of the male-female wage gap as women increase their labor force participation and close the educational gap.[4] Gender convergences in educational achievement and labor force participation were quite rapid over the last three decades, although wage convergence was not. There is some limited evidence for a slight narrowing of the wage gap in the 1980s (Jacobs 1989b). The long-term trend, however, is for considerable stability, even in the face of tremendous growth in women's educational credentials and labor force commitment. Human capital predictions are just not consistent with the long-term trends.

The nearly total segregation of men and women into different occupational and job structures suggests there is a more compelling explanation for this stability. Only rarely do men and women compete for the same jobs. In the North Carolina sample used in this study, most women worked in jobs that were entirely female and most men in jobs that were entirely male. Even taking into account the minority in integrated jobs, the average man was in a job in which 92 percent of his co-workers were male and the average woman was in a job in which 88 percent were female.

Reskin and Roos (1990) show in their important study that in those occupations in which women increased their representation disproportionally in the 1970s, they rarely competed directly with men for positions. Instead, more typically the quality of the job was being eroded so that men had left the job (e.g., printers, bartenders, pharmacists, and insurance adjusters), employment growth was so strong that there was room for entry-level women as men took emerging supervisory jobs (e.g., systems analysts), or both processes were happening simultaneously (e.g., accountants and bookkeepers). In any case, although the occupations integrated, separate, largely sex-segregated labor markets remain. Even the most committed neoclassical theorist would not expect market forces to erode inequality where there is no competition.

To the extent that Reskin and Roos (1990) identify market forces as undermining occupational segregation, it is as a result of the behavior of employers. Employers have on numerous occasions redesigned and often deskilled jobs to save on labor costs. When the attractiveness of jobs is reduced through deskilling and reductions in compensation, they become less attractive to appropriately skilled males and women increasingly fill open positions. These positions can still be quite attractive to women, because of the overall low wages available in traditionally female jobs. For example, although women selling real estate (an integrating occupation) averaged only $6.97 per hour in 1979, this was considerably more than women made in traditionally female jobs that required comparable skills, such as typists ($4.64), general office clerks ($4.90), and even teachers ($6.33) (Reskin and Roos 1990:62). So, while men fled jobs selling household real estate because of their declining earnings, women flocked to these jobs because the wages were higher than in the typically female jobs that were available. Consistent with the findings in my study, Reskin and Roos show, however, that as the proportion of women rise in an integrating occupation, the wage advantages decline.

This study revealed only small human capital differences between men and women and their effects on the wage gap and labor process inequality were essentially trivial. Segregation tended to increase, not decrease, in jobs that required more human capital either in the form of on-the-job training or educational credentials. Human capital investments have little or no consequences in the gendered matching of individuals and jobs.[5]

STATISTICAL DISCRIMINATION: THE DEMAND-SIDE NEOCLASSICAL MODEL

Although the competitive market models that are loosely referred to as human capital theory share an enduring faith in the power of utility maximizing to undermine market and information imperfections, statistical discrimination theory is a generally neoclassical view that presents a set of conditions under which, at least in the short term, discrimination is consistent with market models. The argument is that all employers have to make employment decisions based on imperfect information. That is, it is hard to tell by looking at someone and reading his or her résumé or job application whether he or she will work out as an employee. To minimize the risk of a bad (i.e., costly) job match, employers use certain cues such as education, experience, standardized tests, and interviews to make an educated guess about the potential productivity of a candidate.

Sex and race, it is argued, are often used as cues in the hiring decision as well. What makes this model different from a sociological model of discrimination, or a social closure model based on status, is that the behavior is seen as rational in that it may maximize profits over the long term. Where training costs are high, discriminating against women or African-Americans is economically advantageous if, in fact, the average woman or African-American is less likely to work out in the job. Discrimination is based on employers' perceptions of average differences in group productivity. Although individual women and African-Americans will face unjust discrimination, and employers will miss some potentially fine employees, on average, employers will save money in training costs and lost productivity. This is true only if there are, in fact, group differences in productivity. Thus, the argument is that employers have a strong economic motivation to exclude any workers who they suspect will not work out.

I found very strong evidence that employers allocate African-Americans to jobs that require low educational credentials and have low on-the-job training costs. This skill segregation by race was the strongest measured source of black-white earnings inequality and labor process inequality. The racial composition of jobs is strongly tied to this process of skill-linked status closure. The process of skill segregation, particularly labor process inequality, was important for women and men as well. Gender composition is linked to skill segmentation but also to supervisory and managerial power and internal labor market opportunity. In addition, the degree of gender segregation tends to increase as the quality of the job increases, whereas the pattern for racial segregation is (weakly) in the opposite direction. These findings suggest that processes consistent with the predictions of statistical discrimination may, in fact, be operating to create racial segregation and inequality but that a more pervasive process of status closure characterizes gender segregation and inequality.

This conclusion hinges, however, on the logical adequacy of the statistical discrimination account. There is a strong and a weak version of statistical discrimination theory.

In the strong version, statistical discrimination is the result of actual group differences in productivity and training costs. Are whites more productive as a group? Are women less productive than men? The latter question may be moot at this point since the empirical findings of this study suggest that narrow skill-based discrimination does not account for gender inequality. The former question, however, is important and troubling. There is some evidence that the quality of education typically received by black Americans is lower than that provided to white Americans (Card and Krueger 1990). There is also evidence, however, that industries that employ many African-Americans have higher productivity, even controlling for the human capital composition of the work force, capital investment, and market concentration (Galle, Wiswell, and Burr 1985; Tomaskovic-Devey 1988). It is not possible to conclude that there are, in fact, real productivity differences. The reality that most skills are learned on the job (Berg 1970) strongly implies that racist exclusion, not rational profit-maximizing behavior, leads to skill-based segregation. In any case, as Cain (1986) points out, jobs with high training costs typically have trial periods during which employees may be fired at will. Such trial periods seem to be a much more efficient way of ascertaining the adequacy of a job match than eliminating all candidates of a certain race or gender.

If there are differences by race in current average training costs, which is doubtful, there is something of a catch-22 here. If young African-Americans suspect that they may face skill discrimination, then they may be less motivated to invest their time and effort in acquiring a high-quality education. Certainly the tendency of employers to steer black job candidates away from jobs that provide lengthy and valuable training directly creates a skill disadvantage. The argument here is identical to the argument that human capital models treat women's pre–labor market expectations and plans as individual choices. If individuals can see discrimination and segregation coming, then it would not be surprising if they adjusted their behavior accordingly.

The weak version of statistical discrimination theory is more compelling. Here it is necessary only that employers *perceive* that there are group differences in average training costs to justify their excluding qualified blacks from jobs with significant costs for training.[6] In neoclassical terms, it is a problem of imperfect information. In sociological terms, it is a problem of discrimination. That is, if many employers are prejudiced and act on that prejudice by discriminating against African-Americans when hiring and promoting into skilled jobs, then we would expect labor market patterns to be similar to the statistical discrimination account and consistent with the findings in this study.

Although this version of statistical discrimination is more plausible, it is also theoretically superfluous. In neoclassical terms, if discrimination were only a problem of imperfect information, it would be eroded fairly quickly by market forces. Since the erosion is not rapid and there is no compelling evidence that there are differences in training costs, a more parsimonious approach should focus on the causal process at work— racism—rather than on an economic rationalization of that process— statistical discrimination.

UTILITY OF SOCIOLOGICAL CLOSURE AND STATUS COMPOSITION MODELS

Racism and sexism at work are the results of pervasive status-based processes of social closure in which opportunities for higher-quality jobs are reserved for superordinate-status individuals. Job segregation along racial and gender lines reflects only minimally group differences in human capital acquisition. Racial and gender inequalities are not the result of some vague, lingering, premodern cultural ghost but of contemporary processes that create status hierarchies. Employers take advantage of these hierarchies to exploit cheap sources of labor. Advantaged white male employees and employers struggle to create and recreate their status advantages.

RACIAL INEQUALITY

The finding that racial inequality in the labor process is more narrowly tied to skill and training costs does not mean that social closure processes are necessarily weaker for African-Americans than they are for women. In the employment arena, high-skilled jobs, and particularly employer-provided training, tend to be reserved for white males. Thus, white women and black women, as well as black men, are excluded from access to training. As figure 7.1 shows, this exclusion is more pronounced among black and white women than it is among black males, at least those at the lowest and highest educational levels, who benefit somewhat from their advantaged status as males. Black females are, strikingly, the most excluded from valuable training opportunities.

There is strong evidence that race-based status processes operate at the job level. Although skill-based discrimination is an important source of white advantage and black disadvantage in access to jobs, the racial composition of jobs has a powerful effect on how the labor process is organized. In jobs with many black incumbents, there is a clear tendency for employers to create more routinized and tightly controlled labor processes. This is true even controlling for the human capital, the race of incumbents, and the skill levels of the jobs.

Figure 7.1.   Training time for increasing education levels, by sex and race

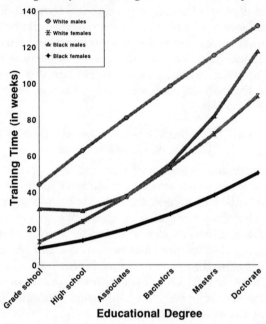

There is also evidence that about 20 percent of the black-white hourly earnings gap is a function of the devaluing of jobs with many black incumbents. In the only other study that has good job-level racial composition measures (Baron and Newman 1990), the effects of racial composition on earnings were even greater than the effects of sex composition. Unfortunately, Baron and Andrew E. Newman did not have access to direct measures of job skill, so it is possible that the strong racial composition effects reported reflect their inability to control adequately for skill segregation along racial lines. Both my study and theirs agree, however, that there is race-based social closure and racial stereotyping in evaluations of jobs.

There is evidence in my findings that there is less pressure to maintain racial segregation in jobs that require the highest educational creden- tials. In figure 7.1 we can see that in jobs that require advanced educational credentials, employer-provided training to black males ap- proaches that provided to white males. This is consistent with theories that suggest that the material bases for status distinctions by race is competition for working-class jobs (Lieberson 1980; Reich 1981; Wood 1986).

There is also strong evidence in this study of direct individual-level racial discrimination in both the organization of the labor process and to a lesser extent wage setting. Even after human capital, job skill, organizational characteristics, and the racial composition of the job are statistically controlled, my findings reveal that some African-Americans are more closely supervised at work and black women continue to be at a wage disadvantage. The experience of direct discrimination, the clear pattern of skill devaluation experienced by black employees, and the generally lower levels of racial segregation (than sex segregation) found in this study all lead me to believe that discrimination in employment is likely to be more transparent along racial than gender lines. That is, black employees' disadvantages are less strongly tied to there being a race-segregated employment structure, and, even though racial segregation is high in a demographic sense, the average black employee is still in a job that is filled mostly by whites.

Since black employees face skill segregation, they are likely to be more highly qualified than their white co-workers. On average, they are older, more experienced, or better educated. In addition, they are more closely supervised. They may even be paid less than comparable white workers in comparable jobs (the evidence for this is limited to women). This pattern of discrimination is no doubt hard to ignore. There is consistent evidence that black employees have lower levels of job satisfaction and organizational commitment than comparable white workers. The findings in this study suggest that this is not the result of some unreasonable "bad attitude" (Fernandez 1987) but that it probably reflects the personal experience of discrimination.

GENDER INEQUALITY

The processes of sex segregation across all dimensions of work are revealed quite powerfully in this study. Women are hired into lower-skilled jobs with less authority and opportunities for promotion. In addition, and consistent with a model of status closure, women in high-skill or high-authority jobs are likely to work mostly with women. The allocation of men and women into different, generally sex-segregated jobs has powerful effects on the organization of the labor process and on earnings. As the percentage of females in a job rises, task complexity, managerial and supervisory authority, and promotion opportunities decline.

At least half and probably closer to 70 percent of the male-female hourly wage gap is a direct function of the sex composition of jobs. Men in female-dominated jobs pay the largest earnings penalty. Typically male jobs have much higher wage rates than typically female jobs. Since wage rates are attached to jobs rather than to individuals, males in female jobs lose their sex advantage.[7]

The pervasiveness of sex segregation may to some extent prevent women from experiencing the associated inequality as sexism. Since women are typically in lower-quality jobs and the quality of a job is a powerful source of satisfaction and commitment, many researchers have expected that women should be less satisfied with their work than men. Researchers have long searched for gender differences in job satisfaction and organizational commitment, but the results have generally been disappointing. Perhaps this is because the field of reference for the vast majority of women is limited to typically female jobs. Thus, women are dissatisfied with jobs that are of low quality relative to other women's jobs. Higher-paying, typically white male work requiring more skills is simply outside most women's frame of reference most of the time.

GENDER AND RACIAL DIFFERENCES IN JOB STRATIFICATION

Since this study has focused on employment-based status processes, it can lead to the incorrect conclusion that race-based social closure is less extreme then gender-based social closure. This would be a misleading conclusion insofar as blacks are exposed to much racial discrimination in the labor market before they are even employed. Black males and females have very high unemployment rates, reflecting their exclusion from many jobs. This is clearly an important indication of black exclusion and white opportunity. Historical patterns of community educational and capital investment are important sources of race-based social closure as well. That black communities often offer fewer job opportunities leads to contemporary social closure processes at the family level in terms of class opportunity. I will return to a discussion of social class inequality later in this chapter.

The sex composition of jobs is more powerful than their racial composition in determining wages partly because the division of household and labor market activity is so different. Because women and men, on average, share the class advantages and disadvantages of their households of origin, they enter the labor market with broadly similar levels of educational credentials and quality of schooling. In addition, because women and men share households and communities, they have nearly identical spatial opportunity structures (Tomaskovic-Devey 1992). Finally, because women and men tend to experience similar family social class and community advantages, the creation of status-based social closure is entirely dependent on the creation of separate divisions of labor in the home and the workplace. Male advantage requires that men and women operate in separate spheres. Since men and women share households and communities, those separate spheres are produced at the job level and in the household division of labor. In addition, since white women in particular represent a large source of cheap skilled labor, there are great incentives for employers to create skilled, typically female jobs to take advantage of their subordinate-status position.

Women and men are generally in different labor queues, vying for sex-segregated employment opportunities. Women compete against other women, and those with better credentials tend to get the better jobs. Men compete with men for a different set of jobs, and again those with better credentials, or the more favored race, tend to get the better jobs. Thus, most men and women never compete for the same jobs and so never directly experience the process by which gender inequality is created. Discrimination against female-dominated jobs and in favor of male-dominated jobs leads to much of the actual gender inequality in the workplace. Blacks and whites, however, are both vying for more integrated jobs. In competitions for good jobs, whites often win, based at least partly on skill-based exclusionary decisions made by employers.

The differences in women's and blacks' direct experiences of discrimination may also explain why women are not more closely supervised than men. Since the labor markets are so segregated, women as a group may not perceive the same level of illegitimacy and unfairness that black workers do. Thus, women may be more willing, or at least less disgruntled, participants in their own exploitation.

Of course, there are other ways in which status processes affect men and women differently than they do whites and blacks. Most important, gender inequality has its fundamental source in household status hierarchies between husbands and wives. These hierarchies are typically, although certainly not entirely, built on an ideology that there are separate spheres and gender differences in competencies, which, if not always legitimated, are largely taken for granted. Thus, men can and do trust their wives to carry out their allotted tasks. The same seems to be true at work. That is, the degree of supervision of men and women in the workplace is tied to class relations, not gender relations. Race-based social closure has never been legitimate or taken for granted, at least not in black households, and there is a long history of white coercion to maintain racial inequality. The high levels of supervision visited on black workers and on white workers in jobs held disproportionately by blacks is likely to be a contemporary version of this coercive status closure. One must wonder whether this process is limited to the American South, with its history of slavery and legal apartheid, or whether it is pervasive in all regions of the country where black-white job competition has exacerbated status distinctions.

HUMAN ACTION AND JOB STRATIFICATION

One clear advantage of social closure and status composition approaches is that they are both profoundly grounded in concrete interactional processes in the workplace. The exclusion of women or minorities need not be conceptualized as a cultural hangover of a premodern era but as a struggle between groups over the monopolization of scarce resources. In this way the process is similar to the common practice whereby groups with educational credentials struggle to exclude those without, or whereby classes who own capital lobby for laws to protect their capital from redistribution by the state or from market competition (Miller and Tomaskovic-Devey 1983; Murphy 1987; Parkin 1979). These forms of social closure are so familiar, and in the U.S. context relatively legitimate, that we take them for granted.

Similarly, the determination of the status composition of a job can be conceptualized as an interactional process, at least partially formed in a struggle over the definition of its "worthiness." When a job is identified as white male, holders of that job have resources beyond skill and formal authority with which to influence organizational rewards. One of these resources may be an unconscious positive evaluation of its worthiness by most members of the organization; other resources are likely to be connected to interactional advantages, worker coalitions, and the like. In both cases social closure and status composition processes are fundamentally embedded in the everyday practices of the people in the organization.

LIMITS OF SUPPLY-SIDE EXPLANATIONS

When I began this study there were two fairly complementary supply-side theories to account for sex and racial segregation at the job level. Human capital theory tries to account for segregation by evaluating differences in investment in human capital and, in the case of sex segregation, male-female household specialization in market and domestic work. This perspective received no support as an explanation of sex segregation and very little support as an explanation of racial segregation. Socialization explanations provide reasonable interpretations of gender differences but are much less satisfying in accounting for why blacks tend to apply for jobs dominated by other blacks. Again, there is little support for a socialization explanation in this study, and, more important, Jacobs (1989a), who rigorously explores the socialization–sex segregation link, finds very little support as well. No matter what investments women make or plans or socialization experiences they have, they tend to end up in female-dominated jobs. When they do not, it is hard to find strong differences in expectations, role models, or the like.

It is likely that socialization plays some role in encouraging women to pursue sex-typical jobs but that socialization is not the primary causal force. Jacobs (1989b) proposes a lifelong social control explanation in which women and men are constantly confronted with reminders and admonitions about gender-appropriate behavior and that this leads to gender segregation in their choice of jobs. This explanation is more consistent with the social closure framework used in this study and also is more intuitively appealing as an explanation of racial segregation.

It is hard to believe that African-American families socialize their children for jobs dominated by blacks and white families socialize theirs for jobs dominated by whites. It is easy to believe, and the evidence in this study consistently supports this, that blacks are reminded of their race at work, are discriminated against in hiring for skilled work assignments, and are more closely supervised than white co-workers. In fact, the only setting where black employees tend to gain managerial power is in segregated jobs held largely by blacks. Thus, the very structure of the labor market and many workplaces may encourage African-Americans to seek out employment in traditional fields where they will encounter fewer hassles. Kanter (1977) certainly suggests that there may be powerful reasons for women to do this as well.

Supply-side theories of segregation, whether based on human capital or socialization explanations, are fundamentally limited by their one-sided perspective. The overwhelming majority of jobs currently in existence are homogenous by race or sex. The organizational, or demand side, of the labor market offers segregated employment options. There are very few sex-integrated jobs to apply for. Black job applicants have more race-integrated jobs available to them, but the vast majority of the best jobs are still held only by or almost only by whites.

On the simplest level, the demographic opportunities for integrated work are low. If everybody wanted, and many workers probably do, the good jobs currently monopolized by white men, there simply would not be enough to go around. The redistribution of these jobs would require a reorganization of the labor process. In the past this simple realization was easy to miss because most social theory systematically ignored the gendered and racial nature of the labor process in most workplaces, focusing instead on class or efficiency considerations. Although jobs are relatively independent of their incumbents in most workplaces, it does not follow that jobs are independent of their typical incumbents' race or sex.

In this study we have seen strong evidence that the sex composition of jobs influences the organization of all areas of the labor process and wages, not only for women but for men. The only arena of the labor process in which there were no observable gender-linked effects was in the level and types of control over work activity. There is, however, a gendered explanation for this absence. Given the other labor process dimensions of women's work—their limited authority, the routinized production processes, and their low promotion opportunities—we would expect their jobs to be more tightly controlled than they are. A possible explanation is that women's subordination is taken for granted, at least partly because of its primary location in the family. Managers can trust women to participate in their own exploitation at a level that many white or black men would reject.

One of the most striking additions of this study to contemporary thinking is that it provides evidence that jobs can take on a "racial" character in the same way that they take on a gendered character. The effects of racial composition on the labor process were every bit as strong in this study as the effects of gender composition. Whether this pattern would be found throughout the United States or is limited to the U.S. South is unclear. The gendered nature of work is a general phenomenon since gender-based status closure is general to U.S. (and other) societies. Racism, with its link to working-class competition, may be more embodied in organizational structures where pressures for race-based status closure are strongest.

The general implication of the gendered and racial nature of jobs, and the general rarity of integrated employment, particularly among better-quality jobs, is that supply-side explanations of segregation are limited. Integrated jobs just do not exist. Blacks and women must overcome the prejudice of employers and co-workers to increase the supply, especially of good-quality jobs. No social science theory seriously argues that labor market entrants can create jobs they want simply because they want them; it would be surprising if this were the case for the racial or sex composition of jobs.

Reskin and Roos (1990), building on the labor queue theories of Lester Thurow (1975), help reconcile supply- and demand-side theories. According to these researchers, there are two labor market queues—the supply side and the demand side—that govern who gets what jobs. On the demand side, jobs are ranked by their desirability and their requirements for credentials. The most desirable jobs are coveted by many labor market entrants, but few have the necessary credentials. These credentials include conventional human capital attributes, such as education and prior experience, but they can also include the socially expected sex or race of incumbents. Firms and managers may vary in the relative importance they give to various credentials—education, experience, sex, race. One of the clear findings of this research is that the importance of sex and race as a demand-side employment characteristic tends to increase with the quality of the job.

Although employers have the primary role in the labor market since they hire and fire, workers' labor market behavior no doubt plays some role as well. There is good evidence that women are more likely to value part-time work and to interrupt their participation in the labor force for household work. These are not, however, important sources of sex segregation at the job level. Other dimensions of work, such as pay, autonomy, and security, seem to be equally valued by men and women (Reskin and Roos 1990) and are important sources and consequences of sex segregation. Further, there is no compelling theory or evidence that black Americans have different values whan whites in evaluating the quality of jobs. Thus, the supply-side queue in the labor market does not seem to be a powerful explanation of segregation outcomes.

Reskin and Roos (1990) show, however, that the supply-side queue is a powerful part of the explanation of changes in segregation. Focusing on sex integration, they show that the process by which male domination of an occupation is reduced tends to include changes in the (demand-side) desirability of a job, which reduces the supply of white male applicants. The job then attracts women, because as a group they have lower opportunities in the labor market and the job is likely to pay more than the average job available to them. When men leave such jobs, women often apply for their vacated positions. Sometimes the deskilling and reductions in compensation that drive men away from jobs are conscious strategies by employers to transfer production to lower-cost female labor.

A final explanation has not been well explored but seems to be the most plausible avenue for future research on the supply-side sources of racial and sex segregation. Most conceptualizations of the process whereby labor is hired view it as a two-way process involving a supply of labor by individuals and a demand for labor by employers. As Mark Granovetter (1973, 1981) points out, however, there is a third necessary process—the person–job matching process. There must be a flow of information about the job to potential workers and about workers to potential employers. Since most jobs are found through fairly informal searches—particularly word of mouth and blind applications—it seems highly likely that job information in both directions is highly gendered and racial in character (Marini 1989).

If employers value most highly recommendations for new employees from current employees and their peers, then there is a high probability that same-sex, same-race candidates will be hired. Similarly, if labor market entrants get much of their information on job openings from their network of acquaintances, both the homogamy of friendship networks and the possibility that job information will be screened for sex and race appropriateness probably will tend to produce job applicants whose race and sex closely resemble those of the labor force.

There is only one study I am aware of that shows how the source of job information or applicant information is linked to the sex and race compositions of jobs. Hanson and Pratt (1991) found that women are more likely to enter male-dominated occupations when they heard of the job from male family members. They also found that women in female-dominated occupations get their job information from other women. Perhaps there is some gender-appropriate screening of job information that grows stronger as the source of the information becomes less familiar. This seems a fruitful avenue for further research.

My study provides fairly strong evidence of status closure processes that are skill-specific for race and more general across many desirable job characteristics for gender. Traditional theories interpret these patterns as employer discrimination. Although I strongly suspect that employer discrimination is an important source of sex and racial segregation and inequalities, the collapse of human capital and socialization explanations leaves us without a compelling supply-side story.

IS THE SIGNIFICANCE OF RACE DECLINING?

There has been much controversy since the publication of William Julius Wilson's influential book *The Declining Significance of Race* (1978) about the intersection of race and class in modern American society. Wilson's thesis is that the castelike status system that produced black disadvantage in the United States is quickly being eroded. Black disadvantage remains, he argues, but increasingly it has a class rather than a status character. The low levels and quality of education in the black community are the historical legacy of past but still recent castelike inequality, and this legacy produces a substantial and intergenerationally transmitted class disadvantage for black Americans. That is, much current black-white inequality and black poverty is a function of *class disadvantage* in increasingly race-neutral labor markets.

According to Wilson, there is a second class-linked source of today's inequality. Investment decisions, whereby new jobs are created, take into account the low educational levels in historically black communities, as well as the increasing inconvenience of urban central cities, and so localities with large black populations are systematically discriminated against for new investments. Such discrimination has primarily a class rather than a racial character.[8]

Wilson's critics argue that racism is alive and well, in hiring, on the job, and in community investment decisions. They are particularly distressed by Wilson's suggestion that racism is no longer a problem for the black middle class (e.g., Feagin 1991).

This study provides some valuable insights into this process of status closure. Since the data in this study are essentially cross-sectional, it is impossible to claim that the degree of race-based status closure is receding and being replaced by class disadvantage. It seems, however, that Wilson's general point that there has been a historical decline in the legal and social acceptability of racism, particularly in education and job assignments at work, is correct. The more controversial issue is the relative importance of class and racial status in the allocation of job-related rewards. It is on this issue that my study has much to say.

Compared with gender inequality, racial inequality is much more clearly tied to class advantage and disadvantage. African-Americans have lower levels of human capital, which explains about a quarter of the racial inequality in both labor process and wage inequalities. The patterns of racial segregation are also closely tied to narrowly defined skill requirements on the job, particularly educational credentials and training-time requirements. There is good evidence that class-based allocation and an interaction between race and class are important sources of both segregation and inequality at work.

It is the interaction between class and race, however, that is most important here. The process described as statistical discrimination throughout most of this study is really a narrowly framed version of old-fashioned racial prejudice. Although women are excluded from jobs based on all dimensions of job quality, blacks are excluded for more narrowly focused reasons having to do with skills. This is still racial discrimination. Its narrower focus on skills suggests that there may, in fact, be some diminution of race-based status closure. Its presence as the most important source of both segregation and inequality, however, suggests that racism is far from dead.[9] It may be that the increasingly class-based nature of black subordination has changed the content of racist practice. That is, black job candidates may be discriminated against based on a class logic. Nonetheless, all (or most) black candidates are ascribed a fictional class background based on their race. Regardless of training, or family background, the result is a tendency to discount the quality of their labor.

As to the second part of Wilson's thesis, that the black middle class is no longer racially disadvantaged and is claiming a new class advantage, there is both positive and negative evidence. Racial segregation is lower in jobs at higher class (power and authority) levels, although few black candidates get admitted to these jobs. Racial segregation is lower in jobs with requirements for advanced degrees as well, although racially balanced integration is quite rare in these jobs. Finally, investments by employers in training time also converge in jobs requiring advanced educational credentials. All of these findings suggest that there is less pressure for status closure in what might be called upper-middle-class positions. They are not, however, absent in such jobs.

In this chapter I have developed the beginnings of an explanation of why dissatisfaction with work tends to be so high among blacks, particularly relative to white women. My explanation hinges on a series of findings throughout this study.

- Black workers are more closely supervised than white workers, not only because of the characteristics of the jobs they hold but also because they are black.
- Black workers are systematically discriminated against in their access to jobs requiring more skill, but they tend to share employment with at least some white workers. This means that the average black worker is formally better qualified for his or her job than the white worker next to him or her.
- Finally, although race segregation is quite high in a demographic sense, because blacks make up a relatively small portion of the labor force, most blacks work in jobs in which the majority of their co-workers are white.

In combination, these three patterns provide a picture of the experiences of many black employees in work settings dominated by white co-workers, white employers, and a white culture. Based on these findings, the experience of racism is likely to be quite profound among many middle-class and less-advantaged African-Americans. In fact, because the black middle class tends to be found in white work situations more as token representatives, even small acts of discrimination are likely to be painfully obvious.

This study has focused on aspects of the labor process that are fairly obvious, such as wages and access to on-the-job training. It is not here but in less obvious aspects of the labor process, such as the intensity of supervision and the degree to which one's work is self- as opposed to manager-controlled, that I found evidence of direct racial discrimination that was not tied to the skill level or racial composition of the job. Although such discrimination is so subtle as to go unnoticed by most white managers with nonracist intentions, it is unlikely to go unnoticed by black workers.

In addition to subtle racism in the labor process, interactional patterns arise at work that generate discrimination. For demographic and historical reasons, most blacks work for white employers and have many white co-workers. All of the social acts of everyday life that produce and signify the superordinance of white status are constant reminders to black workers that they are in a white environment.

It should be clear that the *experience* of racism by black Americans is far from dead, whether or not Wilson is correct that the basis of black Americans' disadvantages are shifting from race-based status closure to a more socially legitimate but no less pressing class disadvantage. It is also clear that skill discrimination and the racial nature of the labor process and wage-setting process still affect very actively the work process for black and white workers alike.

PERSISTENCE OF PATRIARCHY

There is some evidence early in this study and in Jacobs (1989a, 1989b) and in Beller (1984) that the degree of occupational and job sex segregation is declining. Reskin and Roos (1990) warn, however, that this decline is most likely to occur when employers wish to substitute lower-cost female labor for male labor or when technological or labor supply changes deplete the availability of male labor and women flock to the now-available, always attractive but traditionally unavailable jobs. Their gender queue model suggests that much sex integration at the occupational level masks job-level segregation and takes place because males are drawn to jobs with higher skill requirements or higher wages. Whether or not there has been a real decline in job-level sex segregation hinges on the crude comparison of Bielby and Baron's (1986) circa 1970 California sample and the 1989 North Carolina sample used in this study. We clearly do not know enough about changes in job-level segregation to make strong conclusions about the pattern of change.

The persistence of male patriarchal advantage in the labor market seems assured in the absence of aggressive social movement activity and government enforcement. The sex segregation of employment is so widespread that competitive labor market forces do little to redistribute opportunities. Employers do hire women for their low wages, and, in some cases at least, this leads to a short-term integration of occupations but even shorter-term integration at the job level. With natural and perhaps accelerated turnover, males leave declining occupations for greener pastures, and the still largely sex-segregated employment structure provides many opportunities for employment in male jobs at higher wages for a given level of human capital.

The gendered nature of work does not stop with the near-total segregation of male and female jobs. Workplaces become gendered, jobs have typical-sex incumbents, and the organization of work reflects this gendered reality. Men and women in predominantly female jobs perform less complex work than their educational credentials or training time would lead us to expect. They also have less authority over other workers. Most fundamentally, the salaries of typically female jobs are much lower. There is strong incentive for men to avoid such work since their earnings penalty relative to that of similarly skilled men is quite high.

Women often have little choice but to pick from the jobs that hire women. This means that when employers seeking to fill traditionally male jobs start considering women, women flock to these jobs. Men's advantages may be short-lived, however, as employers take advantage of the sex-segregated labor force to (further) reduce the quality of jobs as they become typically female.

The findings in this book concerning sex segregation at work and its consequences for the organization of the labor process and wages are not surprising given the rich case study literature and the findings of comparable worth studies. This study has addressed a few of the methodological limitations of previous research. The conclusion that jobs are gendered is not an artifact of selective case studies or incomplete statistical controls for job characteristics. This study was based on a random sample of an economywide population of jobs. It also has unusually broad measures for job characteristics. The sex composition of jobs does, in fact, influence both labor process organization and the value placed on a job. In addition, previous studies have not been designed to discriminate between sex composition effects and the gender-based status closure processes that allocate women to less desirable jobs. I have found that both operate, both are much more important than human capital processes, and that the sex composition effect is the single most important source of male-female wage inequality.

Although this book is not about households, it is important to recognize that a wife's disadvantage in the labor market is translated into a husband's advantage in the home. On average, husbands have higher earnings potential in the labor market, which gives them resources to back up their status claims in the home. This advantage in the home leads to greater claims on leisure time by husbands and to greater demands for domestic labor from their wives. It also tends to reproduce in each household a secondary labor market position for the wife's paid employment. This may be a rational household allocation of labor under the assumption of marital stability; however, it profoundly disadvantages many women in both their short-term domestic politics and their long-term independence.

A SOCIOLOGICAL THEORY OF JOB QUALITY

When discussing social closure and status composition processes, this study has consistently treated human capital attributes of individuals, organizational resources, and job-related skill opportunities as supplementary or contending explanations for racial and sex inequalities at work. The strong conclusion that both the racial and sex compositions of jobs influence both the organization of the labor process and job earnings enables me to propose a more formal sociological theory of job quality.

Job quality can be conceptualized as those intrinsic and extrinsic aspects of employment that make a job more or less attractive. In this study we have looked at labor process organization and earnings as indicators of job quality. The list could no doubt be extended to include other intrinsic characteristics, such as flexibility, the physical and emotional work environment, and even interpersonal comfort. Although earnings are the primary extrinsic reward attached to jobs, benefits such as pensions, subsidized medical insurance, paid vacations, and the like should be expected to conform to the general model of job quality outlined below.

Figure 7.2 represents a general model of job quality. Depicting primarily the demand side of the labor market, it shows the processes that lead to the differentiation of jobs by their desirability. In this model extrinsic job rewards are hypothesized to be a direct function of the status composition of jobs and the intrinsic organization of the labor process, including opportunities to enhance job skills. The latter conveys the *relative power* of a job, while the former conveys its *relative status*, both within an organizational context. These two factors are independent but typically mutually reinforcing sources of job inequality.

Organizational resources represent the "size of the pie" that organizations have available to distribute to jobs (Tomaskovic-Devey 1989). There is considerable evidence in this and other studies that organizational resources determine compensation and benefit levels both directly and indirectly through their link to intrinsic job characteristics. Product market competition, economies of scale, state policies, the pattern of capital investment, and organizational efficiency all affect the level of these resources (Tomaskovic-Devey 1988). Only the last source is explicitly considered in neoclassical economic theory. All of the remaining

Figure 7.2. Model of job quality

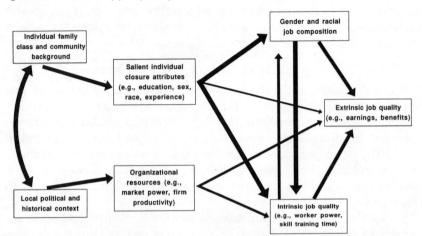

The width of an arrow indicates suspected empirical importance in the United States.
The model is sufficiently abstract to be generalized beyond the United States, but there is
no reason to expect that empirical importance would be similar in other countries.

sources are the result of political and institutional conditions, such as
the state's industrial policy, labor union organization, the vertical and
horizontal integration of firms, and institutional isomorphism. In most
of the industrial world outside the United States, there would be a direct
arrow from political and institutional factors on the far left to intrinsic
job quality. In the United States, direct regulation of the labor process
and compensation practices is weak and tends to specify only minimum
levels of worker safety or wages, not job rights or compensation levels
at specific skill levels. In much of the rest of the industrial world, these
aspects of job quality are regulated by the state and/or are the result of
countrywide union bargaining agreements. The U.S. job structure is
much more anarchic. In fact, in a country with strong state regulation
of employment, much of the middle of figure 7.2 would be reduced in
importance and some causal paths might not be in the model at all. In
Italy, for example, with its strong regulation of compensation practices,
it is likely that sex-based social closure is the basis for all or nearly all of
the gender gap between jobs with low intrinsic and high extrinsic quality
(Bettio 1988; Bianco 1992).

The final part of the model represents the ascribed and achieved
individual statuses to which employers (and other employees) react. In
addition to sex, race, and human capital–like attributes, this box includes other characteristics, such as class background and personal
ambition and talent. It could also include handicaps, sexual preferences,

accents, and even physical attractiveness. This part of the model represents the traditional status attainment approach in sociology (Blau and Duncan 1967; Hauser and Featherman 1977; Bielby 1981). As such, it emphasizes the role of family background and community institutions such as schools and local practices in both the acquisition and value of individual statuses. Unlike the traditional status attainment approach, this model positions family and particular community institutions and practices as embedded in historical and political economic processes. Families will react to perceived local opportunities and constraints based on common practices. Community institutions will tend to reproduce the gender, racial, and class inequalities of the local political economy, forged in local history (Tomaskovic-Devey 1992).

The model outlined in the last section provides a general model of job quality. It is concerned primarily with the job demand side of the labor market, but it is sensitive to individual statuses when it is reasonable to expect some consequences for the quality of jobs. Generally, except for the sorting of people into jobs, the direct effect of individual characteristics on job quality is conceptualized to be quite weak. In the more institutionally regulated economies of the rest of the industrialized world, those effects can be expected to be weaker still. In the more "bazaar" economies of some developing countries (and neoclassical economic theory), these characteristics may be stronger.

The adequacy of this model is primarily a function of empirical examination. Although presented as a general model, it has strongest empirical support from the United States, and for racial composition effects, for the American South. Its application to other historical times and geographical locales will produce refinements and qualifications. In fact, for many activists, the goal of political activity is to reduce or eliminate the causal effects attributed to social closure and status composition processes in this model. In the final chapter we turn to those social mechanisms that are likely to erode these disturbing causal mechanisms.

CHAPTER 8
ORGANIZATIONAL POLICY AND THE EROSION OF WORKPLACE INEQUALITY

A LTHOUGH IT IS COMMON to think of racial and gender inequalities as public policy issues, they are primarily organizational policy issues. Government policy is merely an inducement to help organizations make wise choices. Many firms are already committed to equal opportunity but need help in developing effective equal opportunity agendas. This study should bring home the need for both management and state policy to address gender and racial inequalities at work as more than just matters of preparedness and insensitive discrimination. Gender and racial inequalities are produced in workplaces by processes of exclusion that limit the access of women and minorities to desirable jobs. When a job comes to be organizationally defined as women's work or a minority position, there is frequently organizational discrimination against that job.

Organizational pressures for exclusion and segregation are not simply the result of irrational prejudice. Advantaged employees, including managers, and many employers may have strong interests in excluding women and minorities from desirable jobs. Once a gendered or racial job structure is in place, it is difficult to reverse patterns of inequality. Market mechanisms cannot be expected to erode racial or gender inequalities without strong organizational and public policy initiatives.

ORGANIZATIONAL POLICY ISSUES

Although state and federal governments have traditionally been the arena for eroding white male advantage, many corporations are committed to creating more equitable workplaces. Although there are no doubt many sources of this commitment, achieving equity with only the tools of relative preparedness and attempts to reeducate prejudiced employees cannot succeed. Organizations interested in promoting fairness in hiring, promotion, and pay along racial and gender lines must pay careful attention to the sources of internal sex and racial job segregation and its effects on how the work is organized as well as paid. Are women and minorities excluded from desirable jobs? Do jobs typically held by females or minorities pay less than jobs at comparable skill levels held by white males? Do these jobs offer less training time, fewer promotion opportunities, less task complexity, and less autonomy? If so, it should be no surprise if few women or members of minorities are seen as promising candidates for promotions. Nor should discrimination and comparable worth lawsuits come as surprises.

Organizational policy matters. In this study there is strong evidence that racial and sex segregation decline in firms with more formalized employment relations. Employment relations that rely on traditional assumptions and unmonitored interaction patterns are more likely to produce discriminatory workplace practices. When line managers are accountable to both employees and upper management for complying with formal rules, exclusionary practices are less common. When the employment relationship is characterized by formal job descriptions, including explicit listings of required credentials and experience, where employees are seen as having rights as well as duties (often outlined in an employee handbook or union contract), and when job openings are formally advertised or posted, then exclusions on the basis of sex or race occur less often.

Government or union demands for formal hiring procedures to ensure affirmative action and/or to reduce management caprice are well known, but formalization can also be the result of differences in the cultures of firms or employee activism. The reputation of IBM as an aggressively nondiscriminating employer may be as much a result of its tendency toward formal procedures as of the affirmative action guidelines that come with federal government contracts. Formalization of the employment relationship not only makes it difficult to hide internal promotion opportunities or true job requirements from employees and job applicants, it also produces a paper trail that potentially implicates both managers and firms that discriminate on the basis of sex or race in hiring and promotion decisions.

Formalization is often the outcome of employee struggles for greater job security or fairness. It can be the result of union demands for seniority rules, job posting, and the like, but it can also arise from more modest worker struggles for bureaucratic safeguards. I recently became aware of a good example of this informal process. Some experienced women computer programmers working in the central data-processing office of a Fortune 500 manufacturing company began to notice that while entry-level programming positions were sex-integrated, supervisory positions were held by males. The internal labor market process was such that one day a woman programmer would be sitting next to a male programmer, whom she had probably helped train, and the next day he would be a manager in a private office down the hall. Not only did the women not get promoted but they did not even know when there were job openings, or even an ongoing search, until their male co-workers' promotions were announced. The women responded by planning a lunch meeting among themselves to discuss the problem. Management heard about the plan, however, and forbade the women from meeting. The women prudently decided to hold the meeting off company property. When the managers heard of this plan, they changed their tactics and asked whether they could send a representative. The representative was welcomed and left the meeting with a request that job openings be formally posted in the future so that all qualified applicants could apply. Management agreed, job posting commenced, and the old-boy system of picking only promising males for managerial positions was undermined if not eradicated. In this case a fairly informal and mild organizational effort created a more formalized internal labor market that probably reduced the level of segregation by rank. The example is also interesting in that it was only because the women had worked in sex-integrated programming jobs at the entry level that they were even aware of the discriminatory promotion pattern.

Although formalization of the employment relationship is linked to lower levels of sex and race segregation, it is also linked in many people's minds to the general organizational machinery of bureaucracy. When labor unions or governments require formal procedures to ensure equitable nondiscriminatory outcomes, managers and plant owners often chafe at the "bureaucratic" restrictions. Corporate bureaucracies have recently been blamed by academics and corporate insiders alike for being barriers to innovation and sources of the long-term decline in U.S. competitiveness (e.g., Kanter 1983, 1989; Peters and Waterman 1982).

Bureaucracy is about control. When rules are written, procedures specified, and jobs described, employees' (and often consumers') behavior is controlled. Bureaucratic control is typically aimed at achieving two potentially contradictory goals. The first goal is to produce the organization's product or service at the lowest cost and with the greatest efficiency. The second goal is related to the hierarchical nature of most organizations, specifically the downward exercise of power. Most criticisms of bureaucracies as organizational forms focus on this inflexible, innovation-stifling aspect. It is this second aspect of bureaucracies that typically increases racial and gender inequalities in the workplace. The proliferation of job titles leads to both competition for good jobs and opportunities for both exclusion and segregation.

Organizations intent on reducing discrimination should promote the formalization of employment and promotion rules in order to reduce the supervisory discretion that can lead to gender and racial discrimination. At the same time, firms should strive to produce divisions of labor that are flatter and less specialized. The proliferation of job titles within hierarchical competitive career ladders creates the environment for the discriminatory exclusion of women and minorities from desirable jobs and the creation of jobs that are sex- and race-segregated. Such hierarchies also produce the control-oriented inertia that gives bureaucracies a bad name, and they create a class of advantaged employees with advantages to defend.

Organizations intent on eliminating gender and racial discrimination against people and jobs must be sensitive to this issue of advantage. Policies designed to admit women and minorities into white male preserves will be resisted. The level and intensity of the backlash to affirmative action programs is a good indicator of the underlying threat to advantage. Sexual and racial harassment are also common responses of employees who are threatened by integration (Cockburn 1991; Di-Tomasso 1989; Kanter 1977; Williams 1987).

Cockburn's (1991) study of men's resistance to gender equality in four British firms points out that resistance should be expected but that all policy approaches do not result in the same level of resistance. In two of the organizations she studied, opportunities for more equality were created in part by raising the salaries of the lowest-paid jobs. This policy was supported by trade unions and minority men and had the effect of equalizing the wages of both the men and women in the firms. Although not her point, it also flattened the wage hierarchies in the firms.

Francesca Bettio (1988), after studying occupational sex segregation in Italy, reports that a union and state policy of decreasing wage inequality among jobs has led to Italy having the highest female-male earnings ratio in the industrial world (tied with Sweden). Reducing downward bureaucracy, flattening job hierarchies, and narrowing workplace inequalities are important and probably less controversial mechanisms for eroding racial and gender workplace segregation and inequalities.

In large organizations it is quite common for top managers to have a relatively strong public commitment to equal opportunity but have difficulty acting on it. Directives from the top of the organization must filter down not only through the formal hierarchy but also through the informal power structure (Kanter 1977). Bruce Williams's (1987) study of black workers in a suburban manufacturing plant in the Chicago area revealed that those in the informal power structure of the plant consciously reserved the best jobs for white workers. This power structure included old hands among the production (line) managers and skilled workers. These people had been around a long time, knew how to get things done and how to prevent things from getting done, and were racist. This is an old story and would not be worth repeating except that it puts what follows in context. In this firm there were explicit and public commitments to equal opportunity, and the firm was hiring more new black workers than white ones. As this story demonstrates, a commitment to equality is not enough if skilled and powerful workers resist integration into skilled and supervisory work.

Why do white male workers resist racial and sex integration? In the firm Williams (1987) studied, the line managers feared that their plant would become a "black plant," lose status in the business community, and have trouble recruiting skilled white workers. The fear of integration among skilled workers has a long history, based in part on the management practice of hiring minority and female workers to drive down wages (Wilson 1978; Hartmann 1976; Lieberson 1980; Wood 1986). This study as well as others (e.g., Reskin and Roos 1990) show that the historical record is reflected in contemporary reality. As the proportion minority or female in a job grows, wages do tend to decline.

The importance of line managers in the production of sex- and race-segregated employment structures cannot be ignored. In large companies, it is not top managers or owners or workers who make discriminatory hiring and promotion decisions. Line managers, particularly when they have been promoted from the rank below, have fairly heavy career investments in perpetuating current practices. The sex and racial compositions of the jobs they manage are not pieces of corporate trivia but to some extent measures of their importance as managers and the pedigree of their corporate career. If, in addition, skilled white male workers resist integration through subtle and blatant acts of protest, line managers, unless there is strong pressure from upper management, have little incentive to promote the careers of women and minorities.

With corporate and legal commitments to equal opportunity, managers looking for the path of least resistance between their careers, exclusionary pressures from their white male employees, and equal opportunity requirements, can play a game of passive resistance and withhold information on qualified minority and female job candidates. As John P. Fernandez writes, " 'We won't hire blacks' has become 'Blacks do not have the right qualifications' " (1987:152).

What constitutes the *right* qualifications is often left up to supervisors and first- and second-line managers. In the absence of formal reporting requirements about all job applicants, hiring discretion can be quite wide. McIlwee and Robinson (1992), in their study of women engineers, contrast a male-dominated corporate culture and a formalized corporate culture. In one high-tech firm they studied, the corporate culture was dominated by the male engineers. These engineers tended to be young and were relatively "liberated" in their gender role expectations, yet the competition for projects and promotions was fierce and the women engineers rarely got good projects or promotions. In contrast, another firm was dominated by nonengineers who managed through formal procedures. This firm was much older, the male engineers tended to be conservative about the role of women, and there was more sexual harassment than in the high-tech firm, but women were more likely to be promoted and to have leading roles on major projects. Who controls competitive promotions and job assignments—white male co-workers or managers following formal employment rules—can make quite a difference.

In a recent interview with a young female engineer, I heard a similar story. After getting out of college in the mid-1980s with an electrical engineering degree from a private college, she sent résumés to many corporations. One day while sitting in a local pub with a friend, she mentioned that she had gotten two more rejection letters that day and complained about what a hard time she was having finding an engineering job. Someone at the bar overheard her and, after identifying herself as an equal opportunity personnel manager for a large U.S. business machine company, said that the company she worked for had been unable to find any female electrical engineers. The young woman replied that one of her rejection letters had come from just that company. The manager who was screening the applicants was evidently finding the women unacceptable and then reporting to upper management that there were no female candidates. The young woman and another woman engineer were soon hired in response to strong pressure from above.

Cockburn (1991) contrasted the sexual and racial harassment policies of three companies. All three companies had similar policies forbidding sexual or racial harassment in the workplace, but although they were similar in form, the policies were not implemented similarly. In one, workplace management was committed and aggressive, and harassment was strongly disciplined and publicly pursued. In the other two firms, harassment charges were handled quietly for fear of embarrassment and white male backlash. The aggressive company did have a problem with backlash from white male workers, who complained there was a "thought police." But, as Cockburn reports, in this firm, unlike the other two, employees reported that "they felt the standard of behavior had greatly improved since the equality policy had raised issues of sexism and harassment" (1991:146).

Without strong corporate leadership, it is unreasonable to expect great gains in eliminating gender and racial discrimination where advantaged skilled employees control the work environment. As Bielby and Baron point out (1987:220), "Sex segregation is sustained by behavior as well as structure." Behavior often reflects stereotypes about sex- and race-appropriate behavior and jobs. Social psychological research has demonstrated that such thinking gets stronger when the immediate situation has the greatest personal relevance (Bielby and Baron 1987). Gender and racial integration can be expected to elicit resistance from advantaged workers, particularly when skilled and supervisory jobs are involved.

AFFIRMATIVE ACTION: LIMITS AND PROSPECTS

Affirmative action programs have a dirty name in much U.S. public policy discussion. The previous section should make clear why this is: advantaged workers will resist and feel threatened by competition from minority and female co-workers.

Thomas Sowell (1990) lists three main critiques of affirmative action, which he calls "preferential policies." First, preferential policies seem to work best for the most advantaged in the minority group. Second, they can lead to "institutional mismatches," which lead to high failure rates for preferred minorities. Third, and finally, succeeding because of affirmative action is a "tainted honor." Thus, affirmative action or preferential policies become the majority's explanation for all successes by minorities.

Do preferential policies work best for the most advantaged minorities? It is the case that jobs requiring advanced degrees, although they are rarely racially balanced, are more integrated than jobs requiring fewer skills. Since most affirmative action polices are aimed at the top of the job hierarchy (e.g., engineers, entry-level management), where specific educational or experience requirements are almost always necessary, the vast majority of minorities and women probably receive few direct benefits. It is quite clear that businesses, especially larger ones, have little aversion to hiring minority and female labor; they just hire them in low-skill, low-authority, and low-paying jobs.

Some of the strongest barriers to female and minority hiring and sources of segregated employment structures arise in conjunction with jobs that provide substantial on-the-job training. The issue in this case is not formal qualifications but the investment in workers' skills. If firms do not hire women and minorities into these skill-enhancing jobs or do not provide training to workers in traditionally female or minority jobs, then they are creating substantial qualification inequities in their own work forces. When managers later turn around and say that no minority and female workers are qualified for promotion, corporate responsibility is conveniently forgotten.

Sowell may be correct that affirmative action polices *as typically currently constituted* primarily benefit already advantaged women and minorities. It does not follow that these jobs are the only appropriate ones for affirmative action targeting. Some already advantaged women and minorities may be more advantaged relative to other women and minorities, but it is important not to forget that they are almost always disadvantaged, at least in the workplace, relative to white males. It follows from the critique of affirmative action as a middle-class policy option that affirmative action programs should be aggressively expanded to skilled production and technical work, particularly to those jobs in which firms make significant investments in the skills of their work forces.

Another critique of affirmative action is that there is a structural mismatch. According to this argument, underqualified women or minorities are hired or promoted, struggle in a job that is beyond them, and ultimately fail in large numbers. There is clear evidence from my research that African-Americans and women tend to be more qualified than whites and men in jobs requiring comparable skills. The structural mismatch thesis has been most strongly applied to women and minorities in college (Sowell 1990); it does not seem to have any general applicability in the workplace.

Although skill mismatches may be an occasional result of poorly executed affirmative action programs, I suspect that in the vast majority of cases women or minority group members who break into white or male enclaves do not succeed because of performance pressures stemming from their token status and from co-worker harassment. (I suspect this is true in universities as well.) Kanter (1977) describes this process in some depth. Integration creates boundary heightening by white and male workers, who sterotype, isolate, and not infrequently harass the new minority or female worker.

A pilot told me a story about the first woman pilot at the busy corporate airport where he worked. The other pilots knew from the start she would not be able to cut it. To give her a "fair" chance to prove herself, they had decided not to show her the ropes, to allow her to figure out on her own the controls on planes she had not flown before, and not to introduce her to the control tower and maintenance staffs, although this information was routinely shared with new male pilots. When she finally quit in frustration, no one was surprised. After all, they knew from the start that a woman could not be a pilot. Of course, what they knew did not matter; it was what they did that was decisive. By refusing to share their knowledge, they insured her failure.

One reason the skill mismatch critique of affirmative action is so resilient is that it is embedded in the backlash of the advantaged to integration. The actual skills needed in most jobs are learned on the job. In many white-collar jobs, particularly management jobs, one must talk, listen, and create strategic alliances to get things done and do a good job. The failure of some women and minorities to excel may be blamed on qualification deficits but more likely is the result of harassment and exclusion by workers who refuse to share skills or who interact in strained ways.

Backlashes against affirmative action are often far out of line with the actual amount of preferential treatment that is conferred. This happens for two reasons. The first reason, already mentioned, is that many white and male workers view any career success by minorities and women as the result of affirmative action. Thus, competent job performance is consistently overlooked and belittled in favor of telling stories about unfair promotions.

Within this context of exaggeration, envy, and mistrust emerges the second reason for the backlash. Frequently, many people apply or are in line for a desirable job. Only one person gets the job, and when that person is a woman or minority group member and the job is traditionally held by a white male, accusations of preferential treatment are likely to be widespread. It is true that in the absence of affirmative corporate and government policies, minorities and women would rarely get past discriminatory barriers to such jobs. And occasionally an affirmative action candidate may be hired over a better-qualified white male. Nonetheless, when a single minority or female gets the coveted job, at the most only one white male (whoever was at the top of the traditional job queue) loses out. The political reality is that many white males, including those who had little or no chance of getting the job in the first place, focus their anger and disappointment on their minority and female co-workers. Thus, many more are angered than could ever have actually suffered from "reverse discrimination."

The link between qualifications and reverse discrimination warrants further examination as well. Most skills are learned on the job. Particularly for skilled and desirable jobs, qualifications are reviewed in an effort to find the best job candidates, rather than to identify baseline competency. The key organizational threat of affirmative action is the backlash, not the potential decline in efficiency. For desirable jobs, there is generally a surplus of candidates qualified to learn the job on the job. Many, if not most, of these candidates are capable of performing the work. Competition for a job is therefore often more important for creating a committed, competitive work force than it is for finding the perfect person for any one job (Edwards 1979).

All screening processes are imperfect. The critique that affirmative action leads to suboptimal job-person matches is a false critique. Managers are looking for satisfactory matches and realize full well that most people pick up job-specific skills on the job. If there is resistance from threatened majorities, picking up these skills may be difficult. At the same time, there is no reason to assume that traditional attributes, such as education, recent experience, connections, membership in a certain country club, and being white and male, are used only to screen for efficient job-person matches.

As Kanter (1977), and C. Wright Mills (1956) before her, point out about the best jobs in the biggest corporations, many screening mechanisms are used to find people who look like and will be comfortable with the people at the top. Kanter calls this process *homosocial reproduction*. When Mills wrote, the process was more *WASP homosocial reproduction*. Today it might be more accurate to call it *Anglo-homosocial reproduction*. It seems that where trust is at a premium, similarity to those making job selections is probably at a premium as well. There are, no doubt, glass ceilings above which women and minorities rarely rise. It is also a major premise of this book that advantages are defended by the advantaged. The focus on elite positions, while politically provocative, misses the vast majority of discriminatory practices against people and jobs at the less rarefied levels where most people make a living.

The issue of backlash leads back to the role of leadership. If top management, or owners in the case of small businesses, are aggressive in promoting equality of opportunity, then equality of opportunity can become the norm. In the absence of aggressive leadership from the top, successful backlash and resistance from advantaged employees, including line management, should be expected. Of course, in some circumstances leaders exacerbate the backlash and justify opposition to affirmative action. In the 1990 U.S. Senate race in North Carolina, Senator Jesse Helms, who was running against a black man, Harvey Gantt, ran television ads showing a pair of white hands holding a rejection letter as a voiceover said, "You were qualified, but you didn't get the job because of affirmative action. . . ." Since backlash is to be expected, it is probably not affirmative action that is the main issue but the quality and direction of leadership.

Since there is strong empirical evidence of pervasive undervaluing of the skills of women and minorities, since employers, on average, make lower investments in on-the-job training for women and minorities, and since discrimination in hiring is still a problem in many workplaces (for examples, see Cross et al. 1990 and Turner, Fix, and Struyk 1991), affirmative action programs need to be continued and expanded.

COMPARABLE WORTH

Cockburn (1991) in her study of male resistance asserts that in most organizations there are short and long agendas for equal opportunity. The short agenda often includes a corporate commitment to hire some women or minorities for visible professional or (less commonly) managerial positions. A slightly longer agenda might include an affirmative action program. The long agenda, usually advocated by personnel or equal opportunity officers but rarely by line or top managers, might include attempts to establish equitable compensation standards across jobs in the organization.

The central problem preventing male-female equality is the segregated employment structure, which confines most women of all races and educational backgrounds to female job ghettos. This sex segregation is typically invisible since it is embedded in jobs, not directed at individuals. Sex-segregated employment structures need to be breached and eroded. One way to speed up this process is via comparable worth or pay equity programs. In these programs jobs requiring equivalent skills are awarded equivalent pay to correct for historical inequities that reflect the sex (or racial) composition of the job. In the short term, comparable worth programs create sex-segregated jobs in which there is equal pay. It seems reasonable to expect, however, that as wages rise in typically female jobs, males will begin to enter those jobs.

The racial composition of jobs also affects the character of the work and its compensation but to a lesser extent than the sex composition. The process by which race affects the labor process and compensation policies can be expected to vary dramatically from firm to firm. In firms in which racial segregation at the job level is high, the consequences may be dramatic. The data from my study indicate that racial segregation is particularly high in the state sector. Given the historical defense of racism by southern states, this finding probably should not be surprising (James 1988). In some organizations race-oriented comparable worth programs are necessary correctives.

Comparable worth programs are at the forefront of current strategies promoted by American feminists to improve women's position in the workplace. Comparable worth initiatives attempt to increase the wages of jobs traditionally held by women by making the organizational pay structure more equitable. From this study and many others, it is clear that as the proportion of females in jobs increases, the wages attached to those jobs decline. This discrimination against typically female jobs is independent of individual human capital, job skill, or authority requirements or even the sex of the individual in the job. Male nurses get nurses' wages; female engineers get engineers' wages. It is clear from this study that, at least in the U.S. South, the racial composition of jobs can lead to the devaluing of jobs as well (see also Baron and Newman 1990 and Semyonev and Lewin-Epstein 1989).

One approach is to raise the wages of the poorest-paying jobs relative to the highest-paying ones. This narrowing of wages leads in most organizations to a narrowing of gender and racial inequalities as well. In effect, this is a class-based strategy of pay equalization across skill levels. From a theoretical point of view, this approach recognizes that wages are set not only on the basis of productivity or even labor market forces but also as a result of organizational politics and administrative decisions (Bridges and Villimez 1991). Cockburn (1991) and Bettio (1988) give examples of union-led wage negotiation strategies in Great Britain and Italy that followed this pattern and reduced racial and gender inequalities.

The more common approach in the United States is for an employee or union to institute a lawsuit to achieve comparable worth. In these cases the employee group alleges that certain jobs are undervalued because of their racial or sex composition. Jobs are then evaluated for their compensable characteristics, such as physical difficulty, training time, required experience, required credentials, authority, and the like (see Jacobs and Steinberg 1990 for a review and examples). If, after these compensable job attributes are statistically controlled, it is found that jobs continue to pay less as the percentage of females or minorities in them rises, then the court may order or the organization may elect to raise the pay levels of the jobs that have been undervalued (for extended discussions, see among many others Acker 1989; England 1992; Hill and Killingsworth 1989; Gold 1983; and Killingsworth 1990).

Comparable worth is resisted by employers and rejected by some economists because it seems to undermine the principle that wages are set in competitive labor markets. Economists fear a loss of efficiency; employers fear a loss of control. Of course, wages are only partly set by labor markets, and the job queue is both sex- and race-segregated. Organizational power struggles and administrative evaluations of the worth of jobs are powerful sources of the actual compensation attached to jobs. The segregation of workers and jobs by sex and race, as well as the undervaluing of the skills of minorities and women, make competitive labor market solutions to racial and gender workplace inequalities at best ineffective.

Although pay adjustments to jobs that have been discriminated against are a useful organizational policy, they have been limited in practice by the reality of organizational politics and prejudice. As we have seen, jobs that are typically held by women and minorities tend to get undervalued in the workplace. From a comparable worth perspective, this means that those holding these jobs are not being fully compensated for their skills. This is self-evident when, for example, a secretary gets paid less than a loading dock laborer. It is less evident when the skills are not recognized as skills at all (Acker 1987, 1989).

Steinberg and Lois Haignere (1987) point out that, although two-thirds of U.S. jobs have some form of evaluation mechanism, tasks in typically female jobs are often overlooked. They list twenty-seven invisible skills associated with women's work. Table 8.1 is adapted from that list. Caring for children should be added. Taking care of children in homes, in day-care centers and preschools, and in the public school system is typically women's work and is almost always treated as unskilled or in the case of teachers poorly paid skilled work.

For comparable worth to work, jobs must be evaluated based on their skills. To do this, skills must be identified and given a value. If skills traditionally attached to female or minority jobs are not recognized or not valued, then comparable worth wage adjustments will address only part of the problem. Further, jobs held typically by females or minorities may in fact be less skilled because they are typically held by females and minorities. Chapter 5 provided evidence that as the percentages of females and minorities in jobs rise, supervisory authority, managerial decision-making power, task complexity, and task autonomy all decline. In addition, there are large racial and gender inequalities in access to on-the-job training. A well-executed comparable worth evaluation of jobs will address some of the institutionalized discrimination against jobs that are typically filled by women and minorities, but because of the design of this approach, it is incapable of dealing with skill discrimination against those jobs.

For these reasons, comparable worth initiatives typically turn out to be less far-reaching than critics fear or advocates hope. Organizational politics and the undervaluing of the skills attached to jobs profoundly limit the potential of comparable worth adjustments. This is particularly the case when comparable worth studies take place in the confronta-

Table 8.1. Frequently overlooked skill characteristics of female jobs

Finger dexterity	Stress because of interruptions
Special body coordination	Calming upset or ill people
Scheduling appointments	Gathering informtion from upset or ill people
Coordinating meetings	Stress from concentration (e.g., video display terminal work)
Recordkeeping	Stress from working with terminally ill
Filing	Stress from multiple-role, multiple-boss demands
Writing standard letters	Working with constant noise
Reading forms	Working in a public or otherwise open place
Protecting confidentiality	Answering questions from the public
Working office machines	Answering complaints from the public
Cleaning up after others	Responsibility for inmates, patients, or residents of institutions
Sitting for long periods	Degree of severity of problems of inmates, patients, or residents of institutions
Time pressure	Degree to which new or unexpected problems arise

Source: Adapted from Steinberg and Haignere 1987.

tional domain of lawsuits. This does not mean that pay equity adjustments are bad, just that in practice they erode rather than eliminate wage inequalities associated with the sex or racial composition of jobs.

Mark R. Killingsworth (1990), writing on comparable worth programs implemented in San Jose, California, the state of Minnesota, and across Australia, reports that the pay gaps between men and women were reduced in all three places. In San Jose, the pay gap was reduced by 5.8 percent. In Minnesota and Australia, the reduction was 9.9 percent. In all three cases, however, substantial wage gaps remained, and in Australia, seven years after the adjustments the wage gap had returned to its original level. Clearly, the implementation of comparable worth programs is a political struggle over the distribution of income in a firm and in the economy (Acker 1989).

The Australian case confirms that the effect on compensation of the percentage of females in a job is not merely a historical artifact of women's work being undervalued but the product of a continuing labor process dynamic that undervalues women's work. Since the Australian case was economywide and wages are administered by government and union negotiation rather than set by firms and labor markets, it does not make sense to say that labor market factors bid the wages of typically female jobs back down in the seven years after the comparable worth adjustments. Instead, it seems likely that, in the absence of strong political and administrative requirements, traditional status composition–based pay differentials crept back into the wage system as soon as the political furor died down. Thus, comparable worth programs must be seen as ongoing, not just as political events, if they are to have lasting consequences.

As currently implemented, comparable worth wage adjustments tend to increase the cost of female and minority jobs without reducing the wages of typically male and white jobs. As many people have pointed out, this makes comparable worth expensive from an employer's point of view:

> The basic fact to keep in mind is that comparable worth makes only one change: the price of women's labor to employers increases. Production does not increase. Therefore, because the total amount of goods and services remains constant while women's work receives a larger share of the total, other groups must receive less (Gold 1983:55).

It is possible to reduce the wages of overvalued jobs or of profits to increase the wages of female or minority jobs. In the case of the public sector, where most comparable worth initiatives have taken place, there are no profits to dip into after jobs are reevaluated. This typically leads to some job reductions to cover the cost of the increased wages (Killingsworth 1990). Pay equity initiatives do not logically have to lead to job reductions, however; this is just the path of least resistance. It is difficult to propose wage reductions for any jobs, particularly white and male-dominated skilled work.

In the private sector, comparable worth adjustments could conceivably lead to a larger share of the value produced going to labor. This would be particularly appropriate if employers materially benefited from the discrimination they have practiced against female and minority jobs and individuals. Employers will resist this loss of profits, however. An attractive alternative is for firms to make greater investments in upgrading the skills of those holding typically female and minority jobs and then increase their wages. This would have the effect of reducing organizational skill and wage inequalities. It would also increase the attractiveness of typically female and minority jobs to all workers, thereby reducing segregation. Most important, it would increase the skill levels of the entire labor force, leading to higher productivity across the board. Kanter (1983) provided evidence that companies that are progressive in their human resource practices are actually more productive and profitable. She defined companies as progressive if they had innovations in their job design and quality of work life, human resource development, and affirmative action and equal opportunity practices.

The current role of public policy toward comparable worth initiatives is limited to the courts. Proactive leadership by the public sector, involving self-studies and voluntary comparable worth evaluations, would go a long way toward making gender and racial integration at work the norm. The creation of a countrywide comparable worth policy (as in Australia) for the private as well as the public sector is currently beyond the capacity of any U.S. government entity since wages are administered at the firm rather than the national level. A general federal-level comparable worth law that mandated equal pay for jobs requiring comparable skills, similar to the one that exists in Great Britain, might go far in strengthening workplace equality in the litigious United States.

GENDER-, RACE-, AND CLASS-BASED LABOR MARKET POLICIES

A significant proportion of U.S. racial inequality is a function of inequality in education and labor market experience. To reduce racial inequality requires education and training policies that reduce class inequality in access to education and experience. The key issue is access to skill, through both high-quality education and job-training programs. This is a class issue. It is a matter of how household and community resources are allocated and how they govern life chances. Many U.S. minorities, because of past and current discrimination, grow up in working-class and poor households in disadvantaged communities. When racial discrimination in hiring into skilled jobs is added to their class disadvantages, minorities often find themselves at a profound competitive disadvantage in the labor market. Public policy needs to address the quality of education and access to education. U.S. public policy tends to focus on racial inequality but to be insensitive to class-based inequities. The weakness of class-based equal opportunity initiatives means that racial inequality is strongly reproduced through class inequality.

Gender inequality is only trivially the product of human capital differences. We have already made great strides in promoting equal access to education for men and women (Jacobs 1989b). The current barrier is in access to higher-paying jobs and to jobs that provide significant on-the-job training. Women are already hired into jobs that require advanced education, but they are hired for skilled work only if they invest in their own training through the educational system.

One area in which the United States has clear room for improvement is in job-related skill training, retraining, and the operation of the labor market. The U.S. labor market is basically anarchic. Employers must seek out workers and make uneducated guesses about their skill levels. Workers must seek out employers and sell themselves. In both cases nonproductivity-related attributes, such as race and gender, can be powerful, and misleading, signals about the appropriateness of a job-person match. Employers and employees would be better served with a labor market structure similar to that in Germany, where the government has a role in certifying skill training, providing skill retraining, and matching employees to employers (Janoski 1989). In the current anarchic U.S. system, employers bear the costs not only of training, when they provide it, but also of bad job matches. Employees face discrimination and unnecessarily long job searches. The society pays the price of an underskilled labor force and an underproductive economy.

Now that many corporations are worried about the supply of labor in the future, it may be a good time to recall that most of the skilled white male labor force that is diminishing was trained *on the job*. The tradition of withholding high skill–enhancing jobs for white males needs to be rapidly examined. Corporations should clearly examine their practices. The limited role of federal, state, and local governments in providing training to workers and matching them to jobs is already being challenged because of business dissatisfaction with the quality of the labor force. There is clearly an opportunity for education, training, and worker placement to become less anarchic, more efficient, and less discriminatory.

EROSION OF SOCIAL CLOSURE PROCESSES

Although sex- and race-based social closure processes are widespread in workplaces, they do not have to be pervasive or permanent. There is ample evidence from recent U.S. history that social movements can generate legal and organizational responses that reduce exclusionary practices. Although good-quality, job-level comparisons over time do not exist, there is ample evidence that occupational segregation by both sex and race have declined over the last three decades. I suspect that this is true at the job level within firms as well.

The enforcement of affirmative action programs by the federal government, particularly in the late 1970s, has been a powerful basis for undermining racial and sex segregation. This process has been particularly strong in colleges and universities, where discriminatory admissions policies and the segregation of men and women by majors have been undermined dramatically (Jacobs (1989b). This decline in segregation by major may be reflected in the findings in this study that both racial and sex job segregation tend to be somewhat lower in jobs requiring the most advanced educational credentials. Affirmative action programs have also been important sources for change in the government and in large corporations with government contracts, where equal employment laws are vigorously enforced.

There is evidence in this study that general societal pressures for social closure can vary from place to place. The level of sex segregation tends to be lower in urban areas than in rural areas. Although this was not true for racial segregation in the North Carolina sample, there is evidence from other studies that the level of job segregation is higher in the South than in the North. These findings are consistent with the commonly held notion that concerted educational efforts to reduce status prejudice are important sources of societal change. Such a political process, based on social movement activity, including attempts at reeducation, can create new normative expectations. Other countries, such as Australia, Sweden, and Italy, have eroded gender inequality at work. Egalitarian politics can erode both gender and racial inequalities.

One must not forget, however, that there are real material bases to status closure processes. Whites benefit from the exclusion of blacks from desirable jobs. Discrimination provides opportunities for the superordinate group as it deprives the subordinate group. The material basis for gender-based exclusion from good jobs is somewhat weaker at the household level. On the one hand, husbands have an interest in their wives earning high salaries. On the other hand, there is good evidence that husbands' earnings advantage in the labor market produces a power advantage in the home. Eroding racial and gender inequalities requires first that advantage be eroded. Resistance can be expected in the workplace and the electoral process.

There is strong evidence that the degree of discrimination against blacks rises as the size of their relative population rises. When African-Americans are a larger competitive threat in the labor force, they are more aggressively discriminated against (Blalock 1967; Lieberson 1980). This seems to be true of Hispanics and Asians as well (Tienda and Lii 1987). Thus, attempts at cultural change through antiracist education are most likely to find receptive audiences in those places where they are the least necessary—that is, where the material basis for discriminatory processes are weakest.

The finding in this study that the earnings of all workers decline as the percentage of blacks and/or females in a job rises suggests an additional material basis for status-based social closure. Employers benefit from racism and sexism through their access to a large pool of low-wage workers and their ability to use the sex and racial compositions of employment to create a lower wage job structure. White males benefit as well. One way of thinking about this is that social closure–based segregation "crowds" white males into high-paying positions with high on-the-job training.

A general weakening of status distinctions probably requires both concerted efforts at cultural change and reeducation, as well as a reduction in the material benefits to the superordinate groups. The modern weakening of gender-based status distinctions in U.S. culture has unfortunately been accompanied by a weakening of men's responsibility to support their wives and children (Ehrenreich 1983). When men are less committed to their families, as they increasingly appear to be, there are fewer material incentives for men as husbands to champion gender equality in the workplace and more incentive for them to resist it as workers. In the past, cultural assumptions of male dominance were so widespread that it was unlikely that a man would consider, much less demand, gender equality in the workplace. Now, when there is considerable social movement activity aimed at achieving this demand and the general cultural tendency is toward the diminution of status assumptions based on gender, the material motives of adult males (based on their being in shared households) to support women's equality are weakening.

There are clear indications of a societal tendency to lessen racial prejudice; racial competition tends to be exacerbated, however, during periods of slow or no economic growth. In places of limited employment opportunity and during recessionary periods, racial conflict over jobs is most intense. The history of the working class in the U.S. South is a history of poor whites, often manipulated by economic elites, fighting to exclude poor blacks from the limited economic opportunities afforded by their low-wage economies. The intensification of racial conflict in the deteriorating central cities of U.S. urban centers is a more cosmopolitan example of the same process of racial competition. It is no coincidence that it has been whites in Bensonhurst in Brooklyn, rather than on Fifth Avenue in Manhattan, who have randomly attacked black youths.

Racial competition is most intense among low-wage employees. Thus, in my study I found the levels of racial segregation to be highest in jobs requiring the lowest educational credentials. It is ironic then that it is the most advantaged white male employees in nominally integrated professional and managerial positions who express great fear and complain the loudest about reverse discrimination. It is in their upper-level positions, where competition for jobs is more closely tied to formal credentials, that the routine exclusion of all black candidates is less possible and less necessary. The historical material threat of black labor is to the white working class. When educated black Americans compete successfully for upper-middle-class jobs, they represent a demographically small, although highly visible, threat to middle-class white males.

Eroding gender and racial inequalities in the workplace requires consistent attacks on processes of status-based closure and segregation. Reeducating women and minorities so they are better prepared to enter a competitive labor market will not work. Nor will reeducating white and male employees. They have something to lose and can be expected to defend their advantages. Leadership is required. That leadership can come from many sources. Personnel and equal opportunity offices in the corporate environment should not have to stand alone. They cannot succeed without strong backing from senior management and business owners. Firms that are currently profiting from a segregated employment structure may have something to lose as well. These firms will need incentives from government in the form of strong penalties for discriminating against people and against jobs. Government is not exempt from instituting discriminatory job structures and must be policed as well. Political leadership from workers, unions, corporate elites, and politicians is required if we hope to erode workplace racial and gender segregation and the resulting inequalities.

Appendix
Methodological Issues

THE PLAUSIBILITY OF THIS RESEARCH rests on the reliability and validity of the measures of the sex and racial compositions of jobs. In most previous general population studies, the sex and racial compositions of *occupations*, rather than jobs, was measured. This was usually done by using survey data for the entire United States and aggregating to the national level from reports on individual occupational status. Both public-use samples from the U.S. Census of Population (e.g., Parcel 1989) and from the Current Population Survey (CPS) (e.g., Jacobs 1989a) have been used for this purpose. The strength of this method is that respondents are expected to report only on the general duties and responsibilities of their current job; the sex and racial composition of occupations is arrived at by simple addition within occupational codes. The weakness of this method is that people do not really work in occupations but in concrete jobs in real establishments. The use of job-level measures of sex and racial composition, in place of occupational measures, is clearly more valid.

The second approach to measuring sex and racial composition focuses on jobs but uses a case study methodology. In this case administrative records are used (e.g., Jacobs and Steinberg 1990; Cohn 1985; Baron and Newman 1990). This is clearly a reliable approach to measurement, but, although the focus on jobs is an advance, the case study method leaves the research vulnerable to criticisms that it is not generalizable (Filer 1990). The neoclassical economists take this criticism particularly seriously since the case study literature tends to focus on state-sector (i.e., nonmarket) jobs.

The innovation in the research reported in this monograph and executed in the North Carolina Employment and Health Survey was that it asked employees in a general population to report on the sex and racial compositions of their jobs. Much thought went into developing the survey items and survey protocols for the interviewers to increase the reliability of the measures. Initially, respondents were asked to focus on their primary job, how many hours they worked in a typical week, and for a job description. They were then asked the following three questions: (1) Thinking about the work that you do, in your workplace how many people, including yourself, have the same general *job title* as you? (2) Of these, how many are men? (3) About how many of these are white?

All respondents were able to answer the first question. Four percent failed to provide information on the sex composition of their jobs, and 5 percent did not provide information on the racial composition. An analysis by case identification number indicated that almost all of these nonresponses were in the first week of the survey. This suggests that the problem was less refusal by respondents to provide information than interviewer discomfort with the items.

In training, interviewers were given detailed verbal and written instructions on the goals of the questions and possible problems in interviewing. We anticipated that the most serious problems would involve job titles and job size.

Many jobs do not have formal job titles, suggesting that the first question might simply have asked respondents about their *job* rather than their *job title*. Baron and Bielby (1986), however, report that job titles are important methods for creating sex segregation among otherwise similar jobs in bureaucratic settings. Thus, the formal question used the phrase *job title*, although interviewers were warned that many respondents might need to be probed about their *job*, using more informal language.

The reliability of the second two questions hinges on how well respondents can asses job size. When a person works in a job with ten incumbents, estimates of the number of males or whites are likely to be fairly accurate. When a worker works in a job with one hundred or two hundred incumbents, however, which is quite common among machine operators in factories, the average respondent is less likely to be able to supply a specific number. In these cases, interviewers were prompted to ask for the approximate percentage of whites or males in the job. If the respondent was still hesitant, a series of probes, such as "Is the job all white, 25 percent white, 50 percent white, 75 percent white, or all nonwhite?" was provided for the interviewers to use. Debriefings after the interview stage of the project suggest that these probes were almost never necessary.

Although the success of pretests and the interview process gave us confidence in the method, further comparisons with known population distributions helped us further evaluate the reliability and validity of the sex and racial composition measures. If the sex and racial composition measures are reliable, they should produce estimates of the sex and racial compositions of occupations that are comparable to those that actually exist in the North Carolina population of employed adults.

Tables A.1 and A.2 list the sex and racial compositions of major occupations in North Carolina, based on estimates from the Current Population Survey (merged 1987–88 files) and from the questions on racial and sex composition in the North Carolina Employment and Health Survey. The estimates are nearly identical. In the eighteen comparisons in the two tables, only two estimates are significantly different from each other, based on a test of differences in proportions for two independent samples. For operative and laborer jobs, the Current Population Survey estimate of percent female is 40.1 percent. The job-level sex composition estimate from the North Carolina Employment and Health Survey is 52.3 percent. The job-level racial composition estimate of 21.1 percent among precision production and craft occupations is 7.3 percent higher than the Current Population Survey estimate. The other sixteen estimates are strikingly similar, even when the samples in the occupational groups for the North Carolina Employment and Health Survey were very small.

Since the job-level estimates from the latter survey were nearly identical to estimates of occupational sex and racial composition derived from an aggregate occupational survey, I concluded that the reliability of my indicators approached that of those used in general population studies of the status composition of jobs. There is still some measurement error, of course, but it is not so serious as to produce misleading estimates of status composition. This should be a reassuring finding for readers who were skeptical whether survey respondents could provide accurate information on the sex and racial compositions of their jobs. Toby Parcel, Robert Kaufman, and Leeann Jolly (1991) have recently shown that employee estimates of organizational attributes are less reliable than those of owners and top managers. The results here suggest that employee reports of *job* characteristics may be quite accurate.

Tables A.1 and A.2 as well as the discussion of survey procedures provide reasonably compelling evidence that the sex and racial composition measures on which this study is built are reliable. Measures should be both reliable and *valid*, however, to produce results with which we can feel confident. The face validity of these measures is high,

Table A.1.   Sex composition of major occupational groups in North Carolina

	Current Population Survey estimates, 1987–88		North Carolina Employment and Health Survey estimates, 1989	
	% female	Sample size	% female	Sample size
Total nonmilitary employees	49.6	5,507	51.3	786
Executives, administrators, and managers	40.4	540	40.5	51
Professional specialties	55.8	588	56.1	106
Technicians and support	53.5	144	47.4	32
Sales	56.5	588	49.1	94
Administrative support, including clerical	84.8	838	80.3	153
Service	63.7	653	51.7	74
Precision production, including craft	10.6	713	10.1	101
Operatives and laborers[a]	40.1	1,339	52.3	171

[a]Significant difference between proportions for two independent samples.

in that they replace national aggregate occupational measures of sex and racial composition. This conclusion rests on the theoretical assumption that it is at the *job* level, rather than some more abstract construct level, such as *occupation*, that the casual processes that allocate people to employment positions and through which employment positions are concretely organized and the receipt of wages and benefits takes place. Jobs are paid, jobs are the site of laboring activity, and jobs have incumbents. Occupations are convenient analytical clusters of jobs. As Baron and Bielby (1986) have shown, segregation is generally much higher at the job level than it is at the occupational level.

Face validity is strengthened, however, if we can show that the measures employed here are associated with other known measures of sex and racial composition. Since the measures in the literature are typically the sex and racial compositions of occupations, we should expect that the measures used here—the sex and racial compositions of jobs—should be positively and significantly associated with each other. Since sex segregation is a national phenomenon, and the sex distribution of the population is fairly similar across the nation, we should expect a fairly strong correlation between percent female in the national occupational sample and percent female in the sample of North Carolina jobs employed in this research. Since the spatial distribution of African-

Table A.2. Racial composition of major occupational groups in North Carolina

	Current Population Survey estimates, 1987–88		North Carolina Employment and Health Survey estimates, 1989	
	% nonwhite	Sample size	% nonwhite	Sample size
Total nonmilitary employees	19.2	5,507	21.7	778
Executives, administrators, and managers	6.4	540	9.9	51
Professional specialties	13.8	588	16.8	104
Technicians and support	18.8	144	18.1	32
Sales	10.9	588	14.4	94
Administrative support, including clerical	12.9	838	16.4	153
Service	36.0	653	37.6	73
Precision production, including craft[a]	12.8	713	21.1	100
Operatives and laborers	30.0	1,339	31.7	167

[a]Significant difference between proportions for two independent samples.

Americans varies tremendously, and the degree of segregation does to some extent as well (Fosset, Galle, and Burr 1989), the association between percent black in the national occupational sample and the percent black in North Carolina jobs should be weaker but still positive and significant. These expectations turned out to be correct. The simple correlation between percent female in the job and the corresponding occupational measure at the national level was .62. The simple correlation between percent nonwhite in the job and the corresponding national occupational measures was still positive and highly statistically significant but weaker (.31).

Our confidence in the reliability and validity of the sex and racial composition measures would have been strengthened if a study had been done that compared administrative records with survey responses, but the resources for such a study were not available. Such validity studies are rarely done, but in this case research would probably profit from such a study. In the future it would be desirable to ask respondents to a major national survey such as one of the National Longitudinal Surveys or the Panel Study of Income Dynamics directly about the sex and racial compositions of those in their jobs. Large-scale surveys would allow for more detailed analyses of subgroups such as black women and black men, the analysis of other ethnic groups such as Hispanics, and the modeling of more sophisticated supply-side models that take into account socialization patterns (e.g., whether parents worked in sex-typical occupations and teen-year aspirations) or fixed-effects models (e.g., England et al. 1988). Before carrying out such an expensive and large-scale undertaking, a careful small-scale validation study should be conducted. The reliability and validity tests of the measures in this appendix strongly suggest that the results of a formal validation study would be quite positive. Such a study should also lead, however, to suggestions for improvements in survey administration for future data collection efforts.

SAMPLE DESCRIPTION AND EVALUATION

The North Carolina Employment and Health Survey included interviews with 931 employed North Carolinians aged eighteen and older. The survey included extensive questions on the nature of respondents' jobs, the firms they work for, their insurance coverage, and their physical and mental health.

The sample for the telephone survey was selected through random-digit dialing methods. After contact was made, a census of all employed adults (eighteen and older) in the household was taken and one employed person randomly selected for the interview (using a Kish grid).

In this study, the unit of analysis was often the job rather than the individual. A random sample of employed adults differs slightly from a random sample of jobs. To correct for this difference, jobs were weighted as to the probability of selection by jobs. This weight is simply the number of jobs in a respondent's household divided by the average number of jobs in all households. This reduces the weight assigned to respondents from households with only one job and increases the weight assigned to respondents from households with multiple jobs.

We contacted 1,289 eligible households, from which 931 interviews were completed, for a response rate of 72 percent. This is quite good by current general population survey standards. Of the 190 households we could not contact, at most (154) there was simply no answer, even though at least thirteen attempted contacts were made at all times of the day and on various days of the week. It is likely that these 154 households were ineligible (they had nonfunctioning lines, their homes were recreational homes, their phones were in unoccupied offices, and the like). The other 36 households were probably eligible since most of these (21) had answering machines on at all times. If we assume that the 36 uncontacted households were eligible, then the response rate was still an acceptable 71 percent (931/(1,289 + 36)).

The best test of the representativeness of any sample is its correspondence to known distributions in the population. To evaluate the representativeness of the North Carolina Employment and Health Survey, we compared the sex, racial, age, occupational, and industry distributions to distributions estimated from the Current Population Survey. State-level statistics are not reported by the U.S. Commerce Department so we used public-use tapes and selected all observations of employed North Carolina residents eighteen years or older from the 1987 and 1988 Current Population Surveys. This generated a sample of 5,618 North Carolinians, which is accurate plus or minus 1 percent from the true population distributions.

As table A.3 shows, the NCEHS produced estimates nearly identical to those of the much larger Current Population Survey. Of the twenty-six comparisons, only one proportion (percentage in public administration) is significantly different in the two samples. Overall, the NCEHS is a very representative sample of North Carolina employed adults.

In the analyses in this book the full sample of 931 currently employed North Carolinians was not used. I focused instead on *employees.* The self-employed and those working without pay in a family business were excluded. The largest possible sample size of *employees* was 795.

MISSING VALUES

The samples available for analysis varied in size from chapter to chapter as a function of the data that were missing. Except for the data discussed in chapter 6, data were missing for only a very small proportion of the observations. In all but chapter 6, less than 8 percent of the cases were lost because of missing data. The wage gap models in chapter 6 have an attrition of 20 percent of the cases for all racial and sex groups. The additional attrition here reflects refusals to provide wage information. Although this level of refusal is common in telephone surveys, it is troubling. Since the key innovation in this chapter is that I estimated the effects of sex and racial compositions on earnings inequalities, I was particularly concerned whether the deletion of cases with missing wage data resulted in any differences in the sex or racial compositions of jobs. Table A.4 shows that the sex and racial compositions of jobs in the pay gap models are identical to those in the full sample.

MEASUREMENT AND DISTRIBUTION OF VARIABLES

Table A.5 presents a table of mean values for all variables in the study by sex and race. The table is followed by a series of notes that formally define the measures used.

Table A.3. *Sample distributions for selected variables in the North Carolina Employment and Health Survey (1989) and the Current Population Survey (merged 1987 and 1988)*

	NCEHS	CPS
Sample size	931	5,618
Sampling error at 95 percent confidence level	±.033	±.013
Sex		
Male	52.0%	52.4%
Female	48.0	47.6
Race		
White	82.4	82.4
Black	16.6	15.9
Other	1.0	1.7
Age		
18–25	13.0	17.8
26–40	42.4	42.7
41–60	37.4	33.3
≥ 61	7.2	5.7
Mean	39.7	38.6
Standard deviation	12.9	13.1
Occupation		
Managers and officials	6.5	10.5
Professional and technical	18.8	14.4
Sales	12.7	10.2
Clerical	17.5	14.7
Skilled craft	13.3	11.8
Other manual	20.1	22.8
Service	9.5	11.4
Farmers and farm workers	1.5	2.5
Industry		
Extractive[a]	0.8	3.0
Construction	5.6	7.3
Manufacturing	27.2	28.9
Transport, communications, and utilities	4.2	6.7
Wholesale trade	3.3	4.7
Retail trade	15.5	14.2
FIRE[b]	5.2	4.8
Services	28.1	31.6
Public administration[c]	8.6	2.9

Note: Population is employed North Carolina residents age eighteen and over.
[a]Agriculture, forestry, fisheries, and mining.
[b]Finance, insurance, and real estate.
[c]Significant difference between proportion for two independent samples.

Table A.4.   Percent female and percent black in jobs for chapter 6 analyses and for the full sample

| | Mean percent female | | | Mean percent black | | |
	All jobs	Male incumbents	Female incumbents	All jobs	White incumbents	Black incumbents
Chapter 6	52.30	8.36	88.33	21.39	54.34	13.12
N[a]	654	294	360	654	539	115
All other chapters	52.47	9.46	88.25	21.65	55.41	13.76
Full sample[a]	770	373	425	770	643	147

[a]Missing data on wages reduce sample size for chapter 6 pay gap models below that for the remainder of the study.

Table A.5.   Means and standard deviations for variables not presented in text

Sample sizes	All 654–770	Males 294–373	Females 360–425	Whites 539–643	Blacks 115–147
Job earnings					
Hourly wage	9.93	11.83	8.37	10.33	8.03
	(8.11)	(10.93)	(4.11)	(8.69)	(3.99)
Natural log of hourly	2.15	2.30	2.02	2.19	1.98
wages	(.51)	(.53)	(.45)	(.51)	(.45)
Job-status composition					
Percent female	52.39	8.36	88.33	53.34	47.94
	(44.54)	(18.38)	(21.25)	(44.55)	(44.43)
Percent black	21.39	20.79	21.89	14.35	54.34
	(29.39)	(29.89)	(29.01)	(22.99)	(33.48)
Sex segregation[a]	84.35	90.86	78.94	84.25	84.79
	(29.15)	(28.88)	(28.28)	(29.50)	(27.69)
Racial segregation[a]	71.99	74.19	70.17	62.66	111.96
	(50.88)	(53.02)	(48.92)	(31.50)	(86.37)
Individual human capital					
Education (years)	13.19	13.27	13.12	13.28	12.78
	(2.40)	(2.65)	(2.18)	(2.37)	(2.52)
Firm tenure (years)	7.21	7.20	7.22	7.47	6.02
	(7.60)	(7.98)	(7.29)	(7.70)	(7.06)
Experience[b] (years)	8.48	9.52	7.64	8.70	7.48
	(9.16)	(10.41)	(7.90)	(9.30)	(8.41)
Experience squared	155.65	198.59	120.58	161.97	126.04
	(287.67)	(380.69)	(171.79)	(292.37)	(263.78)
Job characteristics					
Autonomous[c]	0.07	.08	.06	.08	.01
Supervisory authority[d]	1.32	1.56	1.12	1.42	.83
	(1.98)	(2.12)	(1.80)	(2.04)	(1.57)
Job complexity[e]	8.08	8.29	7.91	8.19	7.56
	(1.70)	(1.62)	(1.75)	(1.70)	(1.66)
Closeness of	5.99	5.88	6.07	5.87	6.52
supervision[f]	(1.80)	(1.74)	(1.85)	(1.77)	(1.84)
Union member (yes = 1)	.09	.10	.08	.09	.11
Job required credentials[g]	5.53	5.75	5.35	5.71	4.69
	(2.67)	(2.67)	(2.65)	(2.67)	(2.48)
Prior experience	.66	.73	.61	.68	.60
required (yes = 1)					
Job fragmentation[a]	1.64	1.58	1.68	1.58	1.88
	(1.44)	(1.50)	(1.44)	(1.49)	(1.36)
Relatively large job[a]	.49	.49	.49	.49	.50
	(.31)	(.31)	(.30)	(.30)	(.30)
Firm training program	.18	.20	.17	.18	.20
(yes = 1)					
Weeks to learn job[h]	43.88	62.83	28.42	47.63	26.36
	(65.94)	(79.70)	(46.81)	(70.53)	(32.51)
Firm characteristics					
Formalization[a]	1.72	1.69	1.75	1.70	1.84
	(1.20)	(1.22)	(1.17)	(1.19)	(1.22)
Establishment size[i]	3.88	3.89	3.87	3.85	4.01
	(1.89)	(1.98)	(1.82)	(1.90)	(1.88)

Table A.5. Means and standard deviations for variables not presented in text

Sample sizes	All 654–770	Males 294–373	Females 360–425	Whites 539–643	Blacks 115–147
Out of state ownership (yes = 1)	.17	.19	.14	.17	.14
Subsidiary status (yes = 1)	.17	.15	.18	.17	.15
Part of multi-establishment firm (yes = 1)	.37	.38	.37	.38	.35
Place size[a]	2.19	2.16	2.22	2.16	2.34
	(1.07)	(1.04)	(1.09)	(1.05)	(1.11)
Urban location (yes = 1)	.61	.63	.59	.63	.52
For-profit firm (yes = 1)	.71	.73	.69	.71	.68
Industrial sector (yes = 1)					
Extractive	.008	.014	.003	.008	.010
Construction	.061	.121	.001	.062	.056
Manufacturing	.283	.284	.282	.278	.310
Transportation/utility	.038	.070	.013	.040	.030
Wholesale trade	.034	.050	.021	.035	.030
Retail trade	.152	.121	.177	.161	.112
Business services	.102	.060	.136	.106	.081
Personal services	.022	.028	.018	.021	.030
Social services	.203	.111	.278	.204	.198
Public administration	.135	.141	.061	.085	.143
Market sector (yes = 1)					
State	.264	.237	.286	.256	.298
Oligopolistic	.319	.341	.301	.315	.338
Competitive	.417	.422	.413	.429	.363

Note: Chapters 3 and 5 report descriptive statistics for additional variables.
Standard deviation not reported for dichotomous variables.
[a]Measurement is described in the text.
[b]Experience is measured as age minus education, minus 6, minus current firm tenure, minus .25 for each reported spell of unemployment. In addition, following U.S. Department of Commerce (1987), all experience measures are deflated to take into account average male and female work force interruptions. The deflators for men are age less than 29 = .977, age 30–45 = .947, age 46 and older = .991. The deflators for women are age less than 29 = .947, age 30–45 = .834, age 46 and older = .773.
[c]Coded 1 if does not report to a supervisor.
[d]Six-item scale (reliability = .90) made up of questions about presence and degree of supervisory and managerial authority.
[e]Four-item scale (reliability = .54) made up of questions about task variety, routinization, repetitiveness, and standardization.
[f]Four-item scale (reliability = .64) made up of questions about freedom to discriminate, work-pace discretion, closeness of supervision, and task autonomy.
[g]What level of formal education do you think is needed for a person to do your job? None, some grade school, complete grade school, some high school, high school degree, trade school or apprenticeship, some college, junior college degree, four-year degree, specialized four-year degree, graduate degree.
[h]How long (coded in weeks) would it take a qualified new person to learn to do your job reasonably well?
[i]About how many prople work for your organization at the location where you work? I mean all types of workers in all departments. Response categories: less than 10; 10–25; 26–50; 51–100; 101–500; 501–1,000; 1,001–10,000; more than 10,000.

NOTES

1. The notion that this discrimination is rational may strike some readers, particularly those untutored in neoclassical reasoning, as odd. It is rational only in this sense. To the extent that there are average group differences in labor costs and most employers make hiring decisions with imperfect information, it is difficult to predict accurately how individual employees will work out but comparatively easy to predict, based on average *group* differences over the long term, the probability that the average employee will work out. Thus, if an employer discriminates against all black or female (or young or uneducated) job applicants for a particular job, over the long term, on average, she will save money. Of course, many excellent female and minority workers will be overlooked along the way and some poor-performing white male workers will be hired. These bad individual-level decisions are in the statistical discrimination story an unavoidable cost of making hiring decisions in an imperfect world with imperfect information.

CHAPTER 2

1. Some labor market theory is specifically concerned with occupational processes. See, for example, Berg and Kalleberg 1987.

2. The case weight used to correct for households in which members hold multiple jobs is weight $= j/J$, where j is the number of jobs in the household and J is the average number of jobs across all households.

3. Missing cases were equally distributed by sex and race (males: 20.2 percent; females: 21.4 percent; whites: 20.6 percent; blacks: 21.3 percent, and percent female and percent black in the job were practically identical for those who reported their earnings and those who did not.

4. In this study, percent nonwhite will be routinely referred to as percent black. Nonwhites in North Carolina are overwhelmingly African-American. There are Native American populations in a few rural counties (particularly Robeson and Cherokee) and recently small Asian immigrant populations in the

Charlotte and Raleigh metropolitan areas. In the sample data, 97 percent of the nonwhites are black.

5. It is not clear whether it is desirable in any case. The index of dissimilarity takes as its equality baseline the marginal distribution of the status characteristic in the population. If an organization is all white, then all-white jobs are computed as unsegregated—a clearly unsatisfying procedure. Conversely, if an organization is 50 percent white, well below the population of white employees (78 percent in this sample), then jobs that are 60 or 70 percent white are seen as relatively segregated—even though they are much more integrated than society in general.

6. Only 48 percent of the labor force is female, but females are disproportionately found among *employees*, while males are more likely to be *self-employed*.

7. The formula for the modified (job-level segregation) index of dissimilarity is

Job segregation = $[.5|((p_1/P_1) - (p_2/P_2))|]*100$

where p_1 and p_2 refer to the percent of job employment in status categories 1 and 2 (e.g., male and female respectively) and P_1 and P_2 refer to the percent of total employment in the population in status categories 1 and 2. The formula for the index of dissimilarity is quite similar:

Index of dissimilarity = $[.5(\Sigma|((n_1/N_1) - (n_2/n_2)|)]*100$

where n_1 and n_2 refer to the number of people in the job in status categories 1 and 2 and N_1 and N_2 refer to the total number of people in those status categories in the population and the index is summed over the whole population.

CHAPTER 3

1. In this chapter and the remainder of this study, data presented in the text will be in the form of frequency distributions, cross-classifications, and simple graphs. Conclusions, however, are always based on careful and sophisticated multivariate statistical models. These models can be found in the appendixes to the chapter.

CHAPTER 4

1. Although this chapter focuses on the exclusion of subordinates from valued positions, it should be acknowledged that social closure–produced segregation can create certain short-term benefits for the subordinate group in the form of separate social spheres relatively free from direct competition and domination by superordinates. This temporary haven does, however, reproduce the subordinate-superordinate status distinction.

2. Cohn (1985) points out that the exclusive focus on a single subordinate group can be misleading. In discussing clericals in the United Kingdom, he argues that profit pressures combined with a rise in required skill levels led to the replacement of one low-wage labor force (boys) with another (women). That is, there can be alternative sources of secondary labor. If the wages of white

males are contributing to some level of profit pressure, female, black, young, or immigrant labor may all be functionally equivalent solutions to the problem of how to increase profitability. In this case one might ask which substitution would be less disruptive of ongoing skill requirements, interaction patterns, and status structures in the workplace.

3. This argument is empirically consistent with Cohn's (1985) contention that jobs with many incumbents represent strong cost pressures to hire lower-cost subordinate-status labor.

4. A summated scale combines information from a number of survey questions that all focus on a common concept in order to increase the accuracy of the measure.

5. The majority of employees had zero power. The effect of this skewed distribution was modeled by including a dummy variable (Super) for supervisor versus nonsupervisor in the multivariate models. Since this approach affected only the conclusions about the sex composition of jobs, it is reported only for those models.

6. In statistical models this variable is transformed into its natural logarithm.

7. A more simple metro-nonmetro contrast was explored but was more weakly related to the dependent variables. The size of the place of residence introduces some measurement error to the extent that more rural people commute to work in urban areas than the other way around. Thus, this measurement strategy may tend to understate actual rural-urban differences in employment patterns.

8. Women and blacks may be alternative sources of low-wage, exploitable labor. Following Cohn (1985), we would expect there will be a required skill–large occupation interaction such that lower-skilled jobs that represent high labor costs might be disproportionately filled by blacks. White women, who tend to have higher educational levels than African-Americans, may more often be called upon to fill jobs with large populations and relatively high levels of reading, writing, or other required skills.

9. The oligopolistic, competitive, and state distinction is consistent with Randy Hodson (1978) and James O'Connor (1973), as well as the neoclassical arguments outlined in this book. The operationalization follows Hodson (1984) but has somewhat less detail.

10. There are a number of plausible predictions whereby profit pressures may be linked to job size and job skill level. One predicted interaction, between profit pressure and job size, is modeled by multiplying Relative Number by both the competitive and oligopolistic sector dummy variables. These interactions are reported only in the multivariate statistical models in the chapter appendix. An interaction of skill with job size is modeled by multiplying Relative Number by Required Credentials. Since Cohn (1985) also suggests that absolute as well as relative job size can create profit pressures that lead to employing secondary labor, this interaction is also modeled with a multiplicative term between the credential scale and the absolute number of incumbents in the job (Fragmentation).

11. Again, although not strictly speaking correct, this measure of percent nonwhite will be routinely discussed and interpreted in terms of social closure processes associated with white-black relationships.

12. Again, the formula for the modified (job-level segregation) index of dissimilarity is

Job segregation $= [.5*|(p_1/P_1) - (p_2/P_2)|]*100$

where p_1 and p_2 refer to the percent of job employment in status categories 1 and 2 (e.g., male and female), respectively, and P_1 and P_2 refer to the percent of total employment in the population in status categories 1 and 2.

13. These analyses, because they are about jobs, are weighted to represent a random sample of jobs. As discussed in chapter 2, this corrects for the oversampling of households with one or a few job holders when one samples a random sample of individuals. The formula used is weight $= j/J$, where j is the number of jobs in the household and J is the average number of jobs across all households.

14. Since the dependent variables Percent Female, Percent Black, Sex Segregation, and Race Segregation all have restricted ranges between 0 and 100, they are transformed into logits to make them conform to ordinary least squares (OLS) regression assumptions. The logit transformation is logit $(p) = \ln [p/(1 - p)]$, where p is any variable whose range is between 0 and 1. In theory, this transforms the restricted-range variable into an infinite-range variable. In practice, scores of 0 were set to .01 and scores of 100 were set to .99 to make the natural logarithm defined. Racial and sex segregation scores higher than 100 were also set to .99. All analyses were carried out on untransformed variables as well. In general, substantive and statistical conclusions were identical, although the fit improved for models with the logit transformation.

15. The relative size of the job is weakly positively related to the percent female in the job. Interactions between the job size variables and educational credentials were not statistically significant.

16. The same interaction terms as in note 10 were explored in the logistic regression analyses, but none improved model fit. This suggests that the interactions reported above tell us more about variations from complete segregation than they do about demographically balanced jobs.

17. This finding is at odds with the literature, which argues that there is a glass ceiling at the top of bureaucratic organizations that impedes the upward mobility of blacks. These jobs—upper management in large bureaucracies—are so rare that they play little or no role in the *general population* data examined here. It seems reasonable to expect that racism intensifies again at the very top, where issues of trust and homogamy become increasingly important (Mills 1956; Kanter 1977).

18. An alternative or complementary explanation is that highly educated blacks are relatively rare and so demographic balance is particularly difficult to achieve in jobs that require advanced educational credentials.

19. We do find more sex segregation and fewer sex-integrated jobs in the oligopolistic sector than in either the state or competitive sectors. At the same

time, the state sector has the *highest* racial segregation, the competitive sector the least, and the oligopolistic sector intermediate levels. For these two patterns to be the opposite of each other is clearly not consistent with any general market efficiency explanation about segregation.

CHAPTER 5

1. The labor process measures are all derived from self-reports of employees. This procedure has some advantages and disadvantages for the project at hand. Relative to the *Dictionary of Occupational Titles* and other secondary sources of occupational characteristics, self-reports are much more likely to capture respondents' actual *job*-level experiences than some more aggregate and so more error-prone occupational measures (Glass 1990). In addition, the range of labor process dimensions explored through self-reports is much broader than is available from secondary sources. At the same time, self-reports may introduce more measurement distortion than more objective on-site job evaluations. But even if this were the case, the distortion would have to be seriously correlated with race or sex to affect the conclusions of this study. Denise and William Bielby (1988) and Robert Smith (1979) suggest that, at least for sex, such distortion is unlikely to be a source of bias. In a large study of New York State government jobs, Jacobs and Steinberg (1990) reported that self-reports of job attributes were very highly associated with managers' ratings.

2. There is some overlap in this measure with the variable Promotion Opportunity in the last chapter. This measure is more closely tied to job security and opportunity, while the one in the last chapter was limited to opportunities for promotion.

3. The two variables Supervisory Responsibility and Managerial Power are subscales of the variable Power in the last chapter.

4. Organizational and job segmentation are addressed separately for two reasons. First, previous empirical literature suggests that tendencies toward race- and sex-based segmentation are stronger at the job level than at the organizational level (Hodson 1983). Second, as we saw in the last chapter, sex and racial segregation and job composition are more closely tied to job characteristics than to organizational characteristics.

5. All models are weighted to represent a random sample of jobs, as in the last chapter. All labor process measures are normally distributed except supervisory responsibility and managerial authority. Models were reestimated with logged versions of these two dependent variables, but substantive conclusions were consistent with those based on the nonlogged versions presented in these tables.

6. This is a provisional conclusion in that it is based on a weak statistical assumption—that models are fully specified.

7. Standard human capital measures are used here. These include years of education, tenure with the current firm, labor force experience, and labor force experience squared. The squared term statistically models the well-known decline in the effectiveness of experience late in careers. Labor force experience

is measured in years since starting work minus bouts of unemployment; for women, it is further deflated to take into account average labor force interruptions for age and education categories. This latter approach is quite conservative and ensures that we do not overestimate women's labor force participation. See the methodological appendix for more on this measurement strategy.

8. This is accomplished by building ordinary least-squares multiple regression equations. Each equation adds a new set of variables. Changes in the race and sex coefficients can be interpreted as the result of statistically controlling for the additional block of variables. Thus, when we add human capital variables and racial inequality decreases, we can say that the decrease in inequality reflects human capital processes. Since 130 multiple regression equations, not counting interactions, alternative models, and the like, were estimated to get the results presented in the tables in this chapter, full models are not reported. Interested readers can contact me for further information.

9. This strategy is somewhat different from the core-periphery-state coding in the last chapter. The sectoral coding in this and the next chapter is more detailed than the three-sector contrast and should be a more stringent statistical control since it takes into account not only broad notions of market competition but also to a greater extent industrial variations in technology.

10. Ken Spenner (1985) reviews measures of job skill in the literature and advocates for these three, particularly weeks to learn the job, as plausible measures.

11. This table and table 5.4 report standardized regression coefficients. These coefficients can be interpreted as showing the strength and direction of the association, controlling for other variables in the model. Larger coefficients (negative or positive) imply stronger relationships.

12. The small size of the African-American subsample makes it particularly difficult to find statistically significant status composition effects.

13. Since so few African-American employees have managerial authority, it is possible that such employees work for black-owned firms, but I have no way of knowing definitively if this is the case.

14. Although the effect is nonsignificant for males, it is nearly significant ($p = .052$) and quite nearly identical in size and sign with the coefficients for females.

15. It may be that the results for larger samples of black workers would be more akin to those for the white and full sample.

16. Although the internal labor market effect is not statistically significant among women, it is similar to the effect among men.

CHAPTER 6

1. For the single study that does not provide evidence of a sex composition wage effect after controlling for multiple job characteristics, see Filer 1989.

2. Although studies vary in their approach, the general functional form of the model is

$$w_j = b_0 + b_1 J_j + b_2 PF_j + b_3 PM + u_j$$

where the subscript j indicates the set of jobs; w is the job's hourly (often starting) wage; J is a set of job characteristics; PF and PM are the percent female and percent minority in the job; and u is a random error term.

3. The resultant model can be written as follows:

$$w_i = b_0 + b_1J_i + b_2PF_i + b_3PM_i + b_4HC_i + b_5F_i + b_6S_i + b_7M_i + u_i$$

where the subscript i indicates the set of individuals in the sample of jobs; HC is a set of human capital attributes of the individual; F is a set of firm characteristics; S is 1 if the respondent is female; M is 1 if the respondent is minority; and the other terms are defined as in note 2.

4. Although it would be preferable to estimate separate equations for each group by both sex and race (e.g., black females), the sample is too small for this level of detail.

5. It may be that the elimination of patriarchal and racist tendencies in the labor market will increase the overall bargaining power of the working class and over the long term raise the wages of all employees. Over the short term, however, white men and women benefit from their race and white men and black men benefit from their sex. Black women are doubly disadvantaged.

6. Models estimated separately for males and females and for blacks and whites are more conservative in that any differences in measurement quality or earnings process between men and women and whites and blacks that might produce misleading results in a model estimated for the whole sample are avoided. The model is also conservative in that the progressively smaller sizes of the samples (especially the black subsample) tend to lead to potentially inappropriate conclusions that there are no racial composition effects. For this reason and the comparatively small size of the sample for the entire project, probability levels as high as .10 will be reported in this chapter.

7. The basic model starts with the sex and racial compositions of jobs. The next model controls for human capital variables. The third controls for organizational and job-skill variables, and the final for individual sex and race.

8. The focus on hourly wages is also indicative of a conservative approach. The wage gaps between men and women and between blacks and whites are progressively larger when one looks at weekly, monthly, and yearly earnings. This is because African-Americans (of both sexes) and women (of all races) often end up in jobs in which they work fewer and more unstable hours. The analysis of hourly wage rates understates true earnings inequalities but also relieves us of the sticky problem of evaluating labor supply versus job demand. In the case of male-female differences, there is a clear labor supply component to the hours worked. This is less clear for racial differences, and, as we saw in the last chapter, a great deal of racial inequality has to do with status closure based on the exclusion of blacks from desirable jobs. The generally higher unemployment rates among blacks suggest that limited access to jobs, access to jobs with fewer work hours, as well as access to skilled jobs are all important outcomes of racist labor market processes. In this chapter we find that social closure processes whereby blacks are excluded from higher-skilled jobs are the dominant source of race-based wage inequality. A focus on yearly earnings or unemployment

(with its implications for lifetime earnings) would provide increased evidence of the importance of the process of status closure in creating racial inequality in the United States. All models were also estimated using (log) earnings but led to the same substantive conclusion. See Hodson 1985 for a discussion of the choice of the functional form of earnings in similar models.

9. Previous research on the sex and racial compositions of jobs has either failed to model firm variation (e.g., England et al. 1988) or used only industrial characteristics (e.g., Sorenson 1989a, 1989b). Although the measures in this study represent an improvement over past research, they are still somewhat incomplete. It seems reasonable to assume that some variation in earnings associated with a firm's resources is not captured by these measures. If this measurement error is associated with sex or race, it will lead to some tendency to underestimate the effects of a firm's characteristics on earnings inequalities. The measures for conglomerate status used in the last chapter were not significantly associated with earnings.

10. In general, the results are substantively identical for models in which earnings are untransformed or in the form of a natural logarithm. Only the earnings consequences of the sex and racial compositions of jobs, as well as individual sex and race, are reported in table 6.2. All pooled earnings models as well as final models for sex and racial groups are reported in the chapter appendix.

11. There is a potential problem of multicollinearity between the gender dummy variable and percent female since their zero-order correlation is quite high ($R = .89$). This is not a problem for race and percent black ($R = .51$). Since the addition of the gender dummy variable to the model has almost no influence on the percent female coefficients, multicollinearity is probably not a problem in these models for this variable.

12. This assumption is reasonable in the context of most pay equity studies in which the search is only for sex or racial composition effects on administrative wage setting. These studies are conservative, however, in that they ignore the important role of status closure—job and organizational segmentation—in producing male-female and black-white wage inequalities.

Estimates in table 6.3 of the proportion of the male-female earnings gap accounted for by job composition are computed by taking the differences in male and female average percent female and percent black and multiplying them by the metric coefficient in the appropriate wage equation. Complete equations are reported in the chapter appendix, but the coefficients are the same as those reported in table 6.2. The same procedure, using racial differences in percent female and percent black, are used to produce the dollar value estimates for race reported in table 6.3. The formulas for these decompositions are

$$\beta \text{ percent female } (\chi \text{ percent female}_{male} - \chi \text{ percent female}_{female})$$

and

$$\beta \text{ percent black } \chi \text{ percent black}_{white} - \chi \text{ percent black}_{black})$$

where β refers to the statistical estimate of the effect on wages and χ refers to the average percent female or percent black within status groups.

13. The general formula is $\Sigma_i[\beta\chi_{ij}(\chi_{ij\,male} - \chi_{ij\,female})]$ or $\Sigma_i[\beta X_{ij\,white} - \chi_{ij\,black})]$, where X_{ij} refers to ith variables within the j vector of variables and χ refers to the mean values of all Xs for the subsample. For example, the human capital vector of variables includes education, experience, experience squared, and employer tenure.

14. Decompositions using (*ln*) wage models lead to substantially similar interpretations for both the male-female and black-white pay gaps. When separate sex and race equations are used to decompose the wage gap (see the discussion in Duncan 1968; Cain 1980; Sorenson 1989a), the results are nearly identical.

15. The most conservative reading of these data might lead us to accept the hypothesis that the racial composition of jobs has no effect on earnings. I am not willing to do this, however, since these are conservative, or lower-bound, estimates of the contributions of sex and racial compositions to male-female and white-black earnings inequalities. Since the models used to evaluate these effects control for an important array of job characteristics that are themselves influenced by the sex and racial compositions of the jobs, it is quite probable that the actual impact of racial and sex segregation on earnings is underestimated when we fix their contribution to the respective pay gaps at 21 and 56 percent.

16. It is also possible that some estimated job effects may reflect real differences in human capital attributes between women and men and blacks and whites that are not otherwise captured in these models.

17. It should be remembered, however, that these estimates are based on an incomplete set of firm measures and so may underestimate the impact of firm-level segmentation on earnings inequalities.

CHAPTER 7

1. David Card and Alan B. Krueger (1990) have shown that convergence in the quality of schooling between blacks and whites in the South accounts for about 15 percent of the convergence between 1960 and 1980 in returns to education. Theirs is the first direct assessment of the school quality–wage return model from a human capital framework. Although the translation to general differences in school quality is not possible from their work, it suggests that because of past discrimination in educational funding and practices there may be human capital differences between blacks and whites not captured by the empirical models in chapters 5 and 6. It also suggests that only a small part of the changes in the wage gap is associated with educational quality.

2. It is not necessary to accept that there is an explicit link between human capital via productivity and wages. Even if productivity at the individual level is only weakly linked to human capital, and often not directly measured by employers, it still seems reasonable to treat education and experience as important and generally accepted signals of the potential success of workers in a new job or of their current contribution to a firm. This weak version of human capital

theory is consistent with both credentialing accounts in sociology (e.g., Berg 1970; Collins 1979) and the general logic behind statistical discrimination accounts (Arrow 1973a, 1973b; Phelps 1972; Thurow 1975).

3. For recent immigrant minorities, human capital differences between them and the white population would not necessarily lead to this interpretation.

4. The original human capital explanation of gender differences was based on women's lower levels of labor force participation and investment in education (Becker 1957). The closing of the education gap, the tremendous increase in women's labor force participation, and the academic discovery that occupations are segregated and that this affects wages and that husbands' participation rates in housework are low, even when their wives work full time, led to the abandonment of the earlier formulation and its replacement with the new home economics interpretation.

5. Only one neoclassically framed study (Daymont and Andrisani 1984) has found human capital and utility differences between men and women to explain a substantial part (between 44 and 77 percent) of the pay gap. This study, however, focused on a narrow population of recent male and female college graduates at a time in their careers when the pay gap was smallest. More important, the primary explanatory variables were job and labor market preferences and expectations expressed during the high school years and in college majors. As Cain (1986) points out forcefully, one cannot interpret a variables effect as outside the labor market unless one is convinced that its sources are in fact determined elsewhere. In this case the choice of college majors and anticipated adult occupations clearly must have been influenced, at least in part, by knowledge of the sex-segregated employment structure they would confront on leaving school. In general population studies, such as mine, human capital differences tend to explain between 10 and 15 percent of the male-female pay gap (Cain 1986; Marini 1989).

6. Of course, the reality is more complicated, and employers probably require stronger evidence of potential success from blacks than from whites before hiring blacks for high-training-cost jobs. For example, an employer might require a black candidate to have a degree from a more prestigious university or more years of experience. This inflating of sufficient credentials is consistent with the general patterns of skill-based social closure identified in this study. African-Americans have to appear to be more qualified than their white competition to get most jobs.

7. They may, of course, experience some interactional or even slight wage advantage within the job, but the general labor process and base wage rate will be a function of the job into which they are hired.

8. Wilson sees as an implication of this process the rise of a black middle class that increasingly takes advantage of the race-neutral but class-discriminating labor market. This black middle class follows jobs to the suburbs, depleting cities of middle-class blacks to serve as role models, leaders, and the social glue in black communities.

9. Critics might contend that there is no discrimination here at all. Rather,

there is measurement error in the data employed in this and other studies that does not capture the true extent of African-Americans' skill disadvantage relative to that of white Americans. I am not inclined to give this argument much credence, and its similarity to a general racist argument on the nature of skill-based discrimination is self-evident. It would seem that the burden of proof, for those who argue that inequality reflects unmeasured differences in productivity, rests with those who make the argument.

REFERENCES

Acker, Joan. 1987. "Sex Bias in Job Evaluation: A Comparable Worth Issue." In *Ingredients for Women's Employment Policy*, ed. Christine E. Bose and Glenna D. Spitze, 183–96. Albany: State University of New York Press.

———. 1989. *Doing Comparable Worth: Gender, Class, and Pay Equity*. Philadelphia: Temple University Press.

———. 1990. "Hierarchies, Jobs and Bodies: A Theory of Gendered Organizations." *Gender & Society* 4:139–58.

Acker, Joan, and Donald R. Van Houten. 1974. "Differential Recruitment and Control: The Sex Structuring of Organizations." *Administrative Science Quarterly* 19:152–64.

Arrow, Kenneth. 1973a. "Some Mathematical Models of Race in the Labor Market." In *Racial Discrimination in Economic Life*, ed. Anthony H. Pascal, 83–102. Lexington, Mass.: D. C. Heath.

———. 1973b. "The Theory of Discrimination." In *Discrimination in Labor Markets*, ed. Orley Ashenfelter and Albert Rees, 3–33. Princeton: Princeton University Press.

Averitt, Robert T. 1968. *The Dual Economy: The Dynamics of American Industry Structure*. New York: Norton.

Baron, James N. 1984. "Organizational Perspectives on Stratification." *Annual Review of Sociology* 10:37–69.

Baron, James N. and William T. Bielby. 1980. "Bringing the Firm Back In: Stratification, Segmentation, and the Organization of Work." *American Sociological Review* 45:737–65.

———. 1982. "Workers and Machines: Dimensions and Determinants of Technical Relations in the Workplace." *American Sociological Review* 47:175–88.

Baron, James N., and Andrew E. Newman. 1990. "For What It's Worth: Organizations, Occupations and the Value of Work Done by Women and Non-whites." *American Sociological Review* 55:155–75.

Barry, Janis. 1985. "Women Production Workers: Low Pay and Hazardous Work." *American Economic Review* 75:262–65.

Becker, Gary Stanley. 1957. *The Economics of Discrimination.* Chicago: University of Chicago Press.

———. 1981. *A Treatise on the Family.* Cambridge: Harvard University Press.

———. 1985. "Human Capital, Effort, and the Sexual Division of Labor." *Journal of Economic Literature* 3:33–58 (Suppl).

Becker, Henry Jay. 1980. "Racial Segregation among Places of Employment." *Social Forces* 58:761–76.

Beller, Andrea. 1984. "Trends in Occupational Segregation by Sex, 1960–1981." In *Sex Segregation in the Workplace: Trends, Explanations, Remedies,* ed. Barbara F. Reskin, 11–26. Washington, D.C.: National Academy Press.

Berg, Ivar E. 1970. *Education and Jobs: The Great Training Robbery.* New York: Praeger.

Berg, Ivar E., and Arne Kalleberg. 1987. *Work and Industry: Structure, Markets and Processes.* New York: Plenum Press.

Bettio, Francesca. 1988. *The Sexual Division of Labour: The Italian Case.* Oxford: Clarendon Press.

Bianco, Maria Luisa. 1992. "Some Paths Leading Women to Job Segregation: Social Constraints and Actors' Rationality." Paper presented at the International Sociological Association, Stratification Research Committee, Trento, Italy, May 14–16.

Bielby, Denise. 1978. "Career Sex-Atypicality and Career Involvement of College Educated Women: Baseline Evidence from the 1960's." *Sociology of Education* 51:7–28.

Bielby, Denise, and William T. Bielby. 1988. "She Works Hard for Her Money: Household Responsibilities and the Allocation of Work Effort." *American Journal of Sociology* 93:1031–59.

Bielby, William T. 1981. "Models of Status Attainment." *Research in Social Stratification and Mobility* 1:3–26.

Bielby, William T., and James N. Baron. 1984. "A Woman's Place Is with Other Women: Sex Segregation within Organizations." In *Sex Segregation in the Workplace: Trends, Explanations, Remedies,* ed. Barbara F. Reskin, 27–55. Washington, D.C.: National Academy Press.

———. 1985. "Organizational Barriers to Gender Equality: Sex Segregation of Jobs and Opportunities." In *Gender and the Life Course,* ed. Alice S. Rossi, 233–51. Hawthorne, N.Y.: Aldine de Gruyter.

———. 1986. "Men and Women at Work: Sex Segregation and Statistical Discrimination." *American Journal of Sociology* 91:759–99.

———. 1987. "Undoing Discrimination: Job Integration and Comparable Worth." In *Ingredients for Women's Employment Policy,* ed. Christine E. Bose and Glenna D. Spitze, 211–29. Albany: State University of New York Press.

Blalock, Hubert M. 1967. *Toward a Theory of Minority-Group Relations.* New York: Wiley.

Blau, Francine. 1975. "Sex Segregation of Workers by Enterprise." In *Labor Market Segmentation,* ed. Richard C. Edwards, Michael Reich, and David M. Gordon, 257–75. Lexington, Mass.: D. C. Heath.

Blau, Peter Michael. 1977. *Inequality and Heterogeneity: A Primitive Theory of Social Structure.* New York: Free Press.

Blau, Peter Michael, and Otis Dudley Duncan. 1967. *The American Occupational Structure.* New York: Wiley.

Bloom, Jack M. 1987. *Class, Race, and the Civil Rights Movement.* Bloomington: Indiana University Press.

Bonacich, Edna. 1972. "A Theory of Ethnic Antagonism: The Split Labor Market." *American Sociological Review* 37:547–59.

———. 1976. "Advanced Capitalism and Black/White Race Relations in the United States: A Split Labor Market View." *American Sociological Review* 41:34–51.

Bose, Christine E., and Glenna D. Spitze, eds. 1987. *Ingredients for Women's Employment Policy.* Albany: State University of New York Press.

Braverman, Harry. 1973. *Labor and Monopoly Capital: The Degradation of Work in the Twentieth Century.* New York: Monthly Review Press.

Bridges, William P. 1980. "Industrial Marginality and Female Employment: A New Appraisal." *American Sociological Review* 45:58–75.

———. 1982. "The Sexual Segregation of Occupations: Theories of Labor Stratification in Industry." *American Journal of Sociology* 88:270–95.

Bridges, William P., and Robert L. Nelson. 1989. "Markets in Hierarchies: Organizational and Market Influences on Gender Inequality in a State Pay System." *American Journal of Sociology* 95:616–59.

Bridges, William P., and Wayne Villimez. 1991. "Employment Relations and the Labor Market: Integrating Institutional and Market Perspectives." *American Sociological Review* 56:748–64.

Brito, Patricia, and Carol Jusenius. 1978. "Sex Segregation in the Labor Market: An Analysis of Young College Women's Occupational Preferences." In *Women, Work, and Family,* ed. Frank Mott, 57–75. Lexington, Mass.: Lexington Books.

Burstein, Paul. 1985. *Discrimination, Jobs, and Politics.* Chicago: University of Chicago Press.

Cain, Glen G. 1986. "The Economic Analysis of Labor Market Discrimination: A Survey." In *Handbook of Labor Economics,* ed. Orley Ashenfelter and P. R. G. Layàrd, 693–785. Amsterdam: North-Holland.

Caplow, Theodore. 1954. *The Sociology of Work.* Minneapolis: University of Minnesota Press.

Card, David, and Alan B. Krueger. 1990. "School Quality and Black/White Relative Earnings: A Direct Assessment." Working Paper no. 272. Industrial Relations Section, Princeton University.

Chafetz, Janet Saltzman. 1990. *Gender Equity: An Integrated Theory of Stability and Change.* Newbury Park, Calif.: Sage.

Chandler, Alfred Dupont. 1962. *Strategy and Structure.* Cambridge: MIT Press.

Clawson, Daniel. 1980. *Bureaucracy and the Labor Process: The Transformation of U.S. Industry, 1880–1920.* New York: Monthly Review Press.

Cockburn, Cynthia. 1988. *Machinery of Dominance: Women, Men and Technical Know-How.* Boston: Northeastern University Press.

————. 1991. *In the Way of Women: Men's Resistance to Sex Equality in Organizations.* Ithaca, N.Y.: ILR Press.

Cohn, Samuel. 1985. *The Process of Occupational Sex-Typing.* Philadelphia: Temple University Press.

Collins, Randall. 1979. *The Credential Society.* New York: Academic Press.

Corcoran, Mary, Greg J. Duncan, and Michael Ponza. 1984. "Work Experience, Job Segregation and Wages." In *Sex Segregation in the Workplace,* ed. Barbara F. Reskin, 171–91. Washington, D.C.: National Academy Press.

Cowan, Ruth Schwartz. 1983. *More Work for Mother.* New York: Basic Books.

Cross, Harry, et al. 1990. *Employer Hiring Practices: Differential Treatment of Hispanic and Anglo Job Seekers.* Washington, D.C.: Urban Institute Press.

Daymont, Thomas, and Paul Andrisani. 1984. "Job Preferences, College Major, and the Gender Gap in Earnings." *Journal of Human Resources* 18:408–28.

Daymont, Thomas, and Anne Stratham. 1983. "Occupational Atypicality: Changes, Causes and Consequences." In *Unplanned Careers: The Working Lives of Middle-Aged Women,* ed. Lois Banfill, 61–76. Lexington, Mass.: D. C. Heath.

DiTomasso, Nancy. 1989. "Sexuality in the Workplace: Discrimination and Harassment." In *The Sexuality of Organization,* ed. Jeff Hearn, 132–71. London: Sage.

Doeringer, Peter B., and Michael J. Piore. 1971. *Internal Labor Markets and Manpower Analysis.* Lexington, Mass.: D. C. Heath.

Duncan, Otis Dudley. 1969. "Inheritance of Poverty or Inheritance of Race?" In *On Understanding Poverty,* ed. Daniel P. Moynihan, 85–110. New York: Basic Books.

Edwards, Richard C. *Contested Terrain.* New York: Basic Books.

Ehrenreich, Barbara. 1983. *The Hearts of Men: American Dreams and the Flight from Commitment.* Garden City, N.Y.: Doubleday.

England, Paula. 1982. "The Failure of Human Capital Theory to Explain Occupational Segregation." *Journal of Human Resources* 17:338–50.

————. 1992. *Comparable Worth: Theories and Evidence.* New York: De Gruyter.

England, Paula, and George Farkas. 1986. *Households, Employment, and Gender: A Social, Economic, and Demographic View.* New York: De Gruyter.

England, Paula, et al. 1988. "Explaining Occupational Sex Segregation and Wages: Findings from a Model with Fixed Effects." *American Sociological Review* 53:544–58.

Farley, Reynolds, and Walter Allen. 1987. *The Color Line and the Quality of Life in America.* New York: Russell Sage Foundation.

Feagin, Joe. 1991. "The Continuing Significance of Race: Antiblack Discrimination in Public Places." *American Sociological Review* 56:101–17.

Fernandez, John P. 1987. *Survival in the Corporate Fishbowl: Making It into Upper and Middle Management.* Lexington, Mass.: Lexington Books.

Filer, Randall K. 1989. "Occupational Segregation, Compensating Differentials, and Comparable Worth." In *Pay Equity: Empirical Inquiries,* ed. Robert T. Michael, Heidi I. Hartmann, and Brigid O'Farrell, 153–70. Washington, D.C.: National Academy Press.

———. 1990. "Compensating Differentials and the Male-Female Wage Gap: A Comment." *Social Forces* 69:469–73.

Form, William, and David B. McMillen. 1983. "Women, Men and Machines." *Work and Occupations* 10:147–78.

Fosset, Mark, Omer R. Galle, and Jeffrey A. Burr. 1989. "Racial Occupational Inequality, 1940–1980: A Research Note on the Impact of the Changing Regional Distribution of the Black Population." *Social Forces* 68:415–27.

Galle, Omer R., Candace Hinson Wiswell, and Jeffrey A. Burr. 1985. "Racial Mix and Industrial Productivity." *American Sociological Review* 50:20–23.

Gerhart, Barry A., and George T. Milkovich. 1989. "Salaries, Salary Growth, and Promotions of Men and Women in a Large, Private Firm." In *Pay Equity: Empirical Inquiries*, ed. Robert T. Michael, Heidi I. Hartmann, and Brigid O'Farrell, 23–41. Washington, D.C.: National Academy Press.

Glass, Jennifer. 1990. "The Impact of Occupational Segregation on Working Conditions." *Social Forces* 68:779–96.

Gold, Michael Evan. 1983. *A Dialogue on Comparable Worth*. Ithaca, N.Y.: ILR Press.

Goldberger, Arthur. 1984. "Reverse Regression and Salary Discrimination." *Journal of Human Resources* 19:293–318.

Granovetter, Mark. 1973. "The Strength of Weak Ties." *American Journal of Sociology* 78:1360–80.

———. 1981. "Toward a Sociological Theory of Income Differences." In *Sociological Perspectives on Labor Markets*, ed. Ivar E. Berg, 31–57. New York: Academic Press.

Greenberger, Ellen, and Lauranne Steinberg. 1983. "Sex Differences in Early Labor Force Experience: Harbinger of Things to Come." *Social Forces* 62:467–87.

Halaby, Charles. 1979. "Job-Specific Sex Differences in Organizational Reward Attainment: Wage Discrimination vs. Rank Segregation." *Social Forces* 58:108–27.

Hanson, Susan, and Geraldine Pratt. 1991. "Job Search and the Occupational Segregation of Women." *Annals of the Association of American Geographers* 81:221–53.

Hartmann, Heidi I. 1976. "Capitalism, Patriarchy and Job Segregation by Sex." In *Women and the Workplace*, ed. Martha Blaxall and Barbara Benton Reagan, 137–70. Chicago: University of Chicago Press.

Hauser, Richard, and David Featherman. 1977. *The Process of Stratification*. New York: Academic Press.

Hill, M. Anne, and Mark Killingsworth, eds. 1989. *Comparable Worth: Analysis and Evidence*. Ithaca, N.Y.: ILR Press.

Hodson, Randy. 1978. "Labor in the Monopoly, Competitive, and State Sectors of Production." *Politics and Society* 8:141–93.

———. 1983. *Workers' Earnings and Corporate Economic Structure*. New York: Academic Press.

———. 1985. "Some Considerations Concerning the Functional Form of Earnings." *Social Science Quarterly* 14:374–94.

Hodson, Randy, and Paula England. 1986. "Industrial Structure and Sex Differences in Earnings." *Industrial Relations* 25:16–32.

Hodson, Randy, and Robert Kaufman. 1982. "Economic Dualism: A Critical Review." *American Sociological Review* 47:727–39.

Jacobs, Jerry A. 1989a. "Long-Term Trends in Occupational Segregation by Sex." *American Journal of Sociology* 95:160–73.

———. 1989b. *Revolving Doors: Sex Segregation and Women's Careers.* Stanford, Calif.: Stanford University Press.

Jacobs, Jerry A., and Ronnie Steinberg. 1990. "Compensating Differentials and the Male-Female Wage Gap: Evidence from the New York State Comparable Worth Study." *Social Forces* 69:439–68.

James, David S. 1988. "The Transformation of the Southern Racial State: Class and Race Determinants of Local State Structures." *American Sociological Review* 53:191–208.

Janoski, Thomas. 1990. *The Political Economy of Unemployment: Active Labor Market Policy in West Germany and the United States.* Berkeley: University of California Press.

Jaynes, Gerald David, and Robin M. Williams, Jr. 1989. *A Common Destiny: Blacks and American Society.* Washington D.C.: National Academy Press.

Kalleberg, Arne, and Kevin Leicht. 1986. "Jobs and Skills: A Multivariate Structural Approach." *Social Science Research* 15:269–96.

Kalleberg, Arne, Michael Wallace, and Robert Althauser. 1981. "Economic Segregation, Worker Power, and Income Inequality." *American Journal of Sociology* 87:651–83.

Kanter, Rosabeth. 1977. *Men and Women of the Corporation.* New York: Basic Books.

———. 1983. *The Change Masters: Innovation in the American Corporation.* New York: Simon and Schuster.

———. 1989. *When Giants Learn to Dance: Mastering the Challenge of Strategy, Management, and Careers in the 1990's.* New York: Simon and Schuster.

Kaufman, Robert L. 1986. "The Impact of Industrial and Occupational Structure on Black-White Employment Allocation." *American Sociological Review* 51:310–23.

Killingsworth, Mark R. 1990. *The Economics of Comparable Worth.* Kalamazoo, Mich.: W. E. Upjohn Institute.

Laslett, Barbara, and Johanna Brenner. 1989. "Gender and Social Reproduction: Historical Perspectives." *Annual Review of Sociology* 15:381–404.

Lieberson, Stanley. 1980. *A Piece of the Pie: Blacks and White Immigrants since 1880.* Berkeley: University of California Press.

Lincoln, James R., and Arne Kalleberg. 1986. "Work Organization and Work Force Commitment: A Study of Plants and Employees in the U.S. and Japan." *American Sociological Review* 50:738–60.

McIlwee, Judith S., and J. Gregg Robinson. 1992. *Women in Engineering: Gender, Power and the Workplace.* Albany: State University of New York Press.

McPherson, J. Miller, and Lynn Smith-Lovin. 1986. "Sex Segregation in Voluntary Associations." *American Sociological Review* 51:61–71.

Malkiel, B. G., and J. A. Malkiel. 1973. "Male-Female Differentials in Professional Employment." *American Economic Review* 63:693–705.

Marini, Margaret Mooney. 1989. "Sex Differences in Earnings in the United States." *Annual Review of Sociology* 15:348–80.

Marini, Margaret Mooney, and Mary C. Brinton. 1984. "Sex Typing and Occupational Socialization." In *Sex Segregation in the Workplace: Trends, Explanations, Remedies,* ed. Barbara F. Reskin, 192–232. Washington, D.C.: National Academy Press.

Marshall, Ray. 1974. "The Economics of Racial Discrimination: A Survey." *Journal of Economic Literature* 12:849–71.

Marx, Karl. 1961. *Economic and Philosophical Manuscripts of 1844.* Moscow: Foreign Languages Publishing House.

Massey, Douglas. 1990. "American Apartheid: Segregation and the Making of the Underclass." *American Journal of Sociology* 96:329–57.

Michael, Robert T., Heidi I. Hartmann, and Brigid O'Farrell, eds. 1989. *Pay Equity: Empirical Inquiries.* Washington, D.C.: National Academy Press.

Milkman, Ruth. 1980. "Organizing the Sexual Division of Labor: Historical Perspectives on Women's Work and the American Labor Movement." *Socialist Review* 10:95–150.

Miller, S. M., and Donald Tomaskovic-Devey. 1983. *Recapitalizing America: Alternatives to the Corporate Distortion of National Policy.* Boston: Routledge and Kegan Paul.

Mills, C. Wright. 1956. *The Power Elite.* New York: Oxford University Press.

Mueller, Charles W., Toby L. Parcel, and Kazuko Tanaka. 1989. "Foreclosures in Authority Outcome of Black and White Supervisors." *Social Science Research* 18:1–20.

Murphy, Raymond. 1988. *Social Closure: The Theory of Monopolization and Exclusion.* New York: Oxford University Press.

O'Connor, James. 1973. *The Fiscal Crisis of the State.* New York: St. Martin's Press.

Ogbu, John. 1978. *Minority Education and Caste: The American System in Cross Cultural Perspective.* New York: Academic Press.

Padavic, Irene. 1991. "Attraction of Male Blue-Collar Jobs for Black and White Women: Economic Need, Exposure, and Attitudes." *Social Science Quarterly* 72:33–49.

Parcel, Toby. 1989. "Comparable Worth, Occupational Labor Markets and Occupational Earnings: Results from the 1980 Census." In *Pay Equity: Empirical Inquiries,* ed. Robert T. Michael, Heidi I. Hartmann, and Brigid O'Farrell, 134–52. Washington, D.C.: National Academy Press.

Parcel, Toby, Robert L. Kaufman, and Leeann Jolly. 1991. "Going Up the Ladder: Multiplicity Sampling to Create Linked Macro-to-Micro Organizational Samples." *Sociological Methodology* 21:43–79.

Parcel, Toby, and Charles W. Mueller. 1983. *Ascription and Labor Markets: Race and Sex Differences in Earnings.* New York: Academic Press.

Parkin, Frank. 1979. *Marxism and Class Theory: A Bourgeois Critique.* New York: Columbia University Press.

Peters, Tom, and Robert Waterman. 1982. *In Search of Excellence*. New York: Harper and Row.

Pfeffer, Jeffrey, and Alison Davis-Blake. 1987. "The Effect of Proportion Women on Salaries: The Case of College Administrators." *Administrative Science Quarterly* 32:1–24.

Phelps, Edmund S. 1972. "The Statistical Theory of Racism and Sexism." *American Economic Review* 62:659–66.

Polachek, Solomon. 1979. "Occupational Self-Selection: A Human Capital Approach to Sex Differences in Occupational Structure." *Review of Economics and Statistics* 58:60–69.

———. 1985. "Occupational Segregation: A Defense of Human Capital Predictions." *Journal of Human Resources* 20:437–40.

Pugh, D. S., D. J. Hickson, C. R. Hinings, and C. Turner. 1968. "Dimensions of Organizational Structure." *Administrative Science Quarterly* 13:65–105.

Reich, Michael. 1981. *Racial Inequality*. Princeton: Princeton University Press.

Reskin, Barbara F. 1988. "Bringing the Men Back In: Sex Differentiation and the Devaluation of Women's Work." *Gender and Society* 2:58–81.

Reskin, Barbara F., and Patricia A. Roos. 1990. *Job Queues, Gender Queues: Explaining Women's Inroads into Male Occupations*. Philadelphia: Temple University Press.

Roby, Pamela. 1987. "Union Stewards and Women's Employment Conditions." In *Ingredients for Women's Employment Policy*, ed. Christine E. Bose and Glenna D. Spitze, 139–55. Albany: State University of New York Press.

Rogers, David L., and Willis J. Gudy. 1981. "Community Structure and Occupational Segregation, 1960 and 1970." *Rural Sociology* 46:263–81.

Roos, Patricia A., and Barbara F. Reskin. 1984. "Institutional Factors Contributing to Sex Segregation in the Workplace." In *Sex Segregation in the Workplace: Trends, Explanations, Remedies*, ed. Barbara F. Reskin, 235–60. Washington, D.C.: National Academy Press.

Rosenfeld, Rachel. 1983. "Sex Segregation and Sectors: An Analysis of Gender Differences in Returns from Employer Changes." *American Sociological Review* 48:637–55.

———. 1984. "Job Changing and Occupational Sex Segregation: Sex and Race Comparisons." In *Sex Segregation in the Workplace: Trends, Explanations, Remedies*, ed. Barbara F. Reskin, 56–86. Washington, D.C.: National Academy Press.

Rytina, Nancy, and Suzanne Bianchi. 1984. "Occupational Reclassification and Changes in Distribution by Gender." *Monthly Labor Review* 107:11–17.

Semyonov, Moshe, and Noah Lewin-Epstein. 1989. "Segregation and Competition in Occupational Labor Markets." *Social Forces* 68:379–96.

Semyonov, Moshe, Danny R. Hoyt, and Richard Scott. 1984. "Place, Race and Differential Occupational Opportunities." *Demography* 21:259–70.

Smith, Robert. 1979. "Compensating Wage Differentials and Public Policy: A Review." *Industrial and Labor Relations Review* 32:339–59.

Sorensen, Aage. 1983. "Sociological Research on the Labor Market: Conceptual and Methodological Issues." *Work and Occupations* 10:261–87.

Sorenson, Elaine. 1989a. "The Crowding Hypothesis and Comparable Worth." *Journal of Human Resources* 25:55–89.

———. 1989b. "Measuring the Effect of Occupational Sex and Race Composition on Earnings." In *Pay Equity: Empirical Inquiries*, ed. Robert T. Michael, Heidi I. Hartmann, and Brigid O'Farrell, 49–70. Washington, D.C.: National Academy Press.

Sowell, Thomas. 1990. *Preferential Policies: An International Perspective.* New York: Morrow.

Spenner, Ken. 1985. "The Upgrading and Downgrading of Occupations: Issues, Evidence, and Implications for Education." *Review of Educational Research* 55:125–54.

Steinberg, Ronnie, and Lois Haignere. 1987. "Equitable Compensation: Methodological Criteria for Comparable Worth." In *Ingredients for Women's Employment Policy*, ed. Christine E. Bose and Glenna D. Spitze, 157–82. Albany: State University of New York Press.

Subich, Linda, Gerald Barret, Dennis Doverspike, and Ralph Alexander. 1989. "The Effects of Sex Role Related Factors on Occupational Choice and Salary." In *Pay Equity: Empirical Inquiries*, ed. Robert T. Michael, Heidi I. Hartmann, and Brigid O'Farrell, 91–104. Washington, D.C.: National Academy Press.

Szafran, Robert F. 1982. "What Kind of Firms Hire and Promote Women and Blacks: A Review of the Literature." *Sociological Quarterly* 23:171–90.

Thurow, Lester. 1975. *Generating Inequality.* New York: Basic Books.

Tienda, Marta, and Ding-Tzann Lii. 1987. "Minority Concentration and Earnings Inequality: Blacks, Hispanics, and Asians Compared." *American Journal of Sociology* 93:141–65.

Tomaskovic-Devey, Barbara. 1992. "The Good Wife: Husbands and the Homemaker's Job." North Carolina State University. Typescript.

Tomaskovic-Devey, Donald. 1988. "Labor Force Composition, Market Concentration, Structural Power, and Industrial Productivity." In *Industries, Firms, and Jobs: Sociological and Economic Approaches*, ed. George Farkas and Paula England, 66–97. New York: Plenum Press.

———. 1989. "Organizational Stratification and the Size of the Pie: Environmental Constraints on Organizational Income Streams." Paper presented at the annual meeting of the American Sociological Association, San Francisco, August.

———. 1991. "A Structural Model of Poverty Creation and Change: Political Economy, Local Opportunity, and U.S. Poverty, 1959–1979." *Research in Social Stratification and Mobility* 10:289–322.

Trieman, Donald, and Heidi I. Hartmann, eds. 1981. *Women, Work, and Wages: Equal Pay for Jobs of Equal Value.* Washington, D.C.: National Academy Press.

Turner, Margery Austin, Michael Fix, and Raymon J. Struyk. 1991. *Opportunities Denied, Opportunities Dismissed: Racial Discrimination in Hiring.* Washington, D.C.: Urban Institute.

U.S. Bureau of the Census. 1987. "Male-Female Differences in Work Experience, Occupation and Earnings: 1984." *Current Population Reports.* Washington, D.C.: GPO.

Walby, Sylvia, 1986. *Patriarchy at Work*. Minneapolis: University of Minnesota Press.

Wallace, Michael, and Chin-fen Chang. 1990. "Barriers to Women's Employment: Economic Segmentation in American Manufacturing, 1950–1980." *Research in Social Stratification and Mobility* 9:337–61.

Wallace, Michael, and Arne Kalleberg. 1981. "Economic Organization of Firms and Labor Market Consequences: Toward a Specification of Dual Economy Theory." In *Sociological Perspectives on Labor Markets*, ed. Ivar E. Berg, 77–118. New York: Academic Press.

Weber, Max. 1968. *Economy and Society*. Edited by Guenter Roth and Claus Wittich. New York: Bedminster Press.

Williams, Bruce. 1987. *Black Workers in an Industrial Suburb: The Struggle against Discrimination*. New Brunswick, N.J.: Rutgers University Press.

Williamson, Oliver E. 1981. "The Economics of Organization: The Transaction Cost Approach." *American Journal of Sociology* 87:548–77.

Wilson, William Julius. 1978. *The Declining Significance of Race*. Chicago: University of Chicago Press.

Winsborough, H. Hal, and Peter Dickenson. 1974. "Composition of Negro-White Income Differences." *Proceedings of the Social Statistics Section, American Statistical Association* 1971:6–8.

Wolf, Wendy C., and Neil D. Fligstein. 1979a. "Sex and Authority in the Workplace: The Causes of Sexual Inequality." *American Sociological Review* 44:235–52.

———. 1979b. "Sexual Stratification: DIfferences in Power in the Work Setting." *Social Forces* 58:94–107.

Wood, Philip J. 1986. *Southern Capitalism: The Political Economy of North Carolina, 1880–1980*. Durham, N.C.: Duke University Press.

Wright, Erik Olin. 1978. "Race, Class, and Income Inequality." *American Journal of Sociology* 83:1368–88.

———. 1979. *Class Structure and Income Determination*. New York: Academic Press.

INDEX

ABOUT THE AUTHOR

DONALD TOMASKOVIC-DEVEY is a professor of sociology at North Carolina State University. He received his Ph.D. from Boston University in 1984. His research interests include the political, organizational, and interpersonal social practices that create and maintain economic inequality and deprivation; the effects of race, the power of local elites, and dependent development on economic development in the southern United States; and gender and racial inequality in the workplace.